Swords into Plowshares

Italian POWs in Olivia, 1943. *Courtesy of Alice Morgan*

Swords into Plowshares

Minnesota's POW Camps during World War II

Dean B. Simmons

Foreword by George H. Lobdell

Cathedral Hill Books
St. Paul

Cathedral Hill Books, St. Paul, Minnesota

First Edition

Library of Congress Catalog Card Number: 98-96857

ISBN 0-9669001-0-3

Logo design by Chris Pihlstrom and Paul Stuhlfaut

Cover design by Anthony Brandenburg

Cover photos, top to bottom: 1.) German POW, left, with civilian
workers on the Henry (Hank) Peterson farm near Moorhead, *courtesy
of Northwest Minnesota Historical Center*; 2.) German POWs near
Moorhead, *courtesy of Northwest Minnesota Historical Center*; 3.)
German POWs at New Ulm, *courtesy of Brown County Historical
Society*; 4.) German POWs at Remer, *courtesy of Gerald Delin*.

This book is printed on acid-free paper.

. . . they shall beat their swords
into plowshares,
and their spears into pruning hooks. . . .

Isaiah 2:4

Minnesota's POW Camps

Contents

Foreword

When Cornell University's philosopher-historian Carl Lotus Becker was president of the American Historical Association in 1931, he entitled his inaugural address "Everyman His Own Historian."* He started by describing his search for a simple but complete definition of history and then presented his conclusion: "History is the memory of things said and done." If that were so, he reasoned, "then every normal person, Mr. Everyman, . . . would be astonished to learn that he is a historian." This assertion made it clear he believed professional historians had no monopoly on the field of history. "Each day [Mr. Everyman] performs all the essential operations involved in historical research," Professor Becker continued. Any person who writes a letter, keeps a memo, makes a diary entry, or mounts photographs in an album contributes to the memory of things said and done, and is a historian whether or not he or she realizes it.

Then, sadly, Professor Becker observed, in spite of Mr. Everyman's contributions, over the past ages a multitude of events and episodes have vanished from memory and have left no evidence which might allow them to be ever recalled again. Over sixty years later Dean Simmons became aware that the memory of things said and done about World War II prisoners of war (POWs) in Minnesota was fading fast, and he decided to do something to save what could be found about this very interesting episode in his state's history.

When Simmons undertook his project, unintentionally he filled the role of Professor Becker's non-professional "Mr. Everyman" historian. Simmons' undergraduate collegiate majors were German and economics, and his graduate major was international business. He had no formal training as a research historian. Yet, the curiosity which was aroused when a neighbor told him about Italian prisoners of war working near his home in 1943 developed into a research project that resulted in this book, which deserves the history classification library catalogers give it.

Simmons' serious search for information on a subject he knew nothing about began modestly. As an exchange student to Germany during his collegiate junior year, he tried to locate the few former Minnesota POWs for whom he had addresses. Though he found only one such German veteran then, that success was all the motivation he needed to begin an aggressive campaign to find out all he could about POWs who were unintentional residents of his home state during World War II.

Simmons' footnotes and bibliography provide ample evidence that he pursued his thorough research with remarkable energy and persistence. His citations reveal that he studied carefully several excellent books on POWs and dozens of both popular and professional periodical articles to learn how interned enemy captives were guarded, fed, clothed, sheltered and utilized for work in the United States. For knowledge of POWs in Minnesota, he located articles in journals about their employment which led him to local, county, state and farm-association documents and official reports on agricultural and industrial employment. Dozens of stories and feature articles in daily and weekly newspapers provided him with insights into each local situation. He found significant documents which were held in archival depositories such as the National Archives and Records Service, Washington, D.C., Minnesota State Historical Society Archives, St. Paul, National YMCA Archives, St. Paul, Northwest Minnesota Historical Center Collections, Moorhead, Minnesota, the Politisches Archiv des Auswärtigen Amts, Bonn, Germany, and many of Minnesota's local and county historical society records.

Simmons' need to master the mechanics of POW camp affairs was a foundation for his fundamental interest in discovering and reporting what he could find about the human interaction between the prisoners and their guards and the prisoners and the citizens of Minnesota whose lives they affected. He conducted interviews with many Americans and corresponded with those he could not interview. His talks with Howard Hong, the able and sensitive YMCA representative serving the Minnesota POW camps, and his correspondence with Werner Schmiedeberg who had commanded three different camps and had dealt with both German and Italian prisoners, provided him with contemporary, rare, first-person accounts by two Americans with valuable views of POW camp life.

But what of the perspective of the prisoners? On his second visit to Germany when he was a graduate student, Simmons carried with him the addresses of several ex-POWs with whom he had exchanged letters. Happily, he was able to meet seven of these men and record whatever they were willing to share with him.

Though this sample of POW recollections may at first glance seem too small to provide useful insights into the prisoner experience, such is not the case. The reminiscences recorded in "Prisoner Perspectives" represent the views of men whose place and time of capture ranged from North Africa in May 1943 to Germany in March 1945. In America these POWs recalled service in three different base camps and eleven different Minnesota branch camps. Because of the diversity of their experiences both before and after capture these "Perspectives" give us seven unique and valuable views from the prisoner side of the fences in Minnesota. The author implicitly challenges his readers to compare and contrast the experiences of these men and come to whatever conclusions their stories suggest.

Indeed, Simmons deliberately leaves it up to his readers to sort out the themes which his narratives of Minnesota's twenty-one POW work camps contain. He is a "Mr. Everyman" historian who has composed accounts based on what he has been able to find about almost forgotten episodes which took place four decades before he studied German and economics as a college undergraduate. For those who may be interested in a single camp, his footnotes identify sources which may be used by a local "Mr. Everyman" to go beyond the account in a specific chapter. For others, including professional historians, his rich bibliography offers sources to anyone who wants to explore beyond his reports.

Though Simmons intentionally leaves to others "the task of weighing the evidence and building theses upon it," he does emphasize the story of people on both sides of the stockade fences. What he reports may surprise readers who are unfamiliar with the subject of POWs in America. He believes, with ample justification, that the decent treatment received by over 400,000 Axis prisoners in the United States set a new world standard for the humane treatment of captured enemies. His accounts of the interaction between Americans and the prisoners provides us with more examples of tolerance than hostility. Though the POWs were confined, he found the circumstances of their confinement were not harsh and at times were remarkably casual and comfortable. Both camp officials and outside agencies such as the YMCA provided educational materials and recreational equipment. Arrangements were always made for religious observances. Medical care covered both minor ailments and serious problems. Such decent officially ordered treatment reached beyond the POWs' compounds. Since all of Minnesota's camps were established to serve the wartime labor needs of the state, all its POWs worked either for individuals or contractors. Simmons reports few instances of civilian resistance to POWs and many examples of cordial relationships developing between prisoners and Minnesotans.

Dean Simmons as a "Mr. Everyman" historian has achieved his goal of preserving much of "the memory of things said and done" about Minnesota's World War II POWs. He was philosophically sustained in his project not by Professor Becker's speech, about which he knew nothing, but rather by the famous historian Bruce Catton's declaration, "History after all is the story of people." Accept Simmons' challenge to discover why he believes the record he presents confirms that many German POWs and their Minnesota "hosts" learned from their wartime association that once perceived enemies were after all fellow human beings—"just people."

> George H. Lobdell
> Professor of History, Emeritus
> Ohio University, Athens

* Carl Lotus Becker, "Everyman His Own Historian," *American Historical Review*, vol. XXXVII, No. 2 (January, 1932), pp. 221–236; republished in Becker, *Everyman His Own Historian* (F. S. Crofts & Co., New York, 1935); reprinted in paperback under the same title by Quandrangle Books, Inc., Chicago, 1966. Professor Becker delivered this address before the American Historical Association Convention at Minneapolis, Minnesota, December 29, 1931.

Acknowledgments

I am grateful for the help of these people, among many others, in the preparation of this book: Bernadine Thomas, Mildred Coupanger, Myron Heuer, Lorenzo Bakko, Harvey Fleshner, Evelyn Kubat, Dave Palmquist, Muriel Jeske, Charles Crouch, Robert Odegard, Joyce Edmonds, Arnold Whitcomb, Dorothy Steinbeisser, Winifred Murray, Eileen Rockvam, Mrs. Immanuel Lenz, Lawrence Stadther, Beverly Buck, Mark Lauber, Gerald Delin, Jean Ostlund, Bill Marshall, Sister Cordelia Bloch, Mark Peihl, Kelly Zwagerman, Becky Cowing, Edward Pluth, George and Ruth Rauenhorst, Richard Wahl, Russell Sundet, Pauline Schreiber, Jean Nienoord, Korella Selzler, Jane Stull, Ed Shannon, Elaine Olson, Alice Morgan, Arnold Madow, Melvin Tatge, Shirley Hamer, and Mike Amidon.

Special thanks are due to Werner Schmiedeberg and Howard Hong for providing detailed insights about their work in the camps and with the prisoners.

Librarians and archivists at several locations were particularly helpful. These include workers at the Kautz Family YMCA Archives in St. Paul, Minnesota and the Politisches Archiv des Auswärtigen Amts in Bonn, Germany.

Several individuals aided in the search for specific information, made editorial suggestions, and helped establish personal contacts. These include C. B. Rykken, Rüdiger Overmans, Günter Bischof, Gian-Domenico Brocco, and Gail Gavin.

Information and photos were provided by former prisoners Werner Knauer, Karl Becker, Alfred Neber, Ernst Kohleick, Heinrich Waldschmidt, Hans Welker, Kurt Rasokat, Hermann Massing, Karl Becker, Alex Funke, Friedhelm Henkel, Fritz Reinlassoeder, and Hans Kratzheller.

Finally, I owe a large debt of gratitude to George Lobdell, professor emeritus of History at Ohio University, Athens, who provided information about the Minnesota camps, the Algona base camp, and the Algona camp commander, Lieutenant Colonel Arthur T. Lobdell, his uncle.

Chapter 1

POWs in America: an Overview

More than 400,000 German, Italian, and Japanese prisoners of war were interned in the United States during World War II; never before in history had so many military prisoners been massed on this continent. Most were German, about 380,000. American troops took few captives of their own during the first year of the war, but as 1943 approached, many prisoners were transferred from British to U.S. custody because it was difficult for the British to guard, feed, and house them. As a result, plans were under way as early as 1942 for the arrival of 150,000 British-captured prisoners in the United States. Many of the Germans came in two distinct waves, one from the surrender of Afrika Korps troops in 1943, the other in 1944 following the D-Day invasion of Europe.[1]

The War Department was directly responsible for POWs in United States custody, and the Provost Marshal General's office oversaw their internment in the United States. Prisoners were brought from collection points at the front to transshipment locations such as Casablanca and Oran. Ships carrying war materials to Europe, often Liberty class cargo vessels, were used on their return trip to take prisoners to the United States. The ships usually docked at either New York City or Norfolk, Virginia. By the time they arrived, the prisoners had been processed and had undergone medical examinations. The ships usually traveled in convoys; not one vessel transporting prisoners to the U.S. was sunk during the course of the war. British Prime Minister Winston Churchill once traveled safely on a POW transport ship to visit President Roosevelt.[2]

Of the hundreds of base and branch camps for POWs eventually established in the United States, many were located in the South; the mild climate reduced construction and operating costs. The majority of the camps were thus in less-populated areas of the country, and consequently a lower security risk. Although there was plenty of interpretive room in the Geneva Convention, the United States initially adhered closely to its rules, largely because the government wanted to avoid any reason for the mistreatment of U.S. prisoners overseas. Even so, German prisoners in the U.S. were treated differently than

Americans held abroad. Well aware of that fact, the U.S. War Department nevertheless claimed that it did not wish "to adopt the Nazi
principle of hostages," and that "the particular men held by us are not
necessarily the ones who ill-treated our men in German prison camps.
To punish one man for what another has done is not an American
principle."[3]

Close adherence to the Geneva Convention affected prisoners'
food, pay, dress, housing, medical care, work, money, mail, recreation, and reading, essentially "every detail of the prisoner's welfare."
Housing and mess facilities were equivalent to those of the U.S.
troops at base camps in the United States; the only essential difference
was the addition of barbed wire, guards, and high walls. At times, in
fact, Axis prisoners were treated better than black Americans; prisoners sometimes received meals in lunchrooms, for example, while African American soldiers were required to eat in the kitchen. Later in the
war, however, a policy of reduced rations was implemented in response to wartime shortages of food and a general fear of coddling.[4]

Decent treatment and physical care of the POWs did result in
healthy workers, a persuasive reason for the United States to keep
them physically fit. Under the Geneva Convention, prisoners below
the rank of sergeant could be required to work for the enemy, and it
soon became evident how useful they would be in the acute labor
shortages occurring across the U.S. More POWs were used in agriculture than in any other type of labor. Initial civilian opposition to their
use dwindled as they began to work. As soon as it was apparent that
prisoners could function outside their enclosures without posing a
security risk, the full use of their labor became an official objective.[5]

The initial location of many POW camps did not coincide with
manpower shortages, and branch camps were established to expedite
the movement of prisoners to areas that needed help. The branch
camps increased the percentage of prisoners who could be effectively
employed. In May 1944, for example, 73 percent of prisoners available for work in the U.S. were working; by April the following year,
the figure had reached 91.3 percent. POW labor was paradoxically
furthered by the German High Command. In 1944 it conveyed to the
German prisoners in the U.S. that working, instead of sitting idle in
camp, was in the best interest of the German soldier.[6]

Little occasion for the employment of POWs existed before 1943,
partly because of the small number of prisoners, and partly because a
critical farm-labor shortage had not yet arisen. But an adequate supply

of farm labor was a problem during the rest of the war, for obvious reasons: Selective Service, voluntary enlistment, and high wages in war-related industries. The severity of the shortage was evidenced by thousands of foreigners brought from Jamaica, Mexico, and the Bahamas, sometimes so badly needed that they were flown into the country.[7]

By 1944, prisoners were being used in almost every state of the union. Eventually they were employed in forestry, logging, mining, quarrying, construction, food processing, transportation, and trade, but above all in agriculture. Between 1943 and 1946, prisoners farmed every major crop in the United States. They worked, for example, with sugar cane in Louisiana, potatoes and oats in Missouri, fruit and tobacco in Maryland, peanuts in Georgia, and cotton in Mississippi. The general shortage of farm and factory labor became so severe that prisoners were employed without tight security outside their camps. German prisoners, for example, eventually worked outside 511 branch and 155 base camps in 44 states.[8]

An incentive for the prisoners was income. Their standard pay, when working, was 80 cents per day, roughly based on the rate paid to U.S. privates in 1941. Pay was redeemable at the camp canteen, or credited to a trust fund in the prisoner's name. Employers were required to pay the U.S. government the prevailing wage for labor performed by the prisoners, but occasional allowances were given for transportation and housing costs.[9]

Prisoners could not be forced to work more than 10 hours daily, and they were entitled to a rest of 24 consecutive hours every week. Not all jobs were available to prisoners; according to the Geneva Convention, they could not work in "direct connection with the operations of the war." Prisoners were allowed to sort scrap iron in a foundry, for example, but not to work on an assembly line making tank parts. Only after hostilities with a given country were over could its POWs be used for war operations. Italian prisoners, for example, could do military-related work after Italy surrendered in 1943, and Germans could finally work on war-related tasks after VE Day.[10]

Comprehensive care was taken to meet the educational and recreational needs of the prisoners. Agencies including War Prisoners Aid of the YMCA and the International Committee of the Red Cross offered recreational services. As many as 103 U.S. trade schools and universities provided correspondence courses. Inside the camps, prisoners enjoyed recreation halls, libraries, theaters, workshops, religious activities, schools, and many other amenities. One educational effort that had a notable impact on the prisoners was an "Intellectual Diversion Program," designed in 1944 to produce effective de-Nazification tools including newspapers and films. Thousands of prisoners were affected by such re-education attempts. Prisoners were also trained to help with the postwar American military government in Germany; more than a million German ex-POWs worked for the U.S. in Europe after the war.[11]

Overall, POW camp security was not a significant problem, though initially it was of paramount concern because the U.S. had had little experience with security issues before 1943. Records indicate that 2,827 prisoners escaped between 1942 and 1946, including less than one percent of German internees. Against the vast total POW population in the U.S., the rate of escape was small—lower, in fact, than that of the federal penitentiaries. The overwhelming majority of escaped prisoners were recaptured within three days; all but one were apprehended by authorities. There is no record of sabotage or assault by an escaped prisoner in the United States.[12]

Problems did arise inside the camps; there were occasional killings of prisoners by their fellows, and occasional abuses by Americans. An extreme example involved an American guard in Utah, who fired a machine gun at his prisoners, killing several; the guard was later declared insane. As a result of three incidents involving the deaths of alleged anti-Nazis, 14 German prisoners were found guilty of murder. Their death warrants were signed by President Truman, and they were hanged at Fort Leavenworth in July and August 1945, the first foreign war prisoners ever executed in the United States. Dramatic incidents of this sort, however, were rare.[13]

By the end of May 1945, all shipments of prisoners to the United States had ceased; by June 30, 1946, all camps in the U.S. had been officially closed. The repatriation process began in late 1945 and ended in 1946. Factors affecting its speed included the availability of shipping and the supply of civilians for work that had been performed by POWs during the war. Canteen coupons were redeemed, trust funds were liquidated, and the prisoners were issued government checks, usually amounting to about $50.[14]

Repatriated prisoners had no clear knowledge of their destination until after they arrived in Europe. Many were returned directly to Germany; others were given to Belgium, France, Holland, Luxembourg, or Britain. In order to conserve American and British manpower for combat use and to provide France with much-needed home-front labor, 1.3 million prisoners were assigned to the French, mostly from Allied POW camps in Europe. After the U.S. learned from the International Red Cross that French care of prisoners was unsatisfactory, the transfer was halted for a time. France held its German prisoners the longest; by April 1947, over 400,000 German prisoners were still there.[15]

Although some camp locations across the United States can be seen today, most have gradually disappeared over the years. Prisoners still return to their old campsites and visit the people they worked with, and as many as 5,000 former prisoners have moved to the U.S. permanently.[16]

Chapter 2

Minnesota's POW Camps

On September 5, 1943, nearly four years to the day after German military forces swept across Poland to begin World War II, a train from Camp Clark, Missouri, carrying 200 Italian war-prisoners and their American guards, crossed the state border into Minnesota. The train stopped at Olivia; the guards marched 100 POWs to a nearby camp consisting of tents and a small barbed-wire fence. Continuing eastward, the train reached Princeton later the same day, and the remaining prisoners and crew established a second camp on a local farm. So began Minnesota's experience with POW camps. During the next two years, nineteen more camps would be established, eventually housing thousands of Axis POWs.

Events leading to the use of prisoners in Minnesota began within months after the United States entered the war, when concern arose about the state's farm-labor needs. In 1942, Governor Harold Stassen developed an eleven-point program designed to ease labor shortages on Minnesota farms. Stassen's plan included a network of rural placement and recruitment offices and a program whereby older workers would not lose their pensions if they resumed working. It also promoted the extension of day-care facilities by schools and welfare agencies. In July, Minnesota agricultural leaders requested that the induction of farm helpers into the military be put off for the sake of the fall harvest. The Minneapolis *Morning Tribune* claimed that "there are many instances in which the old folks have been left alone on their farms when their sons have been drafted. They'll have to move off their farms, and sell or rent them." Apparently as a result of these concerns, Minnesota boards were allowed to postpone the draft of men needed for the harvest. This policy, and the use of migrant and temporary local labor, alleviated the shortage in 1942.[1]

As 1943 approached, however, bolder actions were taken to confront imminent farm-labor shortages. In February the Minnesota Agricultural Extension Director, Paul E. Miller, was appointed chairman of the state's Farm Help Coordinating Committee (FHCC). Miller quickly developed a "grass roots" program in which responsibility for labor recruitment was delegated to locally established committees as well as agricultural extension agencies and local offices of the United

States Employment Service (USES). The committees, made up of county and local leaders including mayors, county auditors, and agricultural agents, responded effectively to Minnesota's farm-labor needs throughout the war.[2]

An intense campaign to mobilize farm help began with a meeting for county agricultural leaders in Slayton on March 4 and in Mankato the following day. Other meetings were arranged and within the month, three quarters of the state's agricultural region had been informed about new farm-help programs. By April, Miller announced that conventional sources of labor were insufficient; two months later his agency and the state's USES pooled their resources to mobilize farm help. Meanwhile, state officials continued to predict significant shortages in the supply of farm and food-processing workers. In June, Miller was advised that the use of POW labor in Minnesota was permitted, and the Minnesota FHCC, already busy recruiting conventional labor, began to explore the use of war prisoners.[3]

Paul E. Miller, Minnesota Agricultural Extension Director during the war, is shown here in his office reviewing literature about farm jobs for city youth. His eventual leadership as the appointed chair of the state's Farm Help Coordinating Committee proved invaluable in addressing farm-labor shortages in Minnesota throughout the war. *Courtesy of the University of Minnesota Archives*

Meanwhile, some Minnesota draftees were given deferments to aid canneries, and over 1,000 foreigners were recruited from Jamaica, Mexico, and the Bahamas for work in Minnesota. These workers, along with federal troops, helped provide sufficient farm labor for 1943. The use of POW labor was pursued cautiously, since the government was primarily concerned at first with the satisfactory care of prisoners; only the Olivia and Princeton camps were established in 1943. But despite the experimental status of POW labor in its first year, directed more toward future contingencies than immediate needs, Miller continued to believe that prisoners were a "very important potential supply of labor."[4]

The value of 1943's experiments seems to have been established by 1944; in February, Miller praised the local help he had received during the preceding year. In January, meanwhile, state officials were discussing the use of POW labor, agreeing "that an effort should be made to obtain prisoners of war." Soon the first three POW logging camps were in operation in northern Minnesota, and by spring, the state Farm Help Coordinating Committee was very much in favor of exploring the use of prisoners in agriculture. In April, Miller and the state War Manpower Commission (WMC) director, Dreng Bjornaraa, entered into an agreement outlining some of their responsibilities. Funds to support the extension service were provided to the WMC, which through its state director was responsible for their proper distribution.[5]

In response to the growing demand, Miller set about recruiting 4,000 foreign and POW workers for Minnesota. By the first week of June, Miller and Bjornaraa were ready to announce arrangements for seven POW camps in Minnesota. Eventually foreign recruitment produced over 2,000 non-military workers, while POW camps were established in twelve different locations. Some operated continuously into 1945; others closed and reopened the following year. The only new locations established in 1945 for agriculture were in the Red River Valley and at Wells.[6]

The camps established in 1944 marked the beginning of significant and consistent POW use in Minnesota agriculture, food processing, and small business. POW laborers, along with imported workers, helped prevent serious shortages in 1944. The estimated 1,400 German POWs proved their worth; the state extension service concluded after the 1944 season that they would "undoubtedly be used in as large or larger numbers in 1945." In fact, the POWs proved indispensable in 1945, when the state underwent the most critical farm-labor shortages in its history. They were, according to the extension service, a "rather flexible source of labor throughout 1945 when labor was most needed."[7]

Minnesota's POW camps were considered "branch" or "side" camps of larger, permanent base camps. Their establishment, as part of a national network of branch camps, followed the decision to settle POWs in areas needing labor. Prisoners coming to work in Minnesota arrived from several base camps between 1943 and 1945. Concordia, Kansas, was initially the base camp with jurisdiction over the Remer, Bena, Deer River, and Owatonna camps in Minnesota. Because Nazi sentiments reigned there until late 1943, Concordia had acquired the reputation of being "out of control." Omaha headquarters changed the jurisdiction over the Minnesota camps from Concordia to Algona, Iowa, on June 8, 1944, and all Minnesota camps were eventually placed under Algona's control. See appendix 1 for a complete listing of Algona's branch camps.[8]

The permanent camp three miles west of Algona could house 3,000 prisoners; at least 10,000 passed through it during its operation. In June 1944, its command was given to Lieutenant Colonel Arthur T. Lobdell, a World War I veteran who had been brought up from the reserves in 1941. Under Lobdell, Algona adhered closely to the Geneva Convention in its treatment of prisoners. The Standard Operating Procedure (SOP) for Algona branch camps, including those in Minnesota, laid out a regimen for their proper operation. Drafted in July or August 1944 and approved by Col. Lobdell, it represented an earnest effort to create a sound base-to-branch relationship. Algona's SOP is particularly noteworthy for its progressive emphasis on education for the prisoners.[9]

Like all branch camps throughout the United States, each one in Minnesota was essentially a military post. Their goal was the "maximum utilization of German prisoners of war in essential work where there . . . [was] no free American labor, with honesty and utmost economy in use of men and tax money." The branch commander was usually a commissioned officer, but as shortages arose later in the war, non-commissioned officers, such as high ranking sergeants, became commanders. Every camp had a senior "non-com," the first sergeant, in charge of the other American personnel. Additionally there were supply, mess, and motor sergeants; in smaller camps it was not uncommon for two of these roles to be performed by one person. Even though the prisoners did all the cooking, they were supervised by an American mess sergeant. A medical corps soldier took care of minor ailments, but serious illnesses and injuries were treated under contract with a local civilian doctor, known as a "contract surgeon." Like the prisoners themselves, American personnel who worked as guards and administrators in the Minnesota branch camps moved periodically to different assignments and locations. A surgical technician, for example, stationed as a medic at Moorhead for several months in 1944, was eventually reassigned to a ship to help evacuate wounded soldiers from Europe.[10]

Often, work at the camps was considered just another assignment. A former sergeant, second-in-command at the Moorhead branch camp, summed up his duties as "a boring job. Just had to get 'em out in the morning, send them out with the guards, then get ready for them when they came back in the evening. Not much else." Nevertheless, some guards and other personnel made Minnesota their permanent home after marrying locals whom they had met while stationed at the camps.[11]

Military reports evaluating the performance of the U.S. personnel in the camps differ dramatically. There are many references to "good" and "excellent" commanders and officers. Occasional problems did arise however. The commander at the Moorhead camp, for example, was transferred back to Algona for compound duty; the reason given in a military report was that "he has a penchant for addressing civic organizations on prisoner of war matters and is not properly versed in War Department policies to be entrusted to such public appearances." In order to keep the camps operating smoothly, camp commanders struggled with several challenges. When the New Ulm commander addressed a local Rotary Club meeting in 1945, for example, he listed the problems he faced: "first, the American civilian who wants to come to camps and believes he knows how they should be run; second, the American guards in the prison camps; and third, the war prisoners themselves."[12]

Military reports sometimes portray personnel who were not competent, or who were selected under questionable circumstances. One report states that the Concordia base camp commander "had recently replaced all American personnel at these side camps with some of his most inefficient personnel." A visiting military official was briefed by some of the Americans at this camp, and they claimed that they had been literally "shanghaied" to northern Minnesota. The same report notes that there was "too much fraternization between American personnel and the POW," and that some officers, as well as enlisted men, appear to have had "only a fair knowledge of the provisions of the Geneva Convention and POW circulars." Indeed, the quality of American personnel in the camps, sometimes termed the "least skilled," appears to have been a problem nation-wide. One explanation is that soldiers not needed elsewhere were assigned to low-priority projects such as the POW program. A guard's role at the camps in some ways resembled that of a custodian.[13]

Fortunately, at least one American is living who was intimately involved in their administration. Werner P. Schmiedeberg, commander at three camps and a motor maintenance functionary at others, preserves not only an American official's view of the camps but an immigrant German's understanding of the prisoners as well. Born near Hamburg, Germany in 1920, Schmiedeberg emigrated as a child with his family to the United States in 1929. He was raised in Brooklyn, New York, and entered the U.S. Army in 1942. Following his general military instruction at Camp Lee, Virginia, he received specialized training as a motor maintenance officer at Fort Crook in Omaha, Nebraska. Shortly afterwards, however, the military recognized his potential in other areas and assigned him to a military intelligence school at Camp Ritchie, Maryland, where his coursework included the interrogation of POWs. After Maryland he was assigned to the base camp in Algona, Iowa.

Schmiedeberg had a variety of responsibilities at Algona, often resulting in small assignments outside the compound. He supervised prisoners constructing a silo in Charles City, Iowa, and on another occasion helped salvage and rebuild decommissioned trucks at an Abilene, Kansas depot. Eventually he came to Minnesota, escorting a convoy of prisoners and supplies to Moorhead. In time, his qualifications in motor maintenance brought him to the logging camps in the northern part of the state, where he became the transportation officer at Bena and Deer River. Later he was given control of motor maintenance for all three logging camps in the region. Schmiedeberg's experience in northern Minnesota ultimately led to his appointment by Algona's Colonel Lobdell as commanding officer at Deer River and Grand Rapids. He received his third and last appointment as a camp commander, at Wells in southern Minnesota, after Grand Rapids closed in 1945.

In retrospect, Schmiedeberg places the burden of command at Deer

Ice-fishing shack on Lake Winnibigoshish, February 1945. Schmiedeberg, right, receiving a "tour" from another soldier. At the time of this photo, Schmiedeberg was the commanding officer at Grand Rapids. *Courtesy of Werner Schmiedeberg*

Werner Schmiedeberg in 1996. While he was stationed in Minnesota, Schmiedeberg commanded the Deer River, Grand Rapids, and Wells branch camps. He later escorted convoys of German prisoners back to Europe. *Courtesy of Werner Schmiedeberg*

River and Grand Rapids among the most difficult of his assignments. He had no specific training for his duties, but an efficient regimen for the operation of branch camps had already been laid out at the base camp. The Algona format was followed closely everywhere; independent actions were seldom taken by branch commanders. Schmiedeberg found it necessary at times to work out problems for himself, but he recalls few major difficulties with either the American personnel or the prisoners. Although he spoke fluent German, he chose not to use it in camp, maintaining a comfortable distance between himself and the prisoners. Business was conducted in English, through the prisoners' representative or "spokesman."

Camp spokesmen rarely approached Schmiedeberg with problems, partly because they were capable of solving many themselves. Occasionally, prisoners would voice concerns about violations of Geneva Convention rules, which the Germans were well aware of. More often they complained about work required of them in camp, or about an assignment to a disagreeable outside contractor, although they generally enjoyed working away from the compound. Another common complaint was that the prisoners were not always free for religious observances at times they preferred.

Schmiedeberg and his staff were treated respectfully by the prisoners. The respect was mutual; Schmiedeberg recalls no expression of hostility toward the Germans, even after the ill-treatment of U.S. servicemen overseas became widely known. Security was not an urgent concern, largely because the internees chose to live within the constraints established by the military. The general goodwill of local citizens also contributed to the smooth operation of the camps.

Although administrative duties absorbed his own time and energies, Schmiedeberg observes that for other American personnel camp life was often "pretty lonely . . . particularly in the branch camps, and not very rewarding." The life was "a little strained," given the close living quarters and limited facilities. Free-time diversion for American staff-members was largely limited to bars and restaurants in nearby towns.

Finishing his work as branch-camp commander at Wells in the late fall of 1945, Schmiedeberg was transferred to Brooklyn and put in charge of a guard unit accompanying German prisoners on their return trip to Europe. On his first voyage, he and his men escorted 800 German prisoners to France on a Liberty Ship; the prisoners were subsequently loaded onto trains and taken to their final destination. Schmiedeberg recalls that moving POWs was "tedious and dangerous work." He had limited manpower to keep watch over the prisoners, and the French train crews were not accommodating toward the American military. From the start of the trip, Schmiedeberg was aware that the prisoners would be delivered to the French for work in coal mines, but he withheld that information from his own guards because security concerns were enough of a worry. After overseeing a second, much larger transfer of German prisoners to Europe, he returned to civilian life, resuming his prewar position as a machinist at American Machine and Foundry in New York.

During the postwar years he had little opportunity to reflect on his experiences as a camp commander. Family and work responsibilities occupied much of his time, and he was unable to maintain postwar relationships with his former military associates. Nevertheless, he recalls his service in Minnesota as rewarding, because it gave him a critical role in supplying urgently needed wartime labor.

Reflecting on his work in the camps, Schmiedeberg observes today that "there are always assignments a person would rather have . . . but in the army you take what you get."[14]

The care and oversight of the prisoners was accomplished not only through the U.S. military, but by other means as well. The human dimension of the camps is perhaps best seen in the work of War Prisoners Aid, an organization that provided recreational materials as well as educational and moral support. It was the most comprehensive humane service to POWs in Minnesota, overshadowing complementary efforts by the International Red Cross and several religious groups. Minnesota's representative was St. Olaf philosophy professor Howard Hong.

War Prisoners Aid was an agency of the World's Committee of the YMCA, based in Geneva, Switzerland, a neutral location that allowed the committee to serve the needs of imprisoned soldiers on both sides of any conflict. During World War I the YMCA had provided books, music, and religious services to approximately six million prisoners, an undertaking based on the organization's experience in earlier conflicts dating back to the Austro-Prussian War of 1866. Given the ominous signs of approaching world war, the YMCA decided in July 1939 that services to war prisoners would be one of its responsibilities, and it contacted various organizations to "arrive at a clear understanding regarding the eventual role of the YMCA in case of a world conflict." At the start of World War II, the YMCA's services to prisoners began at once, and approval for aid to POWs in the United States was finally granted in 1942.[15]

On March 31, 1942, the U.S. Provost Marshal General, Allen W. Gullion, informed War Prisoners Aid on behalf of the War Department that:

> . . . after careful consideration, it has been decided to accept your offer to have your War Prisoners Aid conduct recreational and welfare activities in the internment camps in continental United States, including the furnishing of libraries and special books, the providing of equipment for trades, the furnishing of materials for athletics, sports and physical education, and the stimulation of cultural and artistic interests such as art, dramatics, and music.[16]

This decision "required lengthy negotiations." By September 1943 the number of POWs interned in the United States was increasing rapidly enough to require the creation of a U.S. Administrative Unit of War Prisoners Aid and a search for additional field-secretaries. The visits from the secretaries were the "basic element of this extensive service."[17]

John R. Mott was head of the World Alliance of the Young Men's Christian Association, the federation of all national YMCA organizations, during World War II. From the beginning of the war Mott concerned himself with aid to interned prisoners, and his work took him to many college campuses as a speaker. On May 12, 1943, he arrived at St. Olaf College; the Northfield *Independent* invited the public to attend and "hear an outstanding speaker." Mott presented his talk entitled "[The] World Outlook and the Grounds for our Hopes"; the St. Olaf *Manitou Messenger* called it "triumphant, positive optimism."

Mott spoke of a movement which "is directed toward bringing in a new order by the removal of the causes of war and disturbances." Mott's final argument for world optimism was that "God, through the Holy Spirit, is summoning us to an unparalleled advance. He is working with us and through us!"[18]

A member of the audience that evening was St. Olaf professor Howard Hong. Following the lecture, Hong approached Mott and expressed an interest in working for the YMCA, particularly in its program for aid to POWs. Shortly thereafter, Mott relayed Hong's interest to the program's General Secretary, Dr. Tracy Strong. As a result, one of the first five secretaries the YMCA recruited for field work in the United States was Professor Hong.[19]

Born in North Dakota in 1912, Hong was raised in Willmar, Minnesota, where he graduated from high school. After a brief enrollment in business college, he started coursework at St. Olaf in the fall of 1930, where he eventually graduated with majors in English and philosophy. He began graduate work at the University of Washington, but moved back to Minnesota and received his doctorate in English and philosophy from the University of Minnesota in 1938. He accepted a teaching position at St. Olaf, but took a leave of absence during his first year, having received a grant to study the works of Søren Kierkegaard in Denmark. After a year abroad, Hong arrived back in the United States on the exact day whose consequences shaped his early career, September 1, 1939, the invasion of Poland and the start of World War II. He taught English and philosophy at St. Olaf only briefly before he was contacted by War Prisoners Aid.[20]

Hong gives two reasons for his interest in the program. As an undergraduate he "wrestled" with militarism, and he viewed the work of War Prisoners Aid as a respectable and inviting alternative to active military involvement in the war. Moreover, he had been working on Kierkegaard's *Works of Love*, which has been described as "one of the most elegant descriptions of what the imitation of Jesus—the life of Christian love—should be." The YMCA's work with prisoners, as Hong saw it, had all the essential qualities of such a life.[21]

By the autumn of 1943 Hong had started his job as a "field secretary," traveling to camps scattered over an immense area including the entire Mississippi Valley, from Canada to Arkansas in the south, and from Wyoming in the west to Illinois and Michigan in the east. He could not visit all the branch camps; many, including some in Minnesota, were in operation only a short time, most during the harvest season. Hong initially traveled by train and bus to the camps and to the main office of War Prisoners Aid in New York, where he and other secretaries wrote reports of their visits and aided the movement of camp supplies. In time, however, the field secretaries received automobiles. In his car, Hong carried certain "seed" materials, such as dictionaries and guitars, which the prisoners could start using immediately, a token of the bulk of supplies shipped from the main warehouse in New York.

Tracy Strong, left, with other YMCA officials in Geneva, Switzerland. Strong, the General Secretary of the War Prisoners Aid, was the first YMCA official to contact Hong about becoming a traveling secretary. *Courtesy of Kautz Family YMCA Archives*

These workers are packaging books in the YMCA warehouse at the New York Central Railroad Company in New York City. Over 2 million books and pamphlets were shipped out of this facility, including over 300,000 sent to POWs in the United States.[22] *Courtesy of Kautz Family YMCA Archives*

An advertisement printed by the War Prisoners Aid. *Courtesy of Kautz Family YMCA Archives*

Hong describes his job as an effort to help the prisoners "do what they would do in their best moments." It involved visiting the camps and determining how War Prisoners Aid could improve the internees' lives with educational and cultural materials. The job required Hong to be on the road four to five weeks continuously, working day and night. He received a salary and reimbursement for expenses. The long spells away were strenuous at times for his family, Hong recalls, but he was able to be at home between tours and for holidays.[23]

As the work progressed, Hong was no longer required to use the main War Prisoners Aid headquarters in New York as an office, and he eventually established his own office at home in Northfield, Minnesota. Occasionally he traveled to New York to meet with the other secretaries and to work on program policies. His immediate field-work supervisor, Dr. Ethan Colton, had been a secretary himself during World War I. Colton was an effective director, Hong declares, who often entrusted responsibility and detail to his secretaries. While in Northfield in May 1945, Dr. Colton gave a talk at St. Olaf about the War Prisoners Aid.[24]

During his travels, Hong wrote reports required by the Provost Marshal General for his continuous access to the compounds. These commentaries are an invaluable record of camp life. According to the Maschke Commission—the German government's most systematic effort to track German POWs during World War II—the YMCA documentation is particularly important because it provides a "neutral perspective." YMCA secretaries, the commission asserts, "were objective not only in the sense that they didn't favor a particular party, but rather that they had to report truthfully." A unique feature of the YMCA reports is that they observe both prisoners and the U.S. military together at an exact point in time.[25]

Locating suitable materials for the prisoners often required sustained effort. Hong vividly remembers an instance in Missouri, where he contacted a factory that used pieces of black walnut for gun stocks. He sent the necessary funds and address tags so 5,000 pieces could be mailed out for wood-carving projects. But much of Hong's work was simply to share ideas, and he recalls that "it meant a lot to [the prisoners] that anyone had some interest at all in helping them."

His personal impact on the prisoners, individually and collectively, varied from camp to camp, depending on such factors as the attitude of the camp commander. Some commanders disliked extended contact between Hong and the internees—"We were walking a tightrope," he recalls—but most were helpful, partly because they realized that their job would be eased by Hong's efforts. At many camps, guards initially accompanied him on his visits, but as the camp commanders became familiar with him and his work he was allowed to move freely. In jest he now speculates that his white hair, acquired at an early age, may have helped him overcome the prisoners' natural hesitancy when he first met them.[26]

Hong's general practice was to begin his visits early in the morning, around 7:30 or 8:00. If the camp was his last stop for the day, he would often stay overnight in the compound. Besides serving the prisoners' needs, he often attended their theater performances and other presentations. His academic background brought him special responsibilities; he was North American representative for International Student Services, a book service for prisoners that sometimes went to the length of locating rare or unusual books for a physics or history student. Hong also helped facilitate university correspondence courses for the prisoners, from the University of Minnesota among others, but such arrangements were usually standardized and required minimal effort from him. Additionally, he represented War Prisoners Aid on the National Lutheran Council and the National Council of Churches, which had POW ministries of their own.[27]

Minnesota's base camp in Algona, Iowa, was Hong's favorite. Its head, Col. Arthur Lobdell, was a "superb" commander in Hong's view; Lobdell "wanted conditions that would mitigate . . . the inevitable downpulls" in camp life. The Algona commander recognized that the prisoners had much free time, lived in close quarters, and suffered bouts of boredom, "so he welcomed everything that War Prisoners Aid could do." Since Lobdell had no objection to his lengthy discussions with the prisoners, Hong got well acquainted with them. His arrival with materials when the camp opened in 1944 prompted Lobdell to comment to a State Department official that "the best thing that ever happened to [the] Algona POW camp was Howard Hong." Unfortunately, Hong was not always so well received. In Concordia, Kansas, for example, when he was taking previously arranged photos of prisoners' masonry work, the commander rode up on his horse, demanded the camera, took it away, and removed the film.

Although his responsibilities required visits to camps in a large area of the United States, Hong was a distinct presence in the Minnesota branch camps. He visited at least eleven in 16 documented visits in one-and-a-half years. His help and advice to prisoners was appreciated

Howard Hong, right, presents John R. Mott in 1945 with $3,707 of voluntary contributions from German POWs. For his international church and missionary work, Mott shared the 1946 Nobel Peace Prize with pacifist Emily Greene Balch.[28] *Courtesy of Kautz Family YMCA Archives*

This chapel was established in a barrack at the base camp in Algona. Prisoners with useful trades helped furnish the chapel. A POW with a background as a jeweler made candlestick holders from empty tin cans; paraments were sewn by others. The YMCA offered reliable support for religious activities within the camps.[29] *Courtesy of Friedhelm Henkel*

German prisoners, under the direction of POW Eduard Kaib, used Portland Cement obtained through Howard Hong to make this half-life-sized manger scene at the Algona base camp. It is still displayed at Christmas each year. *Courtesy of Friedhelm Henkel*

by army personnel, local citizens, and the prisoners themselves. His last documented visit in Minnesota was to Wells on August 10, 1945. Shortly afterwards, the General Secretary of War Prisoners Aid, Tracy Strong, asked Hong to transfer his work overseas, and his work as a traveling secretary came to an end.[30]

In November, Hong held a lecture at St. Olaf about his work with the prisoners. The invitation in the college's newspaper stated that "he comes to us with a wealth of experience and knowledge." Hong left the United States in January 1946 to address the needs of German prisoners now back in the British Zone of Germany, pending their return to their homes. In August 1946, he returned to the United States and resumed teaching at St. Olaf, but at the urging of his bishop he left for Germany again in 1947 to aid displaced persons. His family accompanied him during the stay, which lasted over two years. Finally, in 1949, he returned to St. Olaf permanently, to teach and to pursue his much-interrupted study of Kierkegaard. Hong officially retired from his academic duties at St. Olaf in 1978, but taught classes periodically for years afterwards.[31]

The prisoners' gratitude for Hong's efforts is evident in the very last issue of the Algona base-camp POW newspaper for January 1946. "COLLECTION FOR THE Y.M.C.A." is prominently displayed on the last page. Citing a total donation of $8,314.87, the paper concludes that "we can all be very proud of this result." The report is signed by Camp Spokesman Friedhelm Henkel. A half-century later, Henkel, among others, remembers very clearly the services Hong rendered to the Algona prisoners:[32]

> Everything from Dr. Hong. Whether one needed a hearing aid, or glasses were broken, whether a prisoner needed a truss, whether one wanted to study and needed a particular book. Dr. Hong came once a week . . . and he took care of that.[33]

Alex Funke, the Algona camp-pastor, was close to Hong, and as a prisoner once visited Hong at his home in Northfield. Funke recalls his first encounter with Hong at the base camp in Algona:

> And now I have to tell. One day Howard Hong came. A man in uniform and he introduced himself. He came from the YMCA and from the American churches

and he went through the camp with me, and then he said, "how can I support you here in the camp?" Well, then we asked . . . we need sporting equipment, we need books for reading, we need music instruments, and a few weeks later came crate loads of books, and sporting equipment and then a rich cultural life unfolded in the camp. An orchestra originated, a trade school was established with lectures about Möricke, or German authors. . . . a very rich cultural life developed.[34]

Hong helped make camp life more bearable, more humane, and more rewarding than it might have been, for both the prisoners and their American captors. Largely because of him, the Minnesota camps served not merely as POW holding-grounds, but also as institutions meeting the needs of imprisoned soldiers.

"I never worked so hard in my life," Hong exclaims fifty years later. "I like to work, but it was there to do, and there was *good* reason to do it. But that reason was not political, it was not a matter of law, it was a matter of the universally human, you see."[35]

Hong was one of eight visitors, seven full-time and one part-time, who aided over 500 camps in the United States, where the efforts of War Prisoners Aid met with their greatest success anywhere in the world. A YMCA report prepared after the war traced the program's effectiveness to "the high living standards in the United States," and explained that "the physical setup of most U.S. camps was better than that of any other country, affording more facilities, more room and better barracks thus making it easier to plan and carry out any phase of the program."[36]

The work of War Prisoners Aid ended early in the United States; the American camps closed officially on June 30, 1946, followed by the American warehouse a month later. Work continued, however, with POWs elsewhere in the world. Internees in the U.S., a total of over 400,000, were just a fraction of the nearly 6 million men in many countries helped by War Prisoners Aid during and after the war.[37]

While the YMCA secretaries did their down-to-earth work of delivering books, instruments, and other materials, the International Committee of the Red Cross was keeping its own camp visitors busy. According to Germany's Maschke Commission, "the long-standing

Tickets for this 1945 theater presentation in Algona, the "Miser," were sold in the camp's canteen for 20 cents. Using materials supplied by the YMCA, painters, hairdressers, and others created this stage and presentation; the hairdressers made wigs for every performer. Several prisoners are shown dressed as women. As a sign of appreciation, the German prisoners gave this professional-quality photograph to their spokesman, Friedhelm Henkel.[38] *Courtesy of Friedhelm Henkel*

Howard Hong in his Lake Superior cabin near Hovland, Minnesota, in 1995. "The point is we could do so little, you see. But if they wanted to do something, then we could help. That was the whole argument."[39] *Author's photo*

friendship between both of these organizations and their presidents . . . would have fruitful consequences for the prisoners." The combined work of the YMCA and the ICRC accounts for the majority of services that reached Minnesota's POWs; monthly meetings between their representatives and other officials helped coordinate their efforts.[40]

Red Cross secretaries, officially known as "delegates," were concerned with whether or not the provisions of the Geneva Convention of 1929 were being honored. From its Geneva headquarters, the ICRC strove for the "continual improvement and diffusion of Geneva Conventions," and thus "intervenes, during armed conflicts, in favor of wounded, sick, prisoners of war, and civilians." Under the direction of Max Huber during World War II, the ICRC forwarded supplies and worked to improve the transmission of messages and letters. Its most visible and extensive service to POWs, however, was expressed in its mission: "To visit the camps and see whether the treatment granted to the inmates was in harmony with the principles of the Convention." Although inspection tours were not explicitly allowed for in the Geneva treaty, the Committee relied on the Convention's Article 88 and on a tradition of past ICRC visits.[41]

The ICRC selected a core group of Swiss national volunteers for these visits, often doctors, competent to answer questions about health, or persons trained in the law, who could efficiently interpret the Convention's provisions. These delegates had to obtain permission to enter the compounds. Once inside, they had no control over the camp's operation; moreover, they had no way to penalize offenders when Convention guidelines were not being met. They were able, however, to "suggest improvements, and to have deficiencies supplied and abuses corrected." Delegates customarily registered their visits before arriving at the camps, a procedure they welcomed since it increased their chances of meeting influential people.[42]

From September 1939 until the end of 1946, the ICRC made over 11,000 visits to POW camps around the world. The delegates were generally well received by camp commanders, but their work was shadowed by the ongoing fear that they would not be allowed to return, or to inspect other camps. Since camp conditions could change quickly, two visits to a particular camp were considered better than one. If concerns arose during the first visit, a second would establish whether any corrective action had been taken in the meanwhile. Nevertheless, a shortcoming that these visits shared with those of the YMCA was the delegate's inability to monitor camp conditions over a long period of time.[43]

Like their YMCA counterparts, Red Cross delegates wrote accounts of their visits. The general format of these reports corresponds to the rules of the Geneva Convention, under subheadings such as work, hygiene, and pay. Of the 570 ICRC reports submitted from the United States in 1944 and 1945, eight are from Minnesota, representing seven camps visited during two trips through the state. The ICRC's reports, like the YMCA's, are invaluable eye-witness accounts of camp life, and determinedly objective. Germany's Maschke Commission considered them "of high dependability" and "irreplaceable."[44]

The ICRC's first documented tour of Minnesota, originating at the base camp in Algona, brought a delegate now identifiable only as "Dr. Zehnder" to Fairmont, New Ulm, and Owatonna, on March 9 and 10, 1945. He could not have been in the state long; records place him at a camp in Clarinda, Iowa, five days later. No information is available on Zehnder. He appears to have been a medical doctor, as suggested by his title. Although the written report seems to be his work, he was apparently accompanied by at least one other person, since he refers to "we" and "us."[45]

A second Red Cross trip in September 1945 resulted in five more visits to Minnesota camps. All were made by a "Mr. Schnyder," apparently accompanied, like Zehnder, by at least one other visitor. As before, the ICRC delegates began with a visit to Algona, including a discussion with Col. Lobdell about the Minnesota logging camps. The delegates visited Owatonna, Faribault, and Montgomery on September 13. On the following day they traveled north to report conditions at Deer River and Bena. In the course of the trip they discussed POW work in Minnesota canneries with the president of the Minnesota Canners Association, in Minneapolis.[46]

Exactly how many prisoners passed through Minnesota camps is unknown, but a cautious estimate suggests between 3,500 and 4,500; the use of POW workers peaked just under 3,000 in September 1945. Only the camps at Princeton, Olivia, Wells, and Warren housed Italian prisoners, employed at the beginning and end of the camps' brief history. Their number was just a few hundred, by contrast with Germans, numbering in the thousands. Japanese prisoners were not employed in Minnesota and were not detained at any Minnesota camp. A camp near Savage, Minnesota, is often misunderstood to have been a Japanese POW camp, but it actually housed Japanese-Americans working for the U.S. Army's Intelligence Service.[47]

Most of the Italian prisoners brought to Minnesota were captured in North Africa. The Germans, on the other hand, arrived from many different war zones. A large contingent came from the German Afrika Korps, which surrendered to the British Eighth Army in 1943. Others were sent from Sicily, Italy, and other locations in Europe, including a sizable group from France and Germany following the Normandy Invasion. The age of prisoners from all Axis countries varied greatly, but most would have been in their early to late twenties.

The prisoners themselves had a share in the administration of the branch camps. A senior POW non-com served as their spokesman, approved by the American commander and the majority of prisoners. He acted as an official contact between the Americans and the POWs on matters such as church services. The spokesmen often demanded military-style obedience, and prisoners rarely disobeyed; this behavior was appreciated by the American military since it reflected favorably on their work. POWs with business experience commonly worked in the canteen under supervision of the camp commander and the First Sergeant. In addition, motor maintenance was often entrusted to POWs, who also served as drivers.[48]

For medical and administrative reasons, prisoners were freely transferred back and forth between branch camps and base camps, as well as between branches. Sometimes one camp would "lend" another a large number of prisoners for a short period. Prisoners from Bena, for example, were the majority of POWs used seasonally in Ortonville; they returned to Bena when the Ortonville camp closed in the fall. A permanent transfer occurred in 1944, when the Howard Lake camp closed and its prisoners were the first arrivals at the newly opened Bird Island camp. When seasonal branch camps were closed in Minnesota, the general practice was to return the prisoners to the base camp for the winter months.

The issue of prisoners' health was taken up by non-military agencies. In July 1944, for example, the U.S. Public Health Service toured four of the Minnesota camps and checked on the medical history of the prisoners. The Service was concerned that some of the POWs might have contracted malaria while in North Africa; men who had a past record of the disease and could spread it to a civilian were examined for a revival of the disease.[49]

The prisoners were generally well received by Minnesota citizens. There was a good deal of interaction between them, and locals typically accepted the war-captive as just another laborer. Often the POWs received better treatment and were more highly respected than other seasonal workers in Minnesota, particularly foreign workers, as suggested by the following excerpt from an editorial in the *Blue Earth Post*, March 23, 1944:

> Personally, we shall miss the Jamaicans, in case none are brought in. We watched them at times, and their slow-motion style of work sort of lulled us into a relaxed tempo of our own. Some were so adept at step-saving that if the truck went too far they would stand there, a forkful of peas held in the air, until the truck backed up. We don't know how often this happened throughout the country or area, but we saw it at least once.
>
> In regard to prisoners of war, that is entirely a different question. We see no reason for resentment toward German or Italian prisoners working in our fields. These are men who fought for their own countries, were taken in battle and are subject to international laws regarding prisoners of war.[50]

Of course, the local response to the prisoners was not always affirmative. Taking issue, for example, with the Geneva Convention's rule allowing POW officers to refrain from working, the same editorial at Blue Earth concludes: "We pamper our enemy officers, permit them to strut around with monocle in eye, and later on send them home, to plan a new and bigger war. What humbug!"[51]

The reaction of organized labor was generally one of disapproval, significant enough to prevent the use of prisoners in three cities. An application to establish a camp near East Grand Forks in 1943 was dropped because of union opposition. The president of the Grand Forks Trades and Labor Assembly, claiming that workers would not work next to those they were fighting against, protested the use of prisoners in a local potato hydration plant. Ironically, the prisoners were needed for help in building a warehouse, not at the plant. In Mankato, AFL opposition "barred the way" for the use of POWs by three businesses, including a foundry and a granite company. A request for prisoner labor at Rochester's St. Mary's Hospital in 1944 was not acted on because of union objections.[52]

Nearly two years of combat had passed since Pearl Harbor by the time Axis prisoners arrived in Minnesota. The state's two-and-a-half million inhabitants were preoccupied with war, and the presence of captive soldiers in their midst was simply another sign of the times. For Minnesotans in the small communities and rural areas where the camps were located, the POW experience became a part of their everyday lives.

Minnesota's camps exhibited all the variety of POW camps nationally during World War II. They were established to serve various practical objectives, lasted various lengths of time, and struggled with various difficulties. Their history, as the following chapters are meant to suggest, is not merely a dry recital of bureaucratic successes and failures, but a story about people.

In the balance of this book, the camps are described individually, grouped roughly according to the type of work—in agriculture, canning, multiple industries, and logging—performed by the prisoners. Seven of the camp histories include "Prisoner Perspectives"; each summarizes the present-day recollections of a German POW stationed at a given camp.

Chapter 3

Farm-Labor Camps

Minnesota's seasonal farm-labor camps, established solely for agriculture, benefited greatly from a state-wide network of county organizations that served their labor needs. County extension agents, first of all, had local duties similar to those of Minnesota's extension director Paul Miller, who dealt with farm-labor problems at the state level. Officially the county agents were "responsible for organization of Trade Center Committees, for arranging for volunteer placement officers on recommendation of committees, and for maintaining supervision of placement centers," all established to fill employers' requests for labor.

At the request of the state extension service, county boards of commissioners helped form county farm "labor" or "help" committees, including among others the county auditor and representatives from the county commissioners, the county war board, and the Office of Civilian Defense. The active recruitment of local students and adults, however, was performed by the local Trade Center Committee, which included mayors, newspaper editors, high school teachers, and superintendents.

Local offices of the United States Employment Service worked closely with county agents, in part to relay information on deficits and surpluses of labor. Additionally, there were volunteer "placement officers" throughout the state, as well as so-called "labor" and "office" assistants hired to support the county agent. By the end of 1944, recruitment and placements were made at 736 different Minnesota locations.

One function of the farm-labor committees was to select a "wage board," which set the wages for foreign and POW labor. The county agent served as the chairman. Twenty-eight county wage boards were in operation by 1945, along with a state wage board for potato growers. Standardized farm wages were intended to avoid problems such as arose in Lyon County in 1945, where some "over enthusiastic" farmers paid a significantly higher wage to workers than what the wage board had agreed upon; subsequently, other workers expected the same amount.[1]

The Princeton and Moorhead camps provided labor for large commercial farms. Near Princeton, businessman and farmer Odin Odegard operated one of the largest potato farms in Minnesota; together with another farmer he raised about 700 acres of onions, carrots, beets, cabbage, and potatoes. On an even larger scale, the two truck farms contracting for POW labor near Moorhead totaled over 6,000 acres. The Hollandale camp was established for two short periods to harvest vegetables on several farms amid a 15,000-acre tract drained in the 1920s. The remaining three camps, Ada, Crookston, and Warren, were all established on short notice and nearly simultaneously in late fall 1945 in the Red River Valley. Fears of early frost and massive losses in the potato and sugar beet fields of northwest Minnesota prompted a quick response from the appropriate authorities. All three camps were thus short-lived, but they were of critical importance in harvesting the crops for 1945, the largest in the area's history.[2]

Guards usually accompanied the POWs at Moorhead and Princeton to the workplace, but farmers at the other camps acted as the prisoners' supervisor. To acquire POWs for work, farmers either contacted the labor committee or the county agent directly. The farmer generally provided transportation and paid in advance for a full workday, usually 8 to 12 hours. The U.S. government collected an hourly wage between 50 and 60 cents for the use of each POW.

The Prisoner Perspective in this section is that of a German soldier interned as a teenager in Moorhead. In addition to reminiscing about his stay, he reflects on his unfortunate return home to the Russian zone of postwar Germany.

Princeton

Mille Lacs County

September 5, 1943–October 30, 1943

The Princeton camp, lasting two months, resulted from the first application for POW labor in Minnesota. The process moved quickly soon after state extension director Paul Miller announced on July 20, 1943, that recent changes in regulations would increase the likelihood of prisoners being used in the state. Three days later, farmers Odin J. Odegard and J. W. Thompson presented their application to Miller for a group of 100 Italian POWs. Captain Charles M. Lee of Camp Clark, Missouri, arrived the following week for a two-day inspection of the prospective campsite. He concluded that there was a real need for the prisoners. A standard wage of three dollars a day was agreed upon at a village-hall meeting.[3]

The camp was located on the Odegard farm, an old lake bed of 2,200 acres known as the "Big Bog," ten miles north of Princeton and mostly in Isanti County. With two dogs named Arno and Poocie, brought from Africa as mascots, the Italian POWs arrived on September 5, 1943, just when the local Catholic priest had begun arrangements for their early-morning Sunday Mass. The St. Paul *Dispatch* described how "the buses and the whistle of a train at an unusual time, brought people flocking to the station." The prisoners spent their first night in an onion-drying shed recently built on the farm. The following day they cleared and mowed the area where tents were to be set up for them, and where a fence and electric lights had already been supplied. Odegard's crops had started poorly in the spring, but they were in good condition for the harvest, and the Italians were immediately helpful.[4]

The prisoners worked from 7 a.m. to 6 p.m. daily, harvesting onions and potatoes and loading them on trucks and into warehouses. Fifteen POWs were transported to Princeton in a Model A school bus every day to sort potatoes in warehouses near the railroad. After the onions were pulled, the POWs sorted them according to quality. Potatoes were piled in twelve empty store buildings in Princeton. The prisoners worked alongside other laborers on the Odegard farm, including some area businessmen and over 400 boys and girls who weeded crops.[5]

Italian prisoners on the Odin Odegard farm near Princeton in 1943. They were housed in the tents behind them. The farmhouse is at the rear of the photo; Odegard sits in the foreground. *Courtesy of Robert Odegard*

Italian prisoners posing with a pheasant. *Courtesy of Robert Odegard*

Princeton POWs are shown working with vegetables harvested on the Odegard farm. When they learned of Italy's surrender, they were quoted saying: "now we should work harder to grow more food here in the United States to help feed Italy."[6] *Courtesy of Robert Odegard*

Italian prisoners pause to have their photograph taken. *Courtesy of Robert Odegard*

The county extension officer reported that the prisoners were "life savers" because local students, beginning the school year, were unavailable. As the harvest progressed, there was still a shortage of labor; the school was asked to allow 50 to 60 students to work, but the request was denied because of a possible reduction in school aid. A call for more prisoners went out, and 50 arrived in early October. Thus, POWs were the core of the labor force on the Odegard farm in 1943, harvesting thousands of bushels of vegetables and potatoes.[7]

Soon after their arrival at the camp, the prisoners heard the news of Italy's surrender. According to one newspaper, some "hung their heads and looked downcast, while others smiled and some said they were glad it was over with." The Minneapolis *Star Journal* reported how interpreters and guards reassured the prisoners "that unconditional surrender was the best thing that could have happened to Italy." Some of the men were not easily convinced and "feared reprisals from Germany on their families."[8]

In their spare time, the POWs spent time drawing, wood carving, and playing sports including baseball and soccer. One prisoner perhaps regretted his choice of activity when he broke his leg during a soccer game and was taken to the Fort Snelling hospital. Another prisoner went to Fort Snelling with a fractured vertebra, suffered when a truck tipped onto its side. Despite the incident, the commanding officer of Camp Clark, Missouri, visiting Princeton around that time, was well pleased with the arrangements. The prisoners cooked their own meals at the camp; local visitors, sampling the meat patties the POWs had made, "pronounced them the best hamburger sandwiches they had ever eaten." The prisoners also purchased additional items at their canteen, including beer and cigarettes. On occasion Odegard would give additional packs of cigarettes to the prisoners free of charge.[9]

Odegard maintained that as many as 50 prisoners could be employed on his farm throughout the year, but the POWs stayed only until late October. The Princeton *Union* reported that the men left "apparently in high spirits. They had done a good season's work, and they knew it and they had really enjoyed being in this section of Minnesota." The camp at Princeton never reopened. During the rest of the war years, the Odegard family reduced the size of their farming operation and recruited a sufficient number of local workers. Despite the brevity of its existence, the Princeton camp helped set a precedent for the efficient, humane use of POW labor in Minnesota.[10]

At the closing banquet, Odin Odegard stands in the middle directly behind the Italian cook. On Odin's left is the camp commander, and on his right is his son Robert. *Courtesy of Robert Odegard*

At the Princeton armory, prisoners and their employers enjoy a dinner before the POWs leave for Missouri. "O.K.," the nickname the prisoners gave Mr. Odegard, is iced on the top of the cake. Odegard, right, poses with the Italian cook directly behind him, holding plates. Captain Harrington, the Princeton camp commander, is seated behind Odegard.[11] *Courtesy of Robert Odegard*

> # Moorhead
> # Clay County
>
> ## May 28, 1944–November 1944
> ## August 1945–November 1945

Paul Horn, a farmer in the Moorhead area since 1929 and a member of the local Farm Help Program, joined Henry (Hank) Peterson in initiating the camp at Moorhead. They had learned of the availability of prisoners in the local newspaper. Horn, who spoke German, traveled with Peterson to Omaha to make arrangements for the reception of POWs. Years later, Horn, who heeded recommendations for the prisoners' housing facilities, asserted that the official arrangements "weren't as strict or as well-planned as they might have been."[12]

May 1944 brought local opposition to the proposed camp location in Moorhead, in a large barn at Twelfth Avenue and Elm Street. Although an earlier meeting that year had showed "favorable sentiment" in the use of prisoners to relieve labor shortages, rumors opposing the camp and its location in town continued to circulate, and Horn concluded that the camp would probably not open if the community mobilized against it.[13]

Alternative plans were made; forty German prisoners arrived under the command of Second Lieutenant Richard M. Blair on May 28, 1944, and spent their first evening at Paul Horn's farm in tents. Additional prisoners came by train from Algona later in May. A substitute for the barn at Twelfth and Elm was found in the warehouse of the Onion Growers Warehouse Association, at Twenty-First Street and Fourth Avenue North. There, the POWs themselves helped install sewer connections and water for the building. Plans were made for a guard tower at this location, but apparently it was never built. The living arrangements were enhanced by a small fish-pool, added to the barracks by the prisoners themselves. Soon after the POWs had settled into their new surroundings, they started work at the Peterson and Horn farms, hoeing and weeding beets and potatoes in summer and harvesting them in the fall.[14]

The Moorhead POWs were only a small proportion of the workers employed in Clay County at the peak of the growing and harvesting seasons. A total of 4,291 workers were counted in 1944, including

German POWs in Moorhead roofing a building on the Hank Peterson farm in 1944. An American guard stands in the upper right. Hong reported in 1944 that "all the men are housed together in a large building formerly used as a warehouse. It is rather dimly lighted, but it is at the same time cool on hot days."[15] *Courtesy of Northwest Minnesota Historical Center*

German prisoners posing around a jeep on the Peterson farm in 1944. Two guards, one wearing a helmet, are standing in the rear. Two more, one with a helmet near the front, the other kneeling at the lower right, are also visible. Henry (Hank) Peterson appears in the center-rear in a dark hat and tie. *Courtesy of Northwest Minnesota Historical Center*

Burial service of POW Franz Hummer at the Algona base camp. A Catholic service was held prior to this in the camp's chapel. Flowers for the funeral were provided by the Algona Flower Club, as requested by camp authorities.[16] *Courtesy of John Slevin, A. T. Lobdell Manuscript Collection.*

Firing-squad salute for POW Franz Hummer at the Algona base camp. In a letter to the Red Cross about the interment, Algona camp commander Col. Lobdell wrote that "it was altogether a very human scene. We regretted the accident." Hummer was the only POW to die in Minnesota.[17] *Courtesy of John Slevin, A. T. Lobdell Manuscript Collection*

some interned Japanese-Americans relocated from the West Coast. Although beets and potatoes absorbed much of their effort, prisoners performed a number of other small jobs for farmers Horn and Peterson. One prisoner liked to work with a tractor; others gardened cabbages and tomatoes. After the day's work, many POWs simply relaxed in camp.[18]

Within a month of the camp's establishment, a minor stir accompanied the death of prisoner Franz Hummer, who drowned on a very hot day when the POWs had been given permission to swim at a gravel pit seven miles southeast of town. The guards had warned the prisoners about the danger of a drop-off and had posted themselves nearby to serve as lifeguards; an American officer was also present. A routine check revealed that Hummer was missing. The Moorhead fire department and police chief arrived with a lifeboat and grappling equipment. After more than two hours, rescuers managed to scoop the body out with a dragbucket located at the gravel pit. Hummer was transported to a Moorhead funeral home and eventually brought to Algona for burial. A six-man coroner's jury ruled the death accidental. The Kossuth County *Advance* reported later that Hummer had given "no outcry or evidence of struggle" and was believed to have been "stricken with cramps." The guards were eventually cleared of any blame.[19]

In his report for August 1944, Howard Hong suggested that the prisoners' leisure time "can in its emptiness be the occasion for undesirable developments." The POWs did have activities outside work, however, including sports all week and church every Sunday, usually alternating between Catholic and Lutheran services.[20]

Later that month, Moorhead's commander Lt. Blair spoke to the Fargo Rotary Club about difficulties with the prisoners. The club reported in its minutes that the prisoners "are head strong and positively refuse to learn a better way of doing anything." Blair answered questions about postwar Germany and Germans in general. Of the prisoners, he asserted, "they are 'cocky' and arrogant. They are deeply resentful of being penned up with barbed wire for they feel that they are the superior race."[21]

A change of command occurred in September, after Col. Lobdell at Algona had received reports of camp conditions below the standards he required, including American soldiers careless in their military courtesy and casual in their appearance. He relieved Lt. Blair of command and replaced him with Second Lieutenant Bertrand Davis on September 28.[22]

In November 1944 the POWs returned to the base camp at Algona; Henry Peterson and Paul Horn had already contacted the Algona authorities in February about acquiring POWs for the 1945 season. To smooth local relations when the 1945 work-year began in July, Moorhead residents were given opportunities to learn about the POW camp being established for its second year. Camp guards included returnees from the war, men who were originally from the Moorhead area or who had entered the service there.[23]

Before the Moorhead camp reopened in 1945, an unusual incident brought to light some local sentiments about the camp. In February a Moorhead citizen wrote a rambling letter to the Department of Justice in Washington, protesting any planned return of German POWs to Clay County. He claimed that 50 percent of the county's residents were "Pro-Hitler" and feared that renewed use of POWs would make his community "a breeding spot for the survival of this Hitler craze." The writer also alleged that "Mr. Peterson was severely beaten by an ex-serviceman for treating these prisoners at nearby taverns." The letter was turned over to the Army, and Col. Lobdell at Algona was directed to investigate the incident.

Algona's legal officer, Lieutenant Arthur Perry, interviewed the letter writer and twelve others, including the mayor, the police chief, and various bar owners and waitresses. The letter writer contradicted himself, was uncertain who Mr. Peterson was and could not confirm that any such person had been assaulted. Two people did assert, however, that they had seen Mr. Peterson buy beer for POWs. Lt. Perry also learned during the course of the investigation that a road-closing near the camp, aggressively enforced by Lt. Blair the previous summer, had irritated city officials; some of the city's "best citizens" had been improperly accused of trespassing. The investigation made it clear that Lt. Blair's poor public-relations policies had generated some ill will toward the camp.[24]

Nevertheless, the camp reopened in August. Labor-saving devices implemented early in the war, such as sweep rakes and hay stackers, helped ensure the satisfactory completion of the harvest in 1945; the extension office demonstrated the use of these devices. The labor supply was sufficient, except for a short time during the sugar beet harvest. Potato picking was largely assigned to women and girls; prisoners were used in vegetable fields, later for potato and beet harvesting.[25]

German POWs and civilian workers pause for a photograph while doing odd jobs on the Hank Peterson farm in 1944. Hermann Massing, second row, third from the right, spent nearly five months on the Peterson farm in 1944. He first worked in Peterson's fields of onions and beets; later, as seen here, he worked as a painter on the farm. He spent most of the remaining time as a prisoner in the southeastern part of the U.S. before his return to Germany in 1946.[26] *Courtesy of Northwest Minnesota Historical Center*

POWs picking onions near Moorhead. *Courtesy of Northwest Minnesota Historical Center*

Moorhead POWs painting a barn on the Peterson farm in 1944. *Courtesy of Northwest Minnesota Historical Center*

POW, left, posing on a tractor with civilian workers at the Peterson farm. *Courtesy of Northwest Minnesota Historical Center*

A few local women and girls were always at the Peterson farm harvesting vegetables, and an amusing incident grew out of their presence there. St. Ansgar Hospital, located just outside Moorhead near the POW camp, employed and housed young girls during the war. Cordelia Bloch, age 16, and a young friend from the hospital often went to the Peterson farm to pick vegetables during their free time from 1:00 to 4:00 in the afternoon. Peterson, a good friend of the Franciscan Sisters who worked at the hospital, allowed them to pick any vegetables they wanted. They were cautioned by one of the nuns not to mingle with the working POWs, but Cordelia and her friend thought the warning was "crazy," since they were not personally at war with the men. The girls started visiting the farm when the nuns were not present. Both could converse in German, and they became acquainted with two POWs named Hans and Kurt.

In the course of several encounters, the girls and the POWs argued over who was going to win the war. "We never lost any war and we won't lose this one," the girls claimed. "This one you will lose," the POWs answered. When an American soldier at the camp saw the girls talking to one of the POWs, he warned the two about conversing with prisoners, so they began meeting in a hidden section of a nearby field.

The farm wife who owned the field confronted them one day, assuming that they were smoking cigarettes. On the next day, the Moorhead police arrived in two cars; they apprehended the girls and the prisoners, placing them in separate cars. At the local jail, they questioned the girls separately and together, threatened to cut their hair off, and gave them fried eggs and potatoes for supper.

The girls were taken back to St. Ansgar Hospital and questioned further by the camp commander and the police. They were restricted to the hospital grounds and forbidden to go into the hospital room of any POW. Apart from a visit by her father addressing her misbehavior, the incident quickly faded into memory for Cordelia.

Partly because the sisters in Moorhead had always been so kind to her, Cordelia entered the Franciscan community in 1947. Years later, in 1979, when she learned of a woman who had been jailed for stealing food for her children, Cordelia thought back to her own prison experience. In 1985 she inquired into visiting procedures at local prisons; soon she started weekly visits to the jail in Little Falls, Minnesota. She brought the prisoners reading material and often shared her own jail experience with them. In 1988 she discontinued her visits when she moved on to another ministry, but she always remembered gratefully how gracious the St. Ansgar Sisters were to her in 1945. Fifty years later, Sister Cordelia wonders what happened to Hans and Kurt, after the incident that had such a strong impact on her own life.[27]

Cordelia Bloch's brush with the law was unusual; no major problems arose during the two terms of POW labor in Moorhead. By the time the prisoners left in November 1945, they had arrived at a smooth relationship with the people they worked for. Security was lax; camp guards arrived in the fields each day with the POWs and watched them from the shade of their trucks. The guards were often at local bars during their time off, and one was eventually court martialed by the camp commander for sleeping during his duty period. According to Peterson, these Americans were like "hillbillies," more trouble than the prisoners.[28]

The only recorded problem with the POWs themselves was a minor act of sabotage when prisoners broke a pump with a sledgehammer; four prisoners responsible for the incident were returned to Algona. In general, however, the prisoners were reliable workers; Horn stated years later that "they were human beings and quite nice people and we got along very well." At times the POWs were given extra food during the day, and sometimes Peterson would bring home cakes the POWs had baked at the camp. Prisoners occasionally went to local bars with guards or farmers. Peterson himself bought beer for the prisoners from time to time, and according to the farm's bookkeeper he was "criticized quite a bit" for that. Undoubtedly he was liked by many of the prisoners.[29] A letter from former POW Alois Sauer in 1948 seems to capture the general sentiment:

> I want to express in these few words my heartiest thanks for everything you did for my comrades and myself when we were still prisoners. You was indeed a true friend and a good master to us, and you will be kept all times in my remembrance.[30]

Letters written to Peterson and Horn after the war document the experiences of POWs both during their stay in Moorhead and after hostilities were over. Bill Horn received at least two letters, but the greatest detail is to be found in those addressed to Hank Peterson over three decades, the majority written during the immediate postwar

Harvey Fleshner, a guard and medic at the Moorhead camp in 1944, standing directly outside the Moorhead compound where prisoners are drying their laundry. Due to his skills as a medic, Fleshner eventually helped evacuate wounded soldiers from Europe.[31] *Courtesy of Harvey Fleshner Collection, Clay County Historical Society*

The POW spokesman, left, is shown with the cook just outside the Moorhead compound in 1944. Empty beer and milk bottles are stacked near the entrance. *Courtesy of Harvey Fleshner Collection, Clay County Historical Society*

years, 1946 through 1948. The ex-prisoners sent wedding and family pictures, reminisced about their experiences in Moorhead, and described the conditions that many Germans faced after the war. Some had returned to broken homes and families. A common concern with rationing and the inability to obtain clothing and other commodities was echoed by all the former POWs, a dilemma inspiring many to ask politely for "care" packages.

One POW exclaimed that his time on the Peterson farm was the "best of my life," and the experience of being invited into Peterson's home was celebrated by another as "a particular joy to my heart." Peterson's former workers wrote not only to express their good wishes, but also to inquire about other POWs, hired hands on the farm, and relatives. One prisoner, having returned to Germany in 1947, conveyed his greetings to Mrs. Peterson in a separate note; he remembered well the time when he was permitted to take a walk with her. A number of letters expressed the writers' desire to return to the United States and work on Peterson's farm or somewhere else.[32]

Some ex-prisoners had returned quickly to Europe and home shortly thereafter; others had spent up to a year and a half in camps in either France or England before returning to Germany. Certain Moorhead POWs sent to France experienced unpleasant treatment. One, injured in an accident and hospitalized, was still there as late as May 1948. His papers had been taken away on his arrival in France, and his parents, having learned of their son's good treatment at Moorhead, wrote to Peterson themselves. Another former prisoner in France, injured while working, was thankful that the injury enabled him to return to Germany sooner than otherwise. Curiously, POWs from Silesia or with relatives there gave the most desperate reports. A POW leader, interpreter for the Moorhead prisoners in 1945, wrote that his parents in Silesia had lost everything. His personal situation was an improvement over theirs, because he had found employment as an interpreter for the Allied armed forces.[33]

The letters written to Peterson after the war create the impression of a camp in which the bond between employer and prisoners transcended that of a mere working relationship. One of Peterson's correspondents was Werner Knauer, whose reminiscences a half-century after his experiences on the farm are summarized below.

Prisoner Perspective
Werner Knauer

At nineteen, Werner Knauer was one of the youngest POWs on the Peterson farm in the fall of 1945. He had become a soldier at seventeen in the fall of 1943 and had been trained for a Flak battery as a radio operator, relaying information to the unit's guns on the location of enemy aircraft. Knauer was captured shortly after the D-Day invasion on June 17, 1944, in Cherbourg, France. He recalls that his unit included 20 recently trained recruits, fairly inexperienced, but unlike many other new soldiers who ran into cubby holes, yelling and screaming.

His unit had occupied a high point on a large hill; when the unit finally retreated under fire, it was reduced to just 30 of its original 180 men. After their capture, Private First Class Knauer and others with insignia suggesting rank were rushed to a nearby barn. For Knauer the moment was the most critical of the war; he feared that he and his fellows would be executed and their bodies disposed of in the barn. An American soldier assumed control of the prisoners, however, and nothing happened. Knauer and his fellows were relieved to have been captured by Americans, since they really feared Canadians, rumored to have had their special units stationed in England for the invasion.

Knauer was taken to England and questioned closely about where he had received his Flak training and about his knowledge of the various functions of Flak units. Next, at Glasgow, Scotland, the POWs were forced to sing marching songs as they disembarked from the landing boats into temporary camps. Knauer eventually boarded the Queen Mary with 2,000 wounded Americans, 4,000 to 6,000 POWs, and a crew of about 1,000. The lunchroom, he recalls, was like that of the "best hotel." U-boat alarms sounded on the trip to the United States, but a U-boat crew on board the ship assured the other prisoners of the improbability of a successful attack.

With the invasion and Europe behind him, it was clear to Knauer that the war had already been lost, but his longest role in the conflict, that of a POW, was just beginning. He traveled from New York to Algona, enjoying a relaxed train-trip after the guards decided that three prisoners to a four-seat section allowed ample leg room. The comfort of the trip was enhanced by cola and cocoa served to the POWs; Knauer and his fellow prisoners simply "couldn't comprehend it."

Starting with their capture in England and continuing until they arrived at Algona, Knauer and the others were segregated many times according to age, name, and type of service. Personal relationships were thus hard to maintain. Walking quickly through a small door and pushed along, Knauer received inoculations in each arm after he arrived in Algona. Frightened, he and others tried to warn the POWs directly behind them but the line was moving too fast. All the POWs eventually became slightly ill, but a doctor assured them that they had not received the "death injection" some had feared.

Soon after Knauer's arrival at Algona, one of the films shown in the camp theater was a documentary, with the mighty Queen Mary docking in New York. Afrika Korps veterans, who had traveled mostly in Liberty Ships, refused to believe the recent arrivals' eager reports of their experiences aboard the Queen Mary. Knauer worked for various farmers around Algona and remembers not a single instance of bad treatment from any of them, although some of German heritage were apparently ashamed of the POWs and avoided any contact. One farmer, however, enraged by a local school teacher who had been portraying the POWs as barbarians, received permission from camp authorities to bring the prisoners to the school. The Germans were lined up in the school yard, and the children were asked to come out and see the young men for themselves.

The branch camps offered even greater freedom than the main camp at Algona. Knauer eventually spent most of his time in branch camps at Tabor and Eldora, Iowa, and at Moorhead in the fall of 1945. Hank Peterson, Knauer recalls, was always friendly with the POWs in Moorhead. Guards were rarely sent with the POW details into the fields. Besides collecting potato bugs from the undersides of the plants, Knauer harvested onions for Peterson. He and others worked alongside migrant Mexicans, who were being paid 50 cents for each sack of onions they harvested. The POWs, aware of this, made an agreement to pick sacks of onions for the Mexicans at 25 cents apiece. Thus, without working, the Mexicans received 25 cents per sack; the POWs, for their part, received U.S. currency. After too many such agreements were made, however, the arrangement was discovered by the employer and the two groups of workers were assigned to separate fields. Knauer very clearly remembers holding his first green dollar in his hands, money he received from Mexicans for sacks of onions he had harvested.

Knauer recalls, rather proudly, that at Moorhead he "learned to eat

This photograph shows many of the German prisoners who arrived in 1945 for work on the Peterson farm. Werner Knauer is standing in the second row, immediately to the right of the prisoner holding the dog. Onions are stacked in the warehouse behind them; the Peterson Farm sales-office sign is partially visible in the upper right of the picture. Hank Peterson is kneeling fourth from left in the front row. *Courtesy of Werner Knauer*

Werner Knauer near his home in Germany in 1995. *Author's photo*

tomatoes." Peterson sent food to the camp with the prisoners, often tomatoes; dishes such as tomato soup became a regular part of the menu. Peterson often supplied so many tomatoes that the prisoners targeted the surplus at a nearby shed housing two horses. The sport ended when the horses escaped after a throwing escapade that left the shed dripping red.

The prisoners' relations with the guards at Moorhead were generally harmonious, according to Knauer. Occasionally the POWs even had a target shoot with the guards' rifles, setting up cans at a distance. Knauer enjoyed playing ping-pong at the camp, and at least once the sport was more than just entertainment. A dentist arrived to pull a tooth that Knauer was to have surrendered in Algona; Knauer was reluctant to have it pulled, so the dentist challenged him to a game of ping-pong. The agreement was that if Knauer lost, the tooth would be pulled. The dentist won, but he was called away to another camp for an emergency. In time, Knauer established a formidable ping-pong team with another POW who was left-handed.

In December 1945, Knauer was released from Algona, shipped to Boston, and put aboard a Liberty Ship. He recalls that sea birds in the sky indicated the ship's imminent arrival at Le Havre in late December. Everything of value was taken from the POWs; after an unpleasant stay in France, Knauer was finally sent back to Germany.

His hometown was located less than a mile from the future East-West German border, on the eastern side; his fiancée lived just over the border in another small town. The couple eventually married and raised two sons. Given the increased security and control at the border, Knauer and his family found it difficult to settle nearby. Facing doubtful employment and an uncertain future, they crossed back and forth twenty times between East and West. After lunch one day in 1952, Knauer and his wife and two sons, aged three and five, crossed to the West for the last time. Although minefields and electric fences had not yet been installed, there was already a barbed-wire barrier. After the final crossing, the family asked themselves one last time whether or not it was the right decision. "I don't regret it," Knauer states assuredly over forty years later. He eventually worked 37 years for an electronics firm in the West. Now retired, he lives just across the former East-West border from the spot where he and his family escaped.

"We were young and dumb," Knauer recalls, speaking of himself and his fellow soldiers during the war. Capture and imprisonment were possibilities that he and other young soldiers never thought of until they happened. Knauer's captivity, however, was memorable, a respite from the brutality of conflict, and a stark contrast to the dreary after-effects of war that he encountered on his return to Europe.

Based on the author's interview with Knauer in Germany on February 13, 1995.

Hollandale
Freeborn County

October 9, 1944–November 1944
September 16, 1945–October 22, 1945

Little information survives the Hollandale camp, in southern Minnesota. There, German prisoners found themselves working the marshland of Freeborn County, ideal for vegetables that require delicate harvesting and handling. Labor shortages were a problem at Hollandale early in the war, so severe in 1943 that the entire town helped 500 other workers harvest the vegetables. Preparations were made to transport workers in from Albert Lea and Austin. A work camp for Boy Scout troops from local cities provided additional help; the boys worked during the week and went home on the weekends to be with their families. By 1944, however, a temporary camp had been established for POWs, and another followed in September 1945.[34]

The prisoners were housed a mile and a half southeast of Hollandale; in addition to the stationary buildings, tents provided room. Farmers, acting as the POWs' supervisors, would simply go to the camp and engage prisoners for work in their fields. On at least one farm, guards were not present and the farmer was required to provide a noon meal for the prisoners. During their stay, POWs harvested potatoes, onions, carrots, cabbage, and sugar beets.[35]

The harvesting operation near Hollandale created some lasting memories for Ernst Kohleick, whose Prisoner Perspective accompanies the St. Charles camp description below. He remembers how carefully the cleanliness and quality of the crops were checked, and recalls that government workers would arrive occasionally for an inspection. The scene presented a radical difference from what the prisoners might have experienced back home, Kohleick recalls, where they would have been grateful just to have *something* to eat. At Hollandale, Kohleick was impressed by the way local farmers constructed devices to aid the harvest. He particularly recalls a homemade mechanism that weighed just the right amount of cabbage to be bagged, simultaneously preparing for the next load.[36]

After the camp closed in 1945, some prisoners were sent back to the base camp at Algona, others to the branch camp at Fairmont.[37]

Shirley Hamer's father hired workers from the Hollandale camp to harvest sugar beets. Here she appears as a young girl with German POW Wilhelm Paecher. Shirley, who still resides near Hollandale, was able to re-establish contact with Paecher in 1996.[38] *Courtesy of Shirley Hamer*

Hollandale prisoners pause for a photograph while picking cabbage in 1945. Former prisoner Ernst Kohleick is pictured on the right. *Courtesy of Ernst Kohleick*

> **Ada**
> **Norman County**
>
> **October 14, 1945–November 1945**

The Ada camp was the most southerly POW location in northwest Minnesota. Before German prisoners arrived in 1945, the Ada area had experienced trouble with labor recruitment. During 1943 and 1944 many farmers suffered damaging losses when they paid for harvesting but were unable to thresh the grains before adverse weather conditions arrived. Continuing rainfall made it difficult for men to earn enough money to warrant their staying in the area. Appeals to the local railroad for extra help were refused, and the lack of organized community effort took its toll. As a partial solution, Native Americans were invited in from neighboring counties to help harvest various crops.[39]

As the 1945 season approached, early surveys suggested that it would not have been necessary to recruit POWs, but they were eventually brought to Ada anyway. Getting help from Ada town-dwellers was difficult; the novelty of victory-farm volunteering had worn off. After area workers left to harvest potatoes elsewhere at higher wages, appeals were made to Governor Edward Thye. Perfect weather offered favorable conditions for the harvest and created the possibility of using POWs for a short time. The decision for the local beet growers to sponsor a camp was soon finalized at a meeting at the local courthouse attended by city and military officials, beet growers, and others.[40]

German prisoners from Algona were rushed to the area to help with the potato and sugar beet harvest. These crops, according to the local newspaper, were among the largest in history. They had been planted for the war effort, and the army acknowledged a particular obligation to help bring them in. Normally sugar beet growers handled their own labor arrangements, but the county agent's office processed time sheets and labor allotments for the POWs. The prisoners were housed at the fairgrounds coliseum in Ada; a dining hall nearby was made available for them. The Germans helped lift and load beets, of which 1,000 acres remained to be harvested when they arrived. Eventually they processed 6,000 tons of beets. In addition to their work at Ada, they provided 185 man-days of labor for neighboring Polk County to the north.[41]

```
┌─────────────────────────────────────────────┐
│                  Crookston                    │
│                 Polk County                   │
│                                               │
│       October 6, 1945–November 7, 1945        │
└─────────────────────────────────────────────┘
```

The use of Ada prisoners in Polk County did not satisfy all the county's labor needs. Situated in the agricultural district known as West Polk County, Crookston experienced labor shortages, widespread in 1944 because rain impeded the grain harvest. Shockers were hard to find, and the need for workers in the sugar beet harvest, the largest in any Minnesota county, was also high. Area men and Mexicans supplied labor, but when the shortages peaked in the Red River Valley in 1945, prisoners were sought.[42]

The farm-labor situation was dismal in 1945. In order to ease the crisis, West Polk County Agent Carl Ash informed other area agents of the conditions in the district in order to increase the number of civilians coming to West Polk for work. An effort was made to organize housewives and other workers, gathered in front of the local post office, for farm help. Many were eventually recruited, along with students who attended classes only half the day. A heavy loss was feared since bad weather during the first three weeks of the harvest season had caused delays. With as much as nine inches of rain falling in some areas in September, it was feared that some harvesting would have to wait until the ground was frozen. Of the five-million-dollar potato crop, twenty percent was in danger of frost in early October. Meanwhile, an appeal was also made to Governor Thye for help in obtaining 2,000 laborers for the sugar beet harvest. The governor was advised that if immediate help could not be found, possibly 200,000 tons of beets would freeze, such that only ten percent of the crop could be harvested. To ease the crisis, arrangements for POW labor were made by County Agent Carl Ash. According to plan, 240 prisoners were to help with West Polk County's potato harvest, and 10 cents per field bag was to be their wage.[43]

Community support was high during preparations for the prisoners' housing and their relocation from Montgomery. Just before the weekend of their arrival, local plumbers, carpenters, and businessmen worked on the prisoners' accommodations in the winter sports arena located in the city, which was ultimately made available for church services as well. All the plumbers from two local companies agreed to give their best efforts to the camp, and they labored two days and one night to finish the project. The plan was to quarter the POWs in double-decker bunks during their stay. Their guards were to occupy the former offices of the Chamber of Commerce. Among the facilities added for the prisoners were lavatories and tables. Many of the bleachers had to be cleared away and the maple flooring lifted. An initial group of 240 German prisoners opened the camp on October 6, followed by another 125 men five days later.[44]

Among the first group was prisoner Hans Kratzheller, who remembers well the curious locals who gathered to observe the Germans arriving at the sports arena. While waiting for their supplies, Kratzheller recalls, the prisoners took time to inspect their new camp. They spotted sports equipment stored at the arena and promptly began racing around on roller skates. After spending a day preparing their accommodations, they started harvesting potatoes on the first workday of the week, when local farmers began selecting small groups of prisoners.

The POWs were surprised they were required to pick only the large potatoes and leave the rest; after they had passed through a field, Kratzheller recalls, it looked as if they had harvested nothing. He remembers that the farmers were very reserved, "almost shy," at first, but later became comfortable partners in a normal farm-labor relationship. Before long, the farmers were bringing extra food to the prisoners for their noon meal and offering them cigarettes. As colder weather arrived, the prisoners were taken from the potato fields to harvest sugar beets.

Since the Germans worked every day of the week, there was little time for other activities; it was dark when they rose in the morning and when they arrived back at the compound in the evening. Catholic Masses were made available, but they lasted only two weeks; few POWs had attended them, since the services were early in the morning before work.[45]

The prisoners worked hard their first day in the fields, accompanied by some of their guards, who worked off-duty, volunteering as many as three hours apiece. The county agent reported that the guards picked 226 bushels in three hours and earned $5.50 for their efforts, a better performance, in his opinion, than that of the prisoners. During the early days of their stay, the POWs worked at 30 area farms; another 50 farms received help as the seven weeks passed. In early

TROST IM GEBET

Katholisches
Mess- und Andachtsbuch
für Soldaten

Herausgegeben
mit
Unterstützung des Bischöfl.
KRIEGS-, NOT- u. HILFSFONDS
vom
KATH. CENTRAL VEREIN
von Amerika

ST. LOUIS, MO.
CENTRAL BUREAU PRESS
1943

A remarkable effort was made to provide religious services to all the prisoners in Minnesota. This was most often arranged through cooperation with the local clergy, but U.S. military and POW chaplains also offered a wide range of services. Former prisoner Hans Kratzheller recalls that Catholic masses at Crookston were arranged by the vicar general of the local diocese. The above title page is from a book for soldiers containing Catholic prayer and reflection, which Kratzheller carried with him while in the camps.[46]

October, good weather increased the prospect of a smooth harvest, and it was completed in fine style, with many official expressions of appreciation to all the parties who helped. The POWs stayed in Crookston until early November. The Crookston *Daily Times* estimated that a final total of 80 area farmers used the prisoners. They brought in 80,777 bushels of potatoes worth $75,000, and 21,148 tons of sugar beets worth $264,100, the last beets harvested just three days before the first frost.[47]

Warren
Marshall County

October 7, 1945–November 6, 1945

While other areas in the Red River Valley experienced shortages, farm labor was in better supply further north in Marshall County during 1944. The county's farmers were able to bring in their harvests, even under adverse weather conditions. Heavy drafting of the county's younger men in 1944, however, warned of the outside labor the area would need in 1945. The shortages would be particularly critical because the young men often maintained the machinery on their farms.[48]

In 1944, the area's high schools closed for two weeks while the students harvested potatoes. Mexican nationals and Texans were brought in. Additional farm help was recruited in neighboring counties, at the Red Lake Indian Reservation, and among local businessmen.[49]

The 1945 harvest presented special complications. The acreage of wheat, flax, potatoes, and sugar beets was large, and the feed crops were all ready for harvest at the same time. Potatoes were picked by high school students, local men, and Mexicans who had already been working with sugar beets. The possibility of using POWs had been discussed in January, but at that time the local commerce club wanted more information on how the camps were operating in other parts of the state. By October 1 the county agent was clearly aware of the upcoming shortage and concluded that POWs had to be secured for the sugar beet harvest. The acute labor problem was magnified by an increased acreage of beets and potatoes, both requiring much manual labor for cultivation and harvest. Moreover, spring work had been delayed, and although efforts were made to keep the Mexicans for the rest of the season, their inexperience in farming practices had prompted them to go elsewhere.[50]

The Warren Commercial Club and the local Farm Labor Committee co-sponsored the camp in Warren. The Commercial Club arranged a meeting of Warren-area businessmen and potato and sugar beet farmers; the consensus was that prisoner labor should be brought in. The monetary deposit required for the camp's establishment and the use of the prisoners was made by local farmers. Arrangements were made to house the POWs at the North Star Bible College.[51]

Under the command of Lt. Harry Wexler, 220 Italian POWs and 23 American military personnel arrived by train on October 7 and set up the camp at the North Star College building. Another 200 POWs were to be employed in the area, but inadequate housing was a problem. Plumbing work was required at the college; many members of the Commercial Club spent the day before the POWs' arrival preparing the building.[52]

The POWs were carefully allocated among the area's farms so that in case of early frost, all the farmers would have the same percentage of crop out of the field. The topping of the sugar beets was finished by November 3; as more favorable weather approached, there was an increasing chance that the harvest would be complete. Initially, nine groups of 20 to 24 POWs and a guard apiece were sent to the fields; eventually twelve details were rotated at two-day intervals for four weeks. The prisoners worked on 54 potato and sugar beet farms, topping 18,000 tons of beets. They saved not only the crops, but the life of one potato farmer, pinned down by a tractor. The POWs working nearby were able to raise the machine just enough to free him in the nick of time; gasoline leaking from the tractor was already on fire when the rescue was made. POW labor resulted in a saving of $200,000 in Marshall County, accomplished through 40,000 man-hours and representing 34 percent of the crop acreage. The prisoners left on November 6 and returned to their base camp.[53]

Chapter 4

Camps Established for Canneries

Supplying prisoners for cannery work was the chief purpose of the camps in this chapter. Typically they were in existence for only two or three months, yet they housed hundreds of POWs at the peak of the canning season. As soon as the season's work was finished, these camps closed, and the prisoners were either returned to Algona or sent to a year-round branch camp.

Cannery camps provided men primarily for processing peas and corn. For the pea harvest, prisoners performed a number of tasks in the cannery building, where a guard was usually on hand. At some canneries they were segregated, while in others they worked in close proximity to civilians. It was also common for small groups of these prisoners to work at the cannery's vineries, where pea plants were brought from the fields, sometimes more than 20 miles from the cannery. At the vineries, POWs were responsible for "pitching" pea plants into machines, which removed the pods from the plants. Following the pea harvest, there was often a short period when the men were available for work on private farms—good timing, since the farmers were harvesting oats, wheat, and barley. Farmers contacted either the local county agent or the nearby cannery to obtain the POWs, and the contractual arrangements were much the same as at the farm-labor camps. The prevailing hourly wage was 50 to 60 cents. Sometimes guards would accompany the POWs, while in other areas, guards remained in a central location to be notified of any problems.

All other procedures varied slightly from camp to camp. Farmers often traveled to the compounds to pick up the men. In other areas, designated individuals drove a predetermined number of POWs to a central location for selection by farmers. If the prisoners were transported to the fields by the U.S. military, the farmer was usually charged accordingly. At Ortonville, for example, the fee depended on the number of prisoners being hauled: five cents per mile for a load of up to nine POWs, and as much as 15 cents per mile for a group of twenty or more. At some camps, however, there was no charge when the men were brought to a nearby town for distribution. Prisoners normally brought their own meals with them to the fields; farmers often supplemented their rations. In some instances, however, POWs brought no meals, and the farmers were required to feed them.

A late attempt to advance the use of POWs on private farms was the formation of so-called "use associations," in which a group of five to seven farmers would negotiate directly with the army for the distribution and employment of the prisoners. Only one county had "use associations" in 1944, but more were functioning in twelve counties by the end of the 1945 harvest season.[1]

As soon as the sweet corn harvest started, large numbers of men returned to the canneries from incidental farm work. Many others worked outside the factory to help harvest the corn. During and after the corn harvest, POWs performed a wide range of tasks for local farmers, including shocking, bailing, and filling silos. With hundreds of POWs available on any given day, the burden on county agents and other officials increased dramatically. Shortly after the harvest, the camps closed for the season.

Vacant buildings of various sorts were used to house the prisoners, including some at local fairgrounds. Old hemp plants were available near Wells and Montgomery, unused since hemp supplies had begun arriving from the Pacific. These hemp factories were among at least seven southern Minnesota plants built early in the war, and some were already undergoing conversion to other uses such as corn drying.[2]

The two Prisoner Perspectives in this chapter are drawn from the reminiscences of German POWs, both captured at an early age in southern Europe.

> # Ortonville
> # Big Stone County
>
> ## July 10, 1944–September 24, 1944
> ## July 10, 1945–November 1945

The county agent's records for this camp provide the best available view of Minnesota POWs as an integral part of a county's labor program. As early as March 1944, local officials were planning for the upcoming work season, and a county-wide meeting was organized. Considerable attention at this meeting was given to whether a POW camp should be established in the Ortonville area for harvesting small grains and sweet corn processing at the Big Stone Canning Company. Although the local wages customarily attracted seasonal labor to the county, surveys confirmed the need for POWs, and steps to bring them in were being taken as summer arrived.[3]

Plans for the use of POWs materialized, wages were determined and barracks were hurriedly finished, with an adjoining house for the American officers. Command of the camp was eventually given to Captain Cliff Jenner. The barracks, which included an athletic field, were better than the POWs had anticipated; they observed, however, that sparrows shared their new quarters. Located adjacent to the plant where the POWs would work, the barracks were financed entirely by the cannery. The POWs jokingly noted in a report that the South Dakota-Minnesota border traversed their dining hall, so they ate their meals in two states.[4]

Applications for farm workers were processed by the county and the assistant USES officer. The county agent issued detailed rules governing prisoner-of-war employment. Farmers were required to pick the men up at 7:30 a.m., provide their noon meal and return them back to camp in the evening. Within ten days of their arrival, the prisoners were already harvesting at least three area farms. Sixty of the POWs brought experience from farms in Germany. Because of late planting, the prisoners were not heavily used at first; from mid-July to August, 30 to 40 POWs went to the fields daily. All the POWs were working hard in early August; the camp commander felt that uninterrupted work might be too strenuous for the men and ordered that they be given a free day. The POWs worked mostly on the larger farms in the northern part of the county, where more help was needed than elsewhere. Work crews from neighboring towns assisted the prisoners, including nearly 100 men from Graceville. After the second week in August, however, all prisoners were turned over to the canning factory.[5]

POWs became an important source of labor for Ortonville-area farmers later in the war. Transients, helpful in prior years, were in short supply in 1944, and Mexican migrants were available only after the POWs had left. Volunteers helped shock several thousand acres, but the POWs were indispensable at the peak of the shocking season. By the time the camp disbanded and the POWs returned to Bena, they had shocked 9,360 acres of grain and worked on 107 different farms, many in nearby counties. Farmers were well satisfied with the work, registering only three complaints.[6]

In April 1945 the manager of the local canning company and the Big Stone County agent were again discussing the need for prisoners. After contacting farmers who had used POWs in 1944, the county agent decided that 150 POWs would be needed. A contract was signed, and a meeting with the War Manpower Commission made arrangements for the camp. On July 10, 1945, forty-one German POWs arrived from Algona. The camp's commanding officer was First Lieutenant Donald P. Copper. The Ortonville *Independent* reported that a "general tightening" of living conditions was to characterize this second season; POWs were to be given no beer, no movies, and no cigarettes or rationed food. The POWs all had experience on farms at home. They were allowed to work up to 12 hours daily.[7]

During the season, a meeting of six county agents and their assistants with the camp commander addressed feeding, transportation, and other conditions of POW use. Guards, for example, were to be used only when a group was sent to a new farmer; subsequently, the farmer himself was to assume the role of guard. The 100 prisoners then available were to be divided into details of a minimum of five men. An eight-hour minimum and a 12-hour maximum were set for the POW workday. Only water had to be furnished to the prisoners, but it was appreciated if the guards were offered a meal. The prisoners' meals were brought out to the farms, and the farmers were charged 25 cents per meal for each prisoner. Farmers who transported POWs were given allowances for doing so.[8]

The initial supply of POWs proved deficient as the need for shockers became more acute, and the camp was enlarged by 50 additional prisoners. These prisoners were soon all booked up and 150 orders for farm help remained unfilled during the first week of August. In an effort to ease the crisis, town crews went into the fields in the evening. The Clinton *Advocate* announced the serious need for additional farm help and stated that "to fail in this task would truly be ungrateful of our people on the home front and a mark against their patriotism." Near the town of Beardsley northwest of Ortonville, "Placement Crew Captains" aided in the distribution of prisoners.[9]

The additional POWs were not enough; another 30 were requested to help in the Montevideo area. At the request of the Montevideo Co-op Canning Company, a meeting of county agents, the Ortonville camp commander, and Col. Lobdell from Algona, agreed that 50 POWs would be transported each day to Montevideo and back. A security payment was required for their use.[10]

Each day a work sheet was presented to the camp commander, who organized groups of POWs for the next day. Through an account at

These POWs were permanently stationed at Bena in northern Minnesota and transferred to Ortonville for the canning season. Hans Welker, whose perspectives are summarized in the Bena section, stands in the second row, second from the left. This photo was probably taken inside the Ortonville compound; a fence stretches behind the prisoners.[11] *Courtesy of Hans Welker*

the local bank titled "P.O.W. Funds," all payments from the farmers were handled by the county agent. The agent's assistant helped send out POW details and collect security deposits in the morning, eventually completing his various errands by phone and car. Meanwhile, the agent himself arrived at the office at 8:30, issued orders for the next day, and canceled old orders. He returned after supper to settle all contracts for that day, and finally finished his work in the evening around 10 or 11 p.m.[12]

Since farm work was still unfinished after the canning season, the county agent requested that the prisoners remain into October. He secured an extension, and prisoners were available for silo filling, late threshing, and other farm jobs. During the 1945 harvest, prisoners shocked 30,000 acres of grain and threshed nearly 20,000 acres, for a total payroll of $21,760.30. A total of 861 farmers in seven counties ordered and received POWs from the Ortonville camp; two counties in South Dakota received 190 prisoners. Due to relaxed rules governing the number of POWs per detail, three to four times as many farmers benefited from their labor in 1945 as in 1944; up to 38 different farmers used POWs each day. The prisoners were generally dutiful, willing to do any job requested. Complaints were few, usually involving the unwillingness of one or two prisoners to work hard. Farmers near the town of Clinton north of Ortonville "appreciated very much the use of this labor." Overall, the competence of the POWs was considered much higher than during the previous year.[13]

The POWs' main project during both summer seasons, however, was to man the cannery, where they were in charge of the entire warehouse detail. Two guards were on the premises; the POWs were easily guarded since they were used only in the warehouse, stacking boxes of cans they received from a conveyor track. There was little contact between civilian workers and prisoners. POWs also performed odd jobs, including welding and other machine work. The company even bid, unsuccessfully, to keep one unusually skillful prisoner in the United States. The work required good physical condition, and the company supplied extra food to the POWs during the 1945 season because the camp's reduced rations were insufficient. Farmers, likewise, found it necessary to augment rations, since the POWs were otherwise unable to perform a full day's work.[14]

> ## Howard Lake
> ## Wright County
>
> ## August 7, 1944–September 1944
> ## July 1945–October 1945

Shortages in Wright County's labor pool brought POWs to Howard Lake. The county had already had trouble finding workers in 1944; by 1945, many had been attracted to high-paying industrial jobs 35 miles away, in St. Paul and Minneapolis, causing a more severe shortage. Thus the Northland Canning Company in Cokato arranged with the Wright County commissioners to house POW laborers at the county fairgrounds in Howard Lake. Twenty-six POWs arrived in early August 1944 and began working shortly afterwards. At this time, Col. Lobdell at Algona had no officers available for branch camp duty, so he appointed Master Sergeant Carl Tisthammer as the commanding officer at Howard Lake. Tisthammer, a veteran of the North African campaign, was probably the first noncommissioned officer appointed as a branch-camp commander in Minnesota.[15]

The Howard Lake camp was unique in that it was populated exclusively with "Anti Nazi" prisoners, who had been threatened and were possibly in danger at other camps. Either the prisoner himself disclosed his anti-nazi position, or he was identified by American authorities. Nothing about Howard Lake made it an unusually favorable site for an anti-Nazi camp. It was chosen simply because the request for prisoners in Cokato coincided with the identification of the first group of anti-Nazi POWs at the Algona base camp, and Col. Lobdell wanted to remove them from Algona as soon as possible.

Many prisoners transferred to Howard Lake had recently been captured in June 1944 in Cherbourg. One group was assembled after three prisoners contacted a German-speaking American sergeant at Algona and requested to be transferred because of some "very strong" Nazi feelings at Algona. A list of other prisoners requesting to leave Algona was placed in the mailbox of a U.S. military chaplain stationed there. Some prisoners appear to have been in immediate danger of their lives. Alfred Neber, whose perspective accompanies the Bird Island camp description, was in danger of being killed by his fellows. Two prisoners, originally from Austria and stationed at the St. Charles

German POWs in their compound at the Howard Lake fairgrounds in 1944. This photo was taken just outside the grandstand, where the POWs' food was prepared. Former prisoner Alfred Neber is second from right. *Courtesy of Alfred Neber*

German POWs working near Howard Lake in 1944. Standing on the far right is former prisoner Fritz Reinlassoeder. *Courtesy of Fritz Reinlassoeder*

camp, were in similar danger before their transfer to Howard Lake. The operation of the camp with its "Anti Nazi" status appears to have gone smoothly, with small exceptions. "Two SS types," for example, were segregated because it was feared that other prisoners might harm them, as recalled years later by a former cannery employee.[16]

Despite the Howard Lake camp's brief life span, serious efforts were made to meet the POWs' recreational needs. Howard Hong visited the camp shortly after its establishment in August 1944. He sensed a "newness" about the place; even the POWs were not familiar with each other. Hong left various items, including a violin, and later sent tools and games. A canteen was available to the prisoners on the fairgrounds. Religious services for the POWs were conducted on Sundays in the grandstand, and prisoners were also transported to the nearby town of Winsted for Catholic Mass, where the priest had a special sermon for them and the nuns sang German hymns. When the Howard Lake theater was closed, the POWs were allowed to view movies at Winsted.[17]

There was little fraternization between POWs and citizens, other than brief interaction with Howard Lake residents who spoke German and worked as interpreters in the fields. Fraternization was even less likely after three local servicemen were killed overseas in June and July 1944 and prisoners were taunted by the citizens.[18]

No major incidents ensued, however; the POWs completed their work at the cannery uneventfully. They also worked for a short time at Johnson Produce in Cokato, processing chickens and eggs. The company experienced a particularly high demand during the war and shipped out hundreds of thousands of eggs weekly.[19]

**Olivia
Renville County**

**September 5, 1943–October 25, 1943
August 23, 1945–November 14, 1945**

Three POW camps opened and closed in Renville County from 1943 through 1945. The first prisoners ever to arrive for work in Minnesota were engaged for Rogers Brothers Seed Company in Olivia, producers of enough hybrid sweet-corn seed to plant over 100,000 acres. A community survey in August 1943 turned up signs of an impending labor shortage, and the company applied for POWs. Although approval was granted by Camp Clark near Nevada, Missouri, local citizens were given the opportunity to voice their concerns to the Renville County Labor Committee at the county courthouse, addressing such issues as the wage scale. The public meeting cleared the way for the POWs' arrival in early September. Accommodations were arranged on the west edge of town, a short distance from the Rogers Brothers factory.[20]

Army personnel arrived with 100 Italian POWs; the unit's two commanders Captain G. B. Howell and Lieutenant J. W. Kent provided information at a Kiwanis Club meeting immediately after their arrival. The Olivia *Times Journal* described the men as "fine specimens of the Roman soldiers, physically and manly. They are not of the Dago type, but keen, alert and outstanding." Since Olivia was one of just two camps operating in the state in 1943, the commanders wanted to make it "a model one in every way." They explained that the average age of the POWs was 21, that many were talented musicians, and that the youngest prisoner was allegedly just 14 years old. Few of the Italians spoke English; communication was aided by two U.S. soldiers of Italian descent. The prisoners were housed along with their guards in tents, and a recreation room was made available in the basement of the local armory. The factory, next door to the camp, contained drying facilities for picked corn. Inside, where both POWs and civilians worked, sorting was performed by some of the prisoners.[21]

The POWs arrived within a week of Italy's surrender, and they reacted in various ways to the news. Certainly there was no more "long live Mussolini" after the day's dismissal, which the prisoners had

Italian POWs on a farm outside Olivia in 1943. The farmer's son is in the foreground. *Courtesy of Dorothy Steinbeisser*

Italian POWs with American foreman George Taylor in the middle. *Courtesy of Dorothy Steinbeisser*

Eileen Rockvam, left, with a German POW in Olivia outside the seed house. The prisoners were impressed with her physical strength and nicknamed her "Super Mouse." Eileen clearly remembers the day when one of the prisoners learned that his parents had been killed in an air raid.[22] *Courtesy of Dorothy Steinbeisser*

German POWs with American worker (middle) near the Rogers Brothers' seed house in Olivia. *Courtesy of Dorothy Steinbeisser*

reportedly shouted in Missouri. Neither the surrender nor the preceding hostilities had any apparent effect on the POWs' good rapport with the community. The local priest, Fr. Henry Pomije, visited the men at their camp shortly after their arrival. Speaking to them in their native language, he said: "We salute you not as enemies, but as friends; not as prisoners, but as your protectors; not as jailed, but as the favored." The prisoners were often heard singing on their way to Mass in the local church. Under the scrutiny of the congregation, the Italians all sat attentively at the front of the sanctuary and listened closely to the service. Once when Fr. Pomije referred to their native country and relatives, "tears sprang to the eyes of the prisoners," as reported by the Olivia *Times Journal*.[23]

At least one local organization was on cordial terms with the prisoners: the Kiwanis club, accompanied by local school teachers, acquainted themselves with the POWs when they toured the camp, and the prisoners prepared an Italian meal of spaghetti for them, served at the Olivia Hotel. Local and area State Guard members also visited the camp in October. The units were in Olivia practicing maneuvers in response to a fictitious "cyclone" that had devastated the town; the Olivia guard were "saboteurs," and the visiting units were responsible for restoring order. An officer who visited the prisoners in camp reported that "many of them had tears running down their cheeks when they spoke of their country." Unit members watched a POW soccer game, and the prisoners greeted the officers with an Italian rendition of the "Beer Barrel Polka."[24]

The Italian POWs at Olivia in the fall of 1943 were productive, picking 1,500 acres of corn by hand, but they had time to enjoy soccer and volleyball at their compound. Their job was done by late October, and they left as they had come, on a special train, bound for Camp Clark in Nevada, Missouri. Following their departure, the local paper reported that "during their stay here they gave to the community a wee bit of Italian life and coloring and they left with our people a favorable impression as to their human quality and characteristics." According to Renville County's extension service, Olivia's use of POWs in 1943 was praised as having "worked out rather successfully," an experience that "should be kept in mind for future programs."[25]

The 1945 growing season promised no acute shortage of workers at first, but as the summer passed, labor became scarce and the demand grew proportionally. Mexican nationals, who had already been employed in early May in the sugar beet fields, reached 200 in

1945. A local firm, the Olivia Canning Company, applied for prisoner labor. In early August it was doubtful that they would receive any prisoners at all, but later in the month 41 German POWs arrived to harvest 1000-odd acres and to can sweet corn. They were housed where the Italians had lived in 1943. A mess hall, a kitchen, and an assembly room had been installed in the old tile factory for the prisoners, improvements that made the location acceptable to the government. Along with the prisoners, Mexican nationals were used by the canning company, which built small cabins near the factory for their accommodation, each with its own kitchen and sleeping facilities. After the POWs had completed their service to the cannery, they worked for Rogers Brothers once again. The group had grown to 88 in the meanwhile and had been joined by boys recruited from Duluth.[26]

Bird Island
Renville County

September 16, 1944–October 1944

New army restrictions on Olivia's Rogers Brothers Seed Company in 1944 called for improved housing, which was established at the fairgrounds in Bird Island five miles to the east. Although Rauenhorst Seed Company, another local hybrid producer, hired Mexicans and boys to detassel its fields, Rogers Brothers began the 1944 season with 50 area women and schoolgirls and then applied once again for POW labor. In mid-September a contingent of 62 German POWs arrived in Bird Island to establish the camp. Later, nineteen more POWs raised the total to 81. The American commander and his wife were set up in a boarding house in town.[27]

The German POWs were taken by truck to the fields and the factory, where they performed the same work as the Italians had in Olivia a year before. The ten-hour workdays involved spreading corn over wire racks, which were placed in a dryer. The corn was then bagged in 100-pound sacks and stacked for shipment. Before the POWs left in early November, they had harvested over 2,000 acres of corn. The second prison camp in Renville County, like the first at Olivia, proved to be a successful and dependable source of labor.[28]

The Rev. Immanuel Lenz, pastor of Olivia's Zion Lutheran Church, visited the POWs nearly every day in the fields and held services for them both years in Bird Island and Olivia. The prisoners all dropped what they were doing and started talking to Pastor Lenz during his first visit to the fields. Instead of attending services in a local church, like the Italians, the German POWs improvised a sanctuary with planks and bricks, and with song books provided by Lenz. Their weekly services were attended by as many as 25 prisoners. Lenz talked with them after the services, and the POWs followed him to the door each time, inviting him to come again. Anxiety about returning home, Mrs. Lenz recalls, occupied the thoughts of many POWs.[29]

In September 1944, George Taylor, field foreman for the Rogers Brothers Seed Company, requested that some of the prisoners write their names and addresses in his book as a memento. Two entries in Ukrainian, each with an address and a name, are from the area of

Kiev. Before these POWs were transferred from the Howard Lake camp, Howard Hong had already noticed that some of them spoke Polish and Russian. Some prisoners included poems and other phrases such as the following from Karl Krings, who had been captured in North Africa:

> Columbus discovered America, if he wouldn't have
> done it, I would never have come to America. Writ-
> ten from a prisoner from the African Army.

Little is known of the seventeen prisoners who left their names and addresses. At least one died shortly after his return to Germany after the war. Another, Alfred Neber, shared his reminiscences with the author in the spring of 1991, in Kindenheim, Germany.[30]

German POWs at the Bird Island fairgrounds in 1944. Former POW Alfred Neber recalls some movies at the local theater in which "there were a number of Germans mowed down with a machine gun."[31] *Courtesy of Dorothy Steinbeisser*

Prisoner Perspective
Alfred Neber

When he was captured July 29, 1943, in Sicily, Alfred Neber had been a soldier for less than a year. He was taken into captivity in an almond plantation, stationed there by his lieutenant to watch the street below. From his post he saw a muzzle fire from behind a tree, and a bullet injured his foot. Dragged up over a pile of rocks he had assembled for protection, Neber took refuge with other wounded German soldiers in a donkey stall. While his wounds were attended to later in the afternoon by a German medical soldier, mortar fire erupted near the location and Neber's unit retreated. Shortly afterwards the wounded Germans heard American voices, and an American soon entered the donkey stall with his finger on the trigger of a machine gun. Noticing that his captives were wounded, the American offered them something to drink. Another soldier came later with a hand grenade, and questioned Neber about the movements of his unit.

From a distance Neber's unit commander Hans Schreiner had watched the Americans take that position and apprehend the wounded soldiers. Neber later learned that Schreiner had written to Neber's mother the following December, explaining in detail the reason for leaving the wounded soldiers behind, and encouraging her not to worry "since the Americans were always a correct and proper enemy." He expressed the intention to visit her later in the month, and asked whether she knew the present location of any other soldiers in the unit.

Meanwhile, Neber and the other wounded spent the night in the donkey stall. The next day they were brought to a field hospital. Neber was sent to Palermo and eventually to Africa on a ship with wounded French, Americans, and Italians. After his injuries were attended to, he was taken to Oran, where he received a blanket, a vest, and the news that he was leaving for America.

From Newport News, Virginia, Neber was transported to Camp Campbell, Kentucky, where he spent Christmas and the winter months before leaving for Algona the following year. His stay in Algona was short because of tension between the POWs with differing political views. Nazi sentiment in Algona, for example, resulted in actions that upset the Americans, such as sowing flowers in the shape of a swastika, or raising a Nazi flag, made of sacks, on a barrack.

Life in a new country, however, offered Neber fresh insights. He saw a functioning society in which there was more than one political party, contrasting with the dogmatic one-party politics of his own land. His curiosity about such differences drew Neber into a close acquaintance with one farmer in particular, named Frankel. Other POWs overheard such words as "Germany," "Hitler," and "army" passing between the two men, and they started to threaten Neber, suspicious of his familiarity with the farmer. Because of the tension, Neber was sent briefly to the camp in Howard Lake, Minnesota, and shortly afterwards to the recently established camp in Bird Island.

With some fluency in English, he was able to assume the role of company clerk, performing desk-work in addition to other camp duties, especially in the kitchen. Neber particularly remembers traveling to Olivia one day to weld a broken typewriter key back together; since he was inexperienced with welding machinery and techniques, the Americans had to finish the job. Neber spent his share of time in the fields with other POWs, helping harvest corn. After work, the Bird Island POWs enjoyed almost any diversion. Neber once objected to the camp sergeant that the propaganda films shown in the local movie theater went too far; the movies involved "a number of Germans that were mowed down," a message that did not enhance camp life.

Neber's time at Bird Island passed quickly and with few notable incidents. He remembers that an older prisoner had been complaining of pains to the camp commander; the POW, who had been trained as a barber, was rewarded by being kept in camp to cut hair. On one occasion, mislabeled dentures arrived for the prisoners. After trying to fit them into their mouths, they realized that the dentures didn't belong to the Bird Island camp at all, and the shipment was sent back to Algona. Pastor Lenz was a constant fortifying presence in camp; Neber and his wife even received a "care" package after the war in 1947 from a student to whom Lenz had given Neber's address. After his stay in Bird Island, Neber was accepted for re-education in New Jersey before his return to Germany. At his interview, officials questioned him as to what kind of political party he wanted for Germany after the war. He replied that he wanted a Christian Social Party, offering his definitions of "Christian" and "Social." These and other responses were apparently acceptable, and Neber was taken into the program. He remembers a series of outstanding speeches, in either German or English, and discussions afterwards. The "re-educated" POWs, Neber recalls, were an elite group handled with special care by the American authorities.

POWs near Algona, Iowa. Alfred Neber is on the far right in the first row. Working in these fields near the base camp at Algona, Neber became well acquainted with a local farmer. He recalls that "others saw me as a traitor." Neber was subsequently transferred to Howard Lake, Minnesota.[32] *Courtesy of Alfred Neber*

Alfred Neber in 1991 holding an atlas he purchased when he was a prisoner. "I got to know people in America, who lived in a democracy. I got to know a country with a multi-party system." *Author's photo*

Preparing for his voyage home, Neber packed his sea sack full of soap and cigarettes. He did not smoke, but he was already aware of the postwar black market developing in Germany. With the money he earned selling these goods, he eventually bought his first pair of shoes and his first suit after the war. Neber left New York on a nine-day journey to Le Havre in a Victory class ship, with hot meals in the ship's cafeteria and films shown every day.

Beginning a new life in Germany in 1946, Neber took a test under French supervision to pursue his goal of becoming a teacher. A written essay was required, exploring the difference between "authority" and "freedom." Neber wrote exactly what he had learned a few weeks earlier in the re-education program in the United States. The concepts were clearly defined; Neber passed the test.

He married over the Christmas holiday in 1946. By 1952 he had passed all his exams and become a teacher. A senior teacher in 1965, he was promoted to an assistant grade-school principalship and eventually became principal of the school in 1972. He remained at this post until his retirement in 1985.

Neber believes that the American authorities showed tremendous foresight in their re-education program, clearly realizing the difficulty of trying to rebuild a former dictatorship. As a result of his exposure to American institutions, he declares, "I tried to educate and raise my students democratically. That I can say." Thus, building on his experiences as a POW, Neber became a teacher and a leader in a new country, and a new democracy.

Based on the author's interviews with Neber in Germany on July 20, 1991 and March 2, 1995.

| Wells |
| Faribault County |
| June 16, 1945–October 1945 |

Wells received prisoners in the summer of 1945, filling an urgent need for manual laborers already evident the previous summer. Action had been taken in 1944 to establish a prisoner camp at Blue Earth, where the city council had authorized electricity and water connections, and a resolution had been passed to install facilities at the local fairgrounds. This plan called for the use of 500 to 600 prisoners, but the shortage in 1944 had been remedied by Mexican labor, so neither POWs nor Jamaicans were needed. In the summer of 1945, however, the Farm Help Committee of Faribault County anticipated a shortage of labor for the fall harvest and decided to explore the POW option. Two official trips to Algona resulted in the decision to set up a camp for general farm and cannery help. The California Packing Company, formerly the Wells Canning Company, was one of the sponsors for the camp. At the height of the season, the company used 75 POWs for each shift at its cannery. The cannery foreman never had any problems with the prisoners, who saluted him when they arrived for work in the morning.[33]

The prisoners were housed in an old hemp mill one-and-a-half miles north of town that had done duty as a drying shed for corn. The POWs expressed disappointment with their accommodations; they weren't fond of the wooden lath floor and the poorly equipped kitchen, and they regretted that toilets had yet to be built and lights added. The necessary work, moreover, "was carried out with rather primitive means." Former camp commander Second Lt. Werner Schmiedeberg acknowledges that the facilities were far from optimal and considered Wells a "make do" camp. The buildings had dirt floors with wooden walkways, and outdoor latrines were built. The small mess hall and kitchen made it necessary for the U.S. Army personnel and prisoners to eat in shifts.[34]

The availability of POW labor was discussed by the camp commander and other officials at two meetings for local farmers, the first in early June, the second in mid-July. About twenty persons at the second meeting learned how to obtain POW help. The time required

The Wells camp, 1945. *Courtesy of Werner Schmiedeberg*

Schmiedeberg conducting a routine Saturday inspection of the enlisted men's quarters at Wells in 1945. *Courtesy of Werner Schmiedeberg*

for the process had recently been reduced from a minimum of 10 days to 24 hours. Farmers were instructed to estimate the number of prisoners needed one day in advance of the job, and to telephone the camp with information on how long the POWs were to work and how far they had to travel. The process was streamlined by the establishment of a labor office at the camp. Besides wages, costs to the farmer included 25 cents a day for meals and an additional 45 cents daily to help pay for the campsite.[35]

Except for a single "roving guard" sent by Commander Schmiedeberg to the various locations where the prisoners were employed, the POWs worked without guards and were treated like any other hired help. On one farm, in addition to helping with the harvest, they built pens and a granary, and even took a hand in raising mink. The POWs on this farm were so enthusiastic about their relationship with the farmer that they sometimes volunteered their services, once even digging the pit for the granary scale.[36]

Prisoners did additional cannery work at the Fairmont Canning Company in Waseca, the Bricelyn Co-op Canning Company in nearby Bricelyn, and the Lake Mills Canning Company in Lake Mills, Iowa. They processed poultry at Lanesboro Produce in Wells, and worked for the Kiester Cooperative Association and the Frost Farmers Elevator. Prisoners also worked for Kansota Farms at Albert Lea. The Faribault County camp placed a total of 1,289 prisoners, performing 8,740 hours of work. Prisoners were also available to farmers in Blue Earth and Waseca counties to the north.[37]

The following report by Howard Hong on the Wells camp, August 10, 1945, is both a precious eyewitness view of camp life and a testimony to the ingenuity and effectiveness of Hong's services.

> I found a certain unusual defeatism in the prisoner of war leaders. Together with energetic Lt. Schmiedeberg we talked about the problem from the angles of leadership and materials. This was one of the camps Col. Lobdell and the Spokesman at Algona were especially desirous that I visit, and I believe we did make some headway in the program of constructive activities.
>
> Constructive Activities: There was no school at all. Some teachers were available, including one whom I had seen a number of times in the camp school at Crowder, and some books, but there was no space for the school, excepting the

mess hall where meals were served in shifts. Our conclusion was to rent one or two breeder houses ($10.00 hauling charge and $5.00 per month each) from the lumber company. If this charge is not allowable against the POW Fund, the bill will be sent to the War Prisoners' Aid of the YMCA, although I offered to leave a check to get the thing started. A breeder house will accommodate about twenty men and a teacher—just right for a class. Fifteen Cassell's dictionaries were among the things I was able to leave with the commanding officer. We then met with the teachers and things seemed inwardly and outwardly propitious for the beginning of the school. The work was slack—between peas and corn—another good omen.

Church services had been held on two Sundays. Local pastors had conducted the services.

A YMCA phonograph and some records had just arrived from Algona. The first thing Lt. Schmiedeberg's sergeant asked upon my arrival was, "What about phonograph needles?" With the confidence of a magician I took a package of two semi-permanent needles (purchase made an hour earlier) from my pocket. For their musical group with two violins, saxophone, and guitar (most of these privately owned) an accordion was the main need for the formation of an active little orchestra. We were all pleased to fill this need from the trunk of my car. They thought that in a fortnight they would have ready a concert of remembered and radio-heard music.

This visit was again "so much for so little." From a few hours of earnest discussion we all hoped that a school and some music would come and that the climate for religious services was bettered somewhat. When I left, Lt. Schmiedeberg said, "You don't know how much you have done. The men will never forget this, I know them."
Howard Hong[38]

Other recreational activities at the Wells camp were soccer and card games. Books were available in the small library; many POWs simply "lay in the sun and read."[39]

Wells was the only location in Minnesota where both Italian and German prisoners worked out of the same camp in the same season. The Germans occupied the camp until late September 1945, when a group of Italian POWs from Weingarten, Missouri, came to replace

Wells camp commander Schmiedeberg and his jeep outside the camp, 1945. *Courtesy of Werner Schmiedeberg*

them. Their arrival must have resembled a circus. Former commander
Schmiedeberg describes the scene:

> The exchange of German POWs and Italian POWs took
> place [on] the same day. I marched the Germans to the train
> station where an American attachment of guards signed for
> and ordered the prisoners aboard a troop train, which took
> them to the Colorado beet fields for the harvest. Everything
> about the morning procedure was very military-like and or-
> derly.
>
> We waited until the afternoon to receive the Italians. As
> the train arrived I was amazed. The POWs were hanging out
> of the windows, wearing an assortment of hats, including
> straw hats, or no hats at all. Bandannas around their necks
> were very popular. As they got off the train, some had suit-
> cases, others brought birds in bird cages, and they were all
> talking at once. The guards seemed not to have any control.
> All told, it was a very non-military sight.
>
> The officer was in a big hurry for me to sign for the Ital-
> ians, but I told him that I couldn't sign until I got a count. This
> took a good hour.
>
> After the count, they just started to pile into several trucks.
> I had to advise them that they had to walk, as the trucks were
> for baggage. Many wore open sandals and slippers of some
> sort—not very comfortable for the march to the camp.
>
> What followed in the next few days surprised me. Many
> women came to see the prisoners, claiming to have lived with
> them in Omaha.[40]

Successful employment of these prisoners seemed doubtful from
the beginning. Eventually, they created minor sabotage problems at
the plant, necessitating stricter administration. Their stay was otherwise productive, but brief; a failure of communication was cited as a
possible reason for the difficulties. The camp closed in mid October.[41]

Montgomery
Le Sueur County

June 10, 1944–October 9, 1944
June 3, 1945–October 21, 1945

The Minnesota Valley Canning Company's needs brought fifty German POWs to Montgomery in June 1944 to prepare the camp at the cannery. Buildings were added to those that had housed Mexican workers in the past. Later in the month, 288 additional POWs arrived; the camp commander was First Lieutenant Robert T. Cumback. Throwing handmade "swastika embellished" leaflets out of their train as it passed through Austin, Minnesota, this contingent made its presence felt before it reached Montgomery. A typical leaflet proclaimed, "Amerikans! Soon the robot bombers will come to your soil. Soon you will feel what war means. Quit the war before it is too late." Other notes contained "bitter attacks against Jews."[42]

A newspaper near the base camp in Algona reported the incident but suggested that "such activities are viewed more with amusement than anything else. The only danger . . . is that a stray one might be found by unthinking persons who might attribute it to some neighbor and start an unjust and cruel 'witch hunt.'" The train had been sealed, and FBI officials were puzzled how the leaflets had been dispersed. On the following day, however, the Austin *Daily Herald* reported that two brothers had seen one prisoner simply throw them out an open window.[43]

Montgomery's peas had been flooded in the spring, and a storm late in June destroyed 600 acres. Since the harvest was too small to keep the plant operating, the peas were brought to Le Sueur for processing, and plans were made to transport workers there. Some prisoners were kept in the area to man the vineries nearby.[44]

A visit from Howard Hong in 1944 revealed the difficulty of setting up constructive activities for the prisoners. Neither the town nor the base camp had been of any help; Algona's preoccupation with other matters was a likely reason. Some progress was made when the prisoners were allowed to swim at Lake Lexington, six miles away, and to play tennis at a nearby city playground. They improvised a soccer ball, using legging leather, and lifted weights made from cannery beet-rollers. Religious services were available in local churches.[45]

While prisoners were occupied at the cannery, plans were made to bring some of them 20 miles north to work at a pea vinery just south of Jordon. By August, preparations were being made for the corn harvest. Severe shortages of labor were a result of late planting, good growing conditions in July, and the beginning of the school year. Mexican labor was unavailable, sent to Oregon earlier in the summer because of the small pea pack. When they were not at the cannery, POWs were sent out in crews of eight for harvesting work. As many as 213 area farmers employed 300 prisoners. The camp was dissolved after the canning season in October 1944, when the POWs left for Faribault, Hollandale, and northern Minnesota.[46]

Col. Arthur Lobdell announced the establishment of a second camp at Montgomery for 1945. A group of fifty POWs came in June; 501 more arrived later in the month, and command of the camp was placed in the hands of Captain Clyde W. Snider. The camp eventually achieved the largest POW population of any in Minnesota, a total of 643 by August. The prisoners were housed at a hemp plant leased by the cannery in the northern part of town. Watch towers and barbed wire were installed; almost all the machinery was moved to make room, and a number of bunk houses were brought from the cannery for additional housing. The cannery was in operation 16 to 18 hours a day, and a supplemental work force of Mexicans and POWs had to be brought from the vineries and fields. Prisoners were also employed at vineries in Scott County.[47]

By mid-July, Le Sueur County's small grain fields had been judged by the Le Center *Leader* as "the best crop by far." Crews of civilian workers were organized and assembled in Le Center, the county seat; drivers were provided with extra gasoline. Prisoners would have been available, but cool weather had extended the pea harvest. In the ensuing confusion, the Le Center *Leader* urged: "Let's work together as best we can, keeping uppermost in mind that all foodstuffs is needed badly by our fighting men, by ourselves on the home front, by people who are our Allies and who are still near starvation from the ravages of war." Harvest crews of 300 men had been organized, but since there were more calls for help than could be filled, the Minnesota Valley Canning Company was asked for POW assistance. By early August, POWs were finally allowed to start field-work and finish the shocking that civilians had begun. A total of 509 POWs in 149 details were sent to thresh or shock in the fields.[48]

The Red Cross made its only known visit to the camp in September,

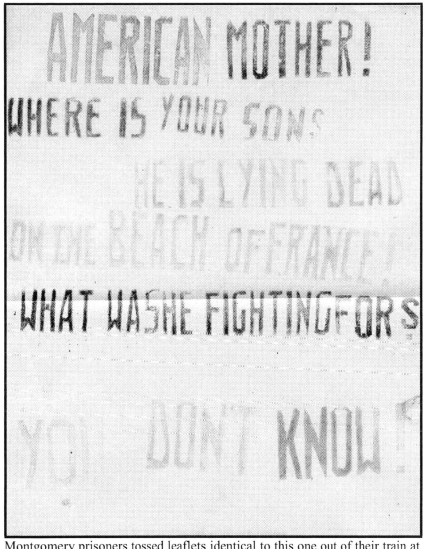

Montgomery prisoners tossed leaflets identical to this one out of their train at Austin, Minnesota, while being transported to the camp in June 1944. This copy was uncovered during a search at the base camp in Algona. They were made from wooden dies and YMCA ink and paper.[49] *Courtesy of A. T. Lobdell Manuscript Collection*

at the peak of the canning season, when a third of the 442 men were harvesting corn and the rest were working 15 to 17 hours daily at the cannery. Classroom instruction had been temporarily canceled, and other leisure activities including ping-pong had been suspended, although the local movie theater was open to prisoners twice a week, and German camp newspapers were available. The commander assured the Red Cross delegate, Mr. Schnyder, that normal working hours would return soon.

The POWs spokesman complained that the camp's rations were not enough for the increased workload. Schnyder concluded, however, that the food was sufficient and the general operation of the camp in good order. Hygiene and discipline were satisfactory. "We had a good impression about this camp," he wrote, conceding that a temporary establishment like Montgomery could not be as well-appointed as a permanent one.[50]

Former prisoner Hans Kratzheller recalls certain useful details of camp life at Montgomery, where he worked in both the fields and the cannery. Relations between the prisoners and the guards were apparently very cordial. Inside the compound, according to Kratzheller, the prisoners befriended the guards, who often came to the barracks for conversation. At the cannery, the prisoners often received better treatment than the Mexicans who worked nearby.

An entertaining interruption of an otherwise typical workday occurred when the camp commander, Captain Snider, arrived for an inspection. Cannery conditions were hot, and the prisoners often chose to work in tee-shirts. When Snider entered the premises he had to inquire which workers were prisoners, since none were wearing their required PW-marked clothing. Visibly disgruntled, Snider approached prisoner Kratzheller and drew a PW on his tee-shirt. The women civilians working nearby began giggling, and proceeded to draw PW letters on each other's clothing with lipstick. Snider stormed out of the factory, to the intense amusement of the workers. On another occasion, the commander tried to monitor the disappearance of sugar from the Le Sueur cannery, but the prisoners smuggled it into camp in their lunch buckets.

Eventually Kratzheller and a number of younger prisoners were transported to a Mankato box factory, where they often received cigarettes and beverages as gifts from the civilian workers. The work lasted only a short time, and as soon as the corn pack was completed, the camp at the old hemp plant began closing down. Before transfer to

Crookston or Algona, a number of POWs were kept at the cannery to wait for seed corn that still needed processing.[51]

Kurt Rasokat, stationed at Montgomery at the same time as Kratzheller, offers the following Prisoner Perspective.

Prisoner Perspective
Kurt Rasokat

Captured on his first day of duty, near Salerno, Italy, Kurt Rasokat helped other POWs and the victorious Americans bury the dead from both sides of the battle. Afterwards he was brought to a church that housed an improvised field hospital. He was sent to Sicily and then to Africa, where, as he recalls, he began to see Americans as people rather than as enemies. He celebrated his twentieth birthday on the Liberty Ship taking him to America.

From Norfolk, Virginia, he was brought to Indianola, Nebraska, where a meal was served the new arrivals in the middle of the night. The camp commander, walking among his new "guests," was pleased to know that they enjoyed what was served them. Six months later Rasokat was transferred to Algona, where a friend from the Indianola camp was waiting for him at the front gate.

Rasokat immersed himself in church activities organized by POW Pastor Alex Funke at the Algona camp. Realizing the importance that the church might have in the early stages of his imprisonment, he surrounded himself with friends similarly involved. Rasokat himself often went from barrack to barrack inviting people to services. In his view, prisoners of various beliefs "became closer" because the camp offered them the chance to improve their understanding of each other.

After working in a number of locations for about two weeks, picking corn and installing drainage spouts, Rasokat volunteered for work at Montgomery with the pea harvest. During his brief stay there, he was allowed to go swimming at a nearby lake and to attend religious services offered by local pastors. His most enduring remembrance of Montgomery was the vanilla ice cream with chocolate syrup that was available in the camp canteen.

Eventually he found himself helping with the sugar beet harvest in Wyoming in the fall of 1945. Brought to Fort Crook, Nebraska, Rasokat was informed of his departure for Europe. His group of POWs traveled through the Rocky Mountains, arrived in San Francisco, and boarded a Liberty Ship. On his copy of a map given to each POW, Rasokat traced the ship's route through the Panama Canal and past Cuba and Jamaica before it docked in England. In low spirits when they arrived, the POWs were hurried off to a camp near Liverpool that addressed the labor needs of a local RAF airport. There were painting projects and various duties in a bicycle factory. Rasokat himself served briefly as the camp barber. The POWs worked completely unguarded and had a good relationship with the English people they served.

Former POW Kurt Rasokat in 1995. While Rasokat was stationed at Montgomery in 1945, the camp housed more prisoners than any other in Minnesota. For most of these POWs, the time at Montgomery was short relative to their overall length of captivity. Even so, Rasokat and the other prisoners found time to participate in a variety of activities available at the camp, including movies, record concerts, and sports. *Author's photo*

Shortly before his return to Germany, Rasokat enrolled in a program called the Norton Camp, established in response to the acute shortage of pastors in Germany. Norton POWs were trained, in both England and Germany, to perform certain ministerial duties. Rasokat was frustrated in his wish to go home to East Prussia. There, as a youth, he had followed the advancing German troops on a bicycle; now the advancing Russians were preventing his return. In the meanwhile he sought the advice of his former camp pastor, Alex Funke, already back in Algona. Funke suggested the diaconate as a career choice; in October 1947, a month after his return to Germany, Rasokat started the necessary five-year course.

As a deacon he spent 32 years in missionary work, which included 24 years at the von Bodelschwingh Institut in Bethel. Later, when Alex Funke became director of the Institut, Rasokat was reunited with his old friend and pastor.

During his four years and four days of captivity, Rasokat learned, as he says, that the people he encountered from different countries were "simple people, human beings like us as well."

Based on the author's interviews with Rasokat in Germany on February 22 and 23, 1995.

> **Faribault**
> **Rice County**
>
> **June 1944–November 1944**
> **March 27, 1945–November 30, 1945**

Negotiations began in April 1944 for a camp in the Faribault area to aid canneries, nurseries, and farmers. The St. James school, closed for two years, was considered as a location, but the school's trustees resisted the idea because repairs would be needed and storing the school's materials would be a problem. Other obstacles presented themselves. Local 37 of the packing-house union, quick to oppose the camp, circulated a resolution on April 10 maintaining that there was no shortage of labor in the area. The union pointed out that escapes of prisoners from other camps had involved "shootings and other commotions," thus "jeopardizing the sanctity" of homes near those camps. The resolution was distributed to local officials, including the county agent and the mayor.[52]

Several members of Local 37 were present at the ensuing city-council meeting to express their convictions. After the discussion, the council decided neither to approve nor to reject the camp because it was the business of the U.S. government, and suggested that objections should be addressed to the canning company itself. By this time, barracks were already under construction on the factory grounds to house workers for the peak canning season. Asked to vote on the camp's acceptance, the local Rotary Club saw "no reason why such a camp should not be started in Faribault." Overwhelmed, the union "dropped the issue" when the city council denied its own jurisdiction. By June, barracks were being set up for the POWs on Russell Square, adjoining the Faribault Canning Company, hastily thrown together so they could be used by the prisoners as soon as possible. German POWs arrived a little later in June.[53]

The main source of work during both seasons was at the Faribault cannery, where the prisoners performed some of the most difficult work in the cooking room, a very hot area where the cans were packed and sealed. In June, a group of twenty was transported to a vinery near Coates in nearby Dakota County. A local paper reported that one POW had pointed to a 16-year-old American youth and inquired "why he wasn't in the army." Prisoners were also brought into neighboring Goodhue County, where they worked alongside Owatonna POWs picking corn for the Goodhue Canning Company.[54]

Beginning in August 1944, Howard Hong visited the Faribault camp at least four times during its two summers of operation. Recreational supplies were already on the way during his first visit, but nothing had yet arrived. Loss of the POWs' pay-coupons in transit complicated the tardy development of the camp's social life. Swimming was available nearby in the Cannon River; swimming trunks for the American personnel were ordered in Northfield.[55]

In November the camp experienced its only known "escape." Two prisoners, cleaning up the canteen after midnight, walked off the grounds "partially drunk on seven or eight bottles of 3.2 beer." They were apprehended by local police when they returned two hours later.[56]

POWs arrived at Faribault again in March 1945; some helped build additional barracks for more POWs. The prisoners reportedly felt less like captives than at Algona. "With good intention, comradeship, and mutual consideration," one wrote in June in the base-camp newspaper, "we will finish this job given to us and get over this dark time." A visit by Howard Hong in May occasioned a discussion of leisure-time activities with the prisoners' spokesman. A church service had been arranged with the pastor of the branch camp in Owatonna. Musical instruments for the prisoners were provided by the YMCA and the International Red Cross. English and German films were shown in cooperation with the Owatonna camp, a major ingredient of the POWs' recreation. The camp leadership was aware of the danger of "an eat-work-sleep existence" in the absence of enough leisure-time activity, but a visit from Hong in early August 1945 revealed progress. A school and an orchestra were in operation by then, and a Catholic priest served not only the Faribault camp but Owatonna and Montgomery as well.[57]

At the Faribault Cannery in 1945, POWs helped pack at least 225,000 boxes of corn, each with 24 cans. They also helped with welding work on the canning grounds. Outside the cannery, they worked at a local nursery, weeding and planting trees and raspberry plants, and grafting buds into seedlings. POW details were also sent out to jobs near Farmington, Hastings, and Rosemount. Returning from that area late on a September night, a bus carrying 27 prisoners struck a tree and overturned after the brakes and steering malfunctioned. Guards and the camp's ambulance rushed to the scene, eight miles out of town. The prisoners received medical attention at camp, and one was transported to Algona because it was feared he had broken a collar-bone. The bus had been late because a prisoner ill with malaria needed special attention during the day.[58]

When work at the cannery had slowed, farmers in counties to the north and east were eager to engage Faribault prisoners. A well-organized bid for prisoner labor was made in Dakota County, where a strong appeal by the county agent had already been made in July for "Crop Corps Youths." One advertisement stated: "It's up to YOU, Young America! . . . There's a real job to be done. NOW, and America is depending on you to help." Such efforts proved insufficient; by early August farmers were advised to place orders for the POWs they needed and to make the necessary deposit at the county agent's office. By October, civilian help had reached a wartime low, and prisoners were soon filling silos, shocking corn, and bailing on area farms. As a result of a meeting to aid vegetable growers in the town of Castle Rock, more than 100 prisoners arrived in separate groups within days to pull and top onions. Near the town of Miesville, prisoners helped gather shocks of grain which had been washed away during heavy storms.[59]

In order to continue using POWs in November, more than 50 farmers formed the "Dakota County Farmer War Prisoner Use Association" and renewed a contract with the Faribault cannery. The plan was a success; after the prisoners left, Dakota County's labor assistant declared that they had "saved the day."[60]

Prisoners were also responsible for harvesting one farmer's 100 acres of sweet-corn seed in Scott County to the north. Adverse weather conditions prevented the use of machines, and it was necessary to pick the entire crop by hand. The farmer received a group of 40 POWs on short notice; they worked five days and picked 75 tons of seed, enough to plant 20,000 acres.[61]

A September 1945 report by Red Cross delegate Schnyder sheds light on the work and recreation of the 411 prisoners in the camp at the time of his visit. Twenty-some labor detachments were harvesting corn on area farms; the remaining prisoners were at the cannery, 126 on the day shift and 97 at night. The peak season allowed little time for recreation, but the prisoners did manage to crowd some soccer and handball, among other sports, into their schedule. Schnyder found the prisoners too numerous for the camp to house them comfortably; he noted, for example, that the canteen was used as a leisure room and a dormitory. Informed that the facility was soon to close and that no changes would be made, he nevertheless concluded his report affirmatively: "The camp was really clean and tidy."[62]

The Faribault cannery's extreme dependence on POW labor must have reflected statewide conditions toward the end of the war. During this trip, Schnyder met at Minneapolis with the president of the Minnesota Canners Association, who much appreciated the prisoners' work and regretted their impending departure. He asked Schnyder if they might be kept in Minnesota to work another year, arguing that "conditions in Germany are too bad currently to send the Germans back there."[63]

Chapter 5

Camps Established for Multiple Industries

Each camp described in this chapter furnished labor for a nearby cannery and functioned additionally as a reliable source of manpower for area businesses and farms. Preliminary arrangements and procedures were similar to those at the cannery camps.

Besides canneries, nurseries, milk processors, ice manufacturers, and makers of brick and concrete products employed these POWs, keeping them occupied when the canning season was over. The employers paid the prevailing wage, usually 50 to 60 cents hourly.

Work outside the cannery allowed these camps to remain in operation much longer than those that lacked it. All, with the exception of St. Charles, were permanent and year-round. Given this stability, camp activities flourished; there were more sporting activities than elsewhere, such as boxing and soccer, and a greater selection of academic courses, including shorthand, mathematics, and languages. Additional free time for the prisoners was occupied with music, including performances by the camp orchestra. Some prisoners spent time writing detailed reports about camp activities and sketching pictures for the two Algona base camp newspapers, published bi-monthly and distributed to camps in four states.

The year-round compounds were set in more attractive facilities than the cannery camps. St. Charles, for example, utilized an old CCC camp in scenic Whitewater State Park; an old transient camp on the banks of the Cottonwood River was used near New Ulm. At Owatonna the prisoners enjoyed the spacious home of a former Minnesota state senator.

Typically, American camp commanders and guards became well known in town, speaking to Kiwanis meetings, Rotary clubs, and other special groups. Local newspapers often provided close coverage of camp events, as well as a continuing forum for citizens' sentiments.

POWs in these year-round camps were more likely than elsewhere to become familiar with their employers and other Americans, as this chapter's three Prisoner Perspectives make clear.

| New Ulm |
| Brown County |
| June 7, 1944–December 1945 |

The New Ulm branch camp, opening in the summer of 1944, supplied labor for area businesses and factories until December 1945. In 1943 the California Packing Company in the nearby town of Sleepy Eye had provided accommodations for many workers; 209 men and boys, seasonal laborers at the cannery, were housed in a building that the company had acquired from near New Ulm. Brown County's labor shortage was increasing by 1944, and the War Manpower Commission certified the area's need for 250 POWs. The prisoners were just one group of laborers among several at the cannery; in addition to the company's American work force, 25 Mexican natives arrived for work in the county the first week of June, and the total had reached 100 by the time the prisoners came.[1]

The POWs' arrival in New Ulm in June 1944 under the eventual command of First Lieutenant Arthur S. Roberts must have had something of the flavor of a homecoming; New Ulm is a town with a strong German heritage. News of the D-Day invasion, a day before the New Ulm camp opened, soon reached the prisoners. The POWs and their escorts stopped in town for directions "and the first thing they spotted along the street was a 'beer' sign which one prisoner apparently read to the rest." The POWs cheered loudly as they passed a few girls. Two local boys, camping in the nearby woods, also encountered some of the early arrivals. The boys were frying eggs when a couple of POWs showed them how to do it "German-European style." The rest of the prisoners arrived by train later in June.[2]

The initial contingent cut down trees and cleaned up the grounds of the old transient camp south of New Ulm, established in the mid-1930s for the unemployed. The cannery paid $50 per week to house the prisoners there. The transients had built facilities, including an artificial lake, expressing the conviction that the area's needy families, like the well-to-do, should have a lake to go to. With its civilian boaters and bathers, the lake was a potential source of trouble, prompting camp authorities to stress the importance of public distance from the prisoners. If civilian contact occurred, extra guards would have to be used, and the prisoners would lose some of their bathing privileges.[3]

After their arrival, the POWs described in their newspaper how they proceeded with zeal "to also create a place here that would be worthy of Germans." The initial effort of cleaning and painting led to the creation of a clubroom, which the skill of various trade-workers turned into a comfortable place. POWs met there for intellectual stimulation and entertainment, including the music of ocarina players, who managed to bring "relaxation and joy."[4]

In July, a month after the POWs' arrival, Howard Hong described the camp as one of the most attractive in the upper Mississippi area, deriving its "beauty through the work of those it housed." Various activities were available. A local German-speaking pastor, J. A. Marxhausen, acting on his conviction that German POWs should be treated just as Americans wanted their own to be treated, offered to provide services to the prisoners. The gesture was welcomed by their spokesman. Pastor Marxhausen also arranged to have the newspaper office collect German storybooks from local citizens for distribution at the camp. Lutheran and Catholic services were held on Sundays and Wednesdays; Hong supplied funds for the purchase of lumber so an altar could be built and carved by the POWs. Classes were planned, with 42 students interested in English and a total of 19 in three other subjects. The teachers included the camp's medical officer. Many POWs played instruments; one apparently played the Hawaiian guitar. A chorus was being formed, and the local Catholic priest found a piano for the POWs, which spurred activities in the camp's chapel.[5]

The main source of employment for the prisoners was the cannery in the neighboring town of Sleepy Eye, which also employed 400 to 500 civilians. Prisoners were used like any other seasonal workers; according to a former supervisor, they were "good kids," doing just enough to get by. School buses transported the POWs from New Ulm to Sleepy Eye for both shifts at the cannery. Whenever workers were needed, the camp was telephoned and the POWs were brought the next day with two guards. The prisoners carried their own lunches, which they were allowed to eat in the plant cafeteria. Tricksters among them would first eat the meat inside their sandwiches, and then show the foreman how little they were receiving for their meals. Sometimes after removing the meat, they took sugar from 100-pound sacks used in the plant, made a thick paste with a little bit of water, and spread it over bread. The POWs found other uses for cannery sugar back in camp; that they managed to brew alcohol was authenticated when one POW arrived at work with an apparent hangover.

According to their foreman, whenever the prisoners got word that they would be searched, sugar was scattered all over the cannery lawn.[6]

The cooking room superintendent at the cannery, who at times provided milk and sandwiches to the prisoners during their shift, claimed they "respected authority" and "were easy to get along with." One prisoner, he recalls, was returned to Algona since he demanded that all other POWs salute him.[7]

The New Ulm POWs were also an important source of labor for small companies in the area. They were instrumental in keeping local brick and tile yards operating at full strength; the needs of three firms kept the men busy into the winter of 1944. The Ochs Brick and Tile Company in Springfield, where 80 to 125 people made bricks during the war, employed New Ulm POWs regularly, although the company's application was initially rejected because of high costs to the government and the low priority rating of the product. When the POWs were brought there and introduced to their work, they were surprised to hear German spoken by the civilian workers. The prisoners figured in a labor dispute at the Ochs plant, when the union demanded their removal if the union's wage demands were not negotiated. It was concluded, however, that the POWs were of no consequence in the dispute, and the firm continued using them.[8]

Besides working at the Ochs factory, the POWs were employed at the American Artstone company plant and in the New Ulm Brick and Tile yards. In order to avoid working there, prisoners were said to have damaged some of the machinery. When the owner's son—himself a POW in Germany—returned from the war and assumed control of the factory, he chose not to use the prisoners since he "was pretty bitter about things." Another New Ulm factory, Elk River Concrete Products, eventually employed some POWs as well. In neighboring Sleepy Eye, POWs plucked chickens at the A. J. Pietrus plant. During the winter, the prisoners thought back to the fall harvest—"the pea and skirt-chasing time"—as they called it, and speculated that not even their hardest-working men could "show any love to the bricks." They were more optimistic about poultry work, in which they imagined "trying to now make a name for themselves as duck pluckers and egg washers."[9]

In summer, the POWs had plenty of opportunity to fish and bathe. For winter sports, they made skis and skates in their workshop. In March 1945, Red Cross delegate Dr. Zehnder arrived to inspect the

SEITENLAGER Nr. 7 - NEW ULM

Sketch of the New Ulm camp in 1945 by a POW, who also drew pictures for a civilian worker at the Sleepy Eye cannery. Minnesota's POWs often submitted articles and drawings similar to this one for publication in the base camp newspaper.[10] *Courtesy of Drahtpost (Algona German POW newspaper)*

New Ulm POWs at the Ochs Brick and Tile factory in nearby Springfield. Prisoners were surprised when they heard civilian workers speaking German. *Courtesy of Brown County Historical Society*

POW twins from the New Ulm camp. Some locals were bothered when some New Ulm residents provided ice cream, beer, and cigarettes to the prisoners located there, particularly when relatives of their own—POWs in Germany— were not receiving such good treatment.[11] *Courtesy of Brown County Historical Society*

camp. He noted one difficulty with the recreational opportunities offered by the camp's location: sewage disposal in the lake was a hygienic problem, becoming a "rather serious disadvantage during the hot and humid season, for the bad odor enters the camp." Zehnder called this defect to the attention of the commanding officer, who assured the delegate "that he would take it up immediately." Otherwise, Zehnder was impressed by the camp's location and commented favorably on the "view of beauty of natural surroundings and the prisoners' living conditions."[12]

Popular concern about the POWs' living conditions, especially the small amount of food they were given, eventually issued in a discussion at a local Rotary Club meeting. The camp's commander, Captain Charles Lawyer, maintained that the POWs were receiving 3,400 calories a day: a warm breakfast, sandwiches and coffee for lunch, and yet another warm meal when they returned to the camp in the evening. Overall, they were well fed, he said, and none of them had lost any weight or had been sick. As to leisure activities, no cigarettes were given to the POWs, but they were able to roll their own with canteen-purchased tobacco. Movies were shown once a week at a charge of 15 cents. Two daily newspapers and four radios were available on the premises. Captain Lawyer was aware that some local people were feeding the prisoners, but in his observation the POWs considered them "suckers" for such treatment. He emphasized that it was his "responsibility to see that they work," and added that "these prisoners are not exactly guests. A few months ago they were shooting our boys over in Germany." A local American army returnee from Germany, adding fuel to the fire, told the Rotary Club that the treatment of prisoners in New Ulm was much better than what Americans received in Europe.[13]

In June additional prisoners arrived, necessitating more tents and stretching the camp's capacity to its limits. The quantity of peas canned in 1945 was the largest in the history of the Sleepy Eye cannery, so great that the plant considered diverting some of its pea crop to nearby canneries. Only one setback appears to have occurred when a quantity equaling 3,000 cases of peas spoiled because there were not enough workers. One local paper voiced the opinion "that those in charge of the factories would be doing a splendid service by allowing the people of the towns and others to go into those fields and salvage all they can use." POWs again worked in the cannery during the corn harvest; the factory produced "a tremendous yield."[14]

The number of New Ulm POWs used in harvesting climbed markedly in 1945. Within two days following the end of their cannery work, prisoners were trucked to three area counties, and the state farm-help supervisor informed all interested parties that the POW farm dispatcher, a former school superintendent, was at their service. The standard method by which farmers acquired help was to group together, nominate a leader, and apply collectively for prisoners. By July 30 ninety-one POWs were working in Brown County, a number that varied daily during the harvest. The local paper called the prisoners "trusties," and suggested that there was no likelihood any would escape. The POWs were supplied without guards, apparently considered unnecessary since there was "little chance of them getting away if they did 'make a break.'" By August, additional prisoners were transferred from Montgomery, and their use at area farms expanded into eight counties.[15]

Starting in the last week of July, newspapers in Redwood County reported that prisoners would soon be available there; farmers were to pick the men up in town and return them at the end of the day. Meetings, including one at the Wabasso library, were arranged to discuss the use of prisoners. By the first week of August a group of POWs was transported daily to Walnut Grove. POW groups of 25 men were sent to Morgan, where the USES had never experienced a greater need for labor. Their guard stood by "to receive reports on misconduct or disorderliness." A commercial club in Morgan handled all the down payments on behalf of area farmers, who in turn reimbursed the organization daily. In the northern part of the county, as many as 20 prisoners a day were transported to Redwood Falls, where the Civic and Commerce Association and the local USES office had teamed up to bring them in. At times, groups numbering up to 20 prisoners moved from farm to farm shocking grain. The Redwood Falls *Gazette* reported that "the men learn rapidly and although they are not seasoned hands, they do get the grain set up." In general, area farmers were "well satisfied with their work."[16]

In Lyon County, one Cottonwood observer commented on the POWs: "I had a true picture of the Supermen. They were ordinary; mostly the pure Aryan type, blond, husky, and healthy. Of course there were some misfits, probably a bit of unclean blood in their make-up, dark-haired, small and wiry." Traveling with the prisoners to and from New Ulm, this American conversed with the men, informing one of them that Russia had declared war on Japan that day. The

A New Ulm prisoner, far left, with other workers taking a break from threshing on the Clifford Jeske farm near New Ulm. The Jeske family maintained contact with some of the prisoners after the war.[17] *Courtesy of Brown County Historical Society*

New Ulm POWs. In a report in their newspaper, they write: "With thoughts at home, faith in the hearts, and a knowledgeable smile on the lips, that's who we are, the prisoners of New Ulm."[18] *Courtesy of Brown County Historical Society*

prisoner replied, "Japs no good, Italians no good, Russians no good," and relayed the information to the others. Farmers had conflicting opinions about the quality of the prisoners' work near Cottonwood; some were pleased, while others claimed that the prisoners were just average. Lyon County made little use of POW labor because of the distance from New Ulm.[19]

Closer to camp, prisoners were made available in Blue Earth County. Lacking transient labor, Sibley County requested New Ulm POWs as well. The county's farmers were required to place their orders for prisoners by 3:00 the day before they were needed and to prepare enough work for an entire day. Soon prisoners were arriving in small groups and working in the vicinity of Gaylord and Winthrop.[20]

Prisoners were used near St. Peter, primarily in the western part of Nicollet County, since workers from the state hospital aided farmers to the east. The demand for New Ulm prisoners dropped off considerably near the end of August, when some never even left the camp. In 1945, the New Ulm POWs threshed at least 6,493 acres in area counties, during a total of 26,197 man-hours.[21]

Although almost all POW working relationships with local farmers went smoothly, one family using prisoners for harvest work in the fall of 1945 became dangerously familiar with a prisoner. New Ulm, with its strong German heritage, was a likely location for the incident. The fence surrounding the camp stood at a distance from the buildings, and it was easily passed through by POWs. On January 15, 1946, two New Ulm residents, Walter Sellner and Catharina Rosenstengel, were charged with aiding prisoner Helmut Lichtenberg to escape, and conspiring to do so.

The court transcripts depict a camp where such an incident might well occur. At night only two guards were on duty, one in the camp office, the other at the gate. POWs worked without a guard, the customary arrangement at New Ulm. Lichtenberg, a young paratrooper captured after D-Day in France, became acquainted with Walter Sellner's mother-in-law, originally from the same area in Germany as the prisoner. Mrs. Rosenstengel, who cooked for the threshers, became acquainted with Lichtenberg while he was threshing on the Sellner farm.

In a letter to Mrs. Rosenstengel, enclosing a drawing, Lichtenberg indicated that he would be able to meet his American friends on a Saturday night at a certain cornfield one-and-a-half miles from camp, in order to visit them at their home. Sellner, the son-in-law, drove to the New Ulm tile yard where the POW was working and arranged the date and time. According to plan, at 8:30 p.m., three hours after head count on October 27, Lichtenberg would go to the cornfield, wait for Sellner's car to turn off its lights, and then exit the field.

The Sellner and Rosenstengel families drove to the site. Before Lichtenberg approached them, three other POWs, apparently waiting for another car, came up to the Americans. Realizing their mistake, they exclaimed in German, "This is not the right car!" Subsequently Lichtenberg came out of the cornfield and joined his hosts. While they did some shopping in New Ulm, he waited in their back seat. At no other time was he left alone. Lichtenberg and the two families visited all evening, and the POW spent the night with them.

The visit continued on Sunday afternoon after some of the family had gone to church. Lichtenberg made it clear that he was to be returned to camp by 5:30 p.m. for roll call. In good time, five family members drove him through the main gate of the camp, which had no sentry, and were stopped by a guard.

Grilled by the camp authorities, the family initially claimed that they had picked Lichtenberg up that afternoon, but later admitted that they had met him the previous evening in the cornfield. They expressed various levels of concern about their actions; Lichtenberg had assured them in his letter that nobody would get into trouble. Mrs. Rosenstengel made known her belief that the POWs were not treated well. All protested that they had no intention of aiding a permanent escape. Mrs. Rosenstengel's chief motive had been the hope that the POW would get in touch with her relatives in Germany.

Lichtenberg was immediately put in solitary confinement for fourteen days, with a bread and water diet. In court martial proceedings that followed, he was punished with six months of solitary confinement after it became clear that his final story did not coincide with his earlier statements, or with those of his hosts.

Court proceedings for the two accused Americans established that no "un-American" or "unpatriotic" acts had been committed. Mrs. Rosenstengel, an American by marriage, offered the defense that she didn't read the paper and didn't listen to the radio. Asked whether she knew she had done wrong, she answered, "Well, in a way I did and in another way I didn't realize it was so bad." Given the two defendants' plea of "no contest" and the nature of the facts presented, the court imposed fines of $300 each, and lectured Sellner and Mrs. Rosenstengel on the importance of observing laws of Congress passed in time of war. The testimony suggests that more than one such nocturnal escapade took place at the New Ulm camp, but the whole truth will never be known.[22]

By the end of August, the New Ulm prisoners were eager to return home. The commander of the camp, Captain Charles Lawyer, discussed their attitude at a Kiwanis club meeting in Mankato. He declared that "the Nazis . . . still think they are a 'master race,' jeer at those who can be induced to show them favors, work best and seem happiest under rigid, impersonal discipline." He concluded, however, that the prisoners "are good workers . . . [and] have shown little inclination to attempt escape."[23]

Two months later, in the final weeks of December 1945, the New Ulm camp closed after a year and a half of continual operation, and the last remaining prisoners were transferred. It was among the last three camps to close at the war's end; only Deer River and Owatonna outlived it. Shortly after the facilities were emptied, the local Jaycees were making plans to convert them into temporary housing for returning veterans and their families.[24]

> **Fairmont**
> **Martin County**
>
> **June 5, 1944–July 1944**
> **September 2, 1944–December 14, 1945**

Martin County's camp had a long life, beginning in 1944 when the Fairmont Canning Company engaged POWs and other foreign workers for canning-related work. In May 1944, the necessary plumbing extensions were installed at the fairgrounds; the POWs were scheduled to leave in mid-September so the county fair could still be held. The Fairmont cannery had planned for a total of 1,100 foreign workers, including 630 from the West Indies and 325 POWs. For its facilities the cannery purchased $10,000 worth of equipment—dining tables, blankets, mattresses, and bunks—and eleven barracks from an airport in Estherville, Iowa, used previously for Air Force training at a junior college.[25]

The prisoners began arriving on June 5, 1944, and were housed in the 4-H building at the fairgrounds. Noticing a local newspaper representative with a camera, the first contingent of 30 to 40 POWs waved their arms and jumped on boxes to get a better view. The Fairmont *Daily Sentinel* noted how "one huge German picked up a mattress and held it, Atlas-like over his head." The guards eventually moved them so they would not be photographed. Two days later, two truckloads of POWs arrived, bringing the total to 100. The prisoners, carrying pocket dictionaries, tried to interpret what was said to them by the local people. POWs were quoted as saying, "It will soon be over and we can go home again. We're coming back here to live, in 1950. Fairmont is very beautiful. It looks like a park."[26]

Two weeks after their arrival, 20-odd prisoners were sent to the nearby town of Winnebago to set up facilities for workers arriving from Barbados. The prisoners were fed at a local café, an hour before it opened to the general public. One prisoner was asked if he would like to escape. "Why should we want to escape?" he replied. "We are being better cared for here than under Hitler's program. We had to work there so why not work here where we are paid sufficient for our needs, are well fed and housed. It would be foolish, indeed, to try to escape." The Fairmont cannery recruited Barbadians for work near Winnebago, but it preferred war prisoners and Mexicans. "Only as a last resort," the Winnebago *Times* reported, "will the Jamaicans be returned here by the company for help. Because they are so slow moving, these islanders are not considered top rate help."[27]

Within a month of the camp's establishment, some signs of trouble arose with the American personnel who were stationed there. The first commander misused government transportation, associated with his enlisted men "in an inappropriate manner," and had an improper association with local women. He was replaced. Additionally, two enlisted men were returned to Algona for allowing one or two prisoners to sneak out of camp to visit young women, and for illegally carrying notes between POWs from Fairmont to Algona.[28]

The prisoners quickly made themselves comfortable in their camp—too comfortable, it seems, since their incidental encounters with local people prompted increased attention to security. Guards took a camera away from one citizen. Two local women sneaked under the camp fence to get closer to the POWs, and were thrown out. "It just isn't policy," the camp's commanding officer declared, "for anything in skirts—or slacks—to come waggling feminine figures around there."[29]

Such incidents angered Americans both locally and overseas. Sitting under an apple tree somewhere in France during a lull in the fighting, a corporal came across a Fairmont paper of June 15, 1944, reporting the attention given by local women to the POWs. "This is my home state," he wrote to the paper.

> I'm five thousand miles from my father and mother. I gave up EVERYTHING that makes life worthwhile to do my part to stop these Germans from destroying these worthwhile things and look at the sympathy being shown those barbarians back there. If only those who are carrying on flirtations and making personal contact with those prisoners would stop long enough to visualize the hardships we are encountering in subdueing [sic] these barbarians, they might at least understand why such things irk the soldiers who are guarding them, even though no consideration is given us as we sweat to take them from their fox-holes. . . . the prisoners you are slipping food to and also flirting with, took the food and lives of helpless and innocent families who love the same kind of life and freedom as you and I do.[30]

Other citizens questioned the prisoners' treatment at the cannery, incensed that the POWs received a roll and a cup of coffee in the morning. A canning company official responded by emphasizing that the POWs ate breakfast at 6:00 and were not relieved for lunch until 3:00 in the afternoon.

An "escape" from the Fairmont camp occurred in early July; the two escapees, who were also charged with "irregularities in their correspondence," were sentenced to 20 days' confinement. Unsettled relations between the POWs, their guards, and the local population were to persist for the remainder of the camp's existence.[31]

In July, the company's barracks at the plant north of town, large enough to house several hundred workers, were set on solid concrete foundations and modernized with plumbing, sewer connections, and electricity. They had been designed for seasonal laborers but were suitable for year-round use. Meanwhile, the POWs had damaged the Four-H building where they were initially housed, and were permanently removed from it. Reportedly they stole kitchen utensils, marred walls, removed partitions, and scattered 20,000 pounds of waste paper stored at the fairgrounds, apparently when they were searching for something to read. They promised to clean up the paper, but never did. At a scrap drive meeting shortly thereafter, one local citizen commented that "if the Nazis could cause such destruction under guard of United States soldiers, think what they would do if they were loose."[32]

Military records indicate that the camp closed for a short time in July and August. By the time it resumed operations in September under the command of Captain Joseph E. Gaitskill, the POWs were sleeping on army cots scattered over the floors of an old inn and its adjacent cottages, closed a few years previously, at nearby Interlaken Park. The new location had been established within 24 hours after a call was made to Algona. "The idyllic Interlaken Park," as described by the POWs, was an area where the "warm sun spreads its rays over a peaceful nature." A ten-foot woven wire fence was erected "to protect the prisoners from predatory females and other wild animals," and the local deputy sheriff was on duty at the camp to prevent civilian interference. The public was warned repeatedly to stay away from the POWs.[33]

It appears, however, that at times the challenge was to keep the prisoners away from civilians. Late one September evening, three POWs managed to exit the compound. On a road south of town, a civilian recognized the men as prisoners and apprehended one of them. The other two fled back to camp, apparently making their way across nearby Amber Lake in a rowboat, using boards for paddles. The captured prisoner, described in the local paper as a "19-year-old boy," refused to disclose the names of the other two. Explaining the incident, he stated: "We heard the music across the lake at Amber Inn. It was a nice night, so we thought we'd go." He was first taken to the county jail and later transferred to the base camp at Algona for punishment.[34]

On October 15 the prisoners were finally moved to barracks near Fourth and State Streets in Fairmont, which had formerly housed Mexican workers.[35] A POW characterized this latest move in the base-camp newspaper:

> Each change carries with it expectation and surprise, and the surprise surpassed every expectation, above all the 'charm' of the muck, which is just like the mud in Russia.[36]

According to this prisoner, the POWs had to rid the barracks of the "unimaginable" dirt and food-refuse left by the Mexicans, who had "wreaked havoc" on this place. Moreover, the neighborhood was unattractive; a glance through the barbed wire revealed a factory with its "eternally smoking and sooting chimney," a couple of wooden houses, bare trees, nothing "which could have pleased the eye." The barracks themselves were eventually acceptable "after water, soap, and brushes had got rid of the last traces of the Mexicans."[37]

As elsewhere, the POWs in Fairmont were an essential supplement to the labor supply. The War Manpower Commission recruited in the area, but local women had trouble finding care for their children, and local high-school boys were involved with football practice. The work performed by the POWs varied seasonally. They packed peas at the cannery in June, and eventually worked in the Winnebago cannery as well. The Winnebago plant received 40 prisoners each day. They worked on the labeling machines and in other "safe" areas; the local paper reported that "the prisoners have no access to open cans, so it is utterly impossible for them to slip anything into the cans even if they desire to do so." They eventually helped harvest and pack corn in August and September. At the Fairmont cannery, they were separated from civilian workers by a wire enclosure. Later in the year, commercial fishing and snow shoveling were suggested as ways to occupy them during the winter.[38]

Howard Hong visited the camp in January 1945, and mentioned the rapport at church services between the local pastor and the POWs, with attendance sometimes exceeding 60 percent. Classes in mathematics, shorthand, and English were being offered. Fifty books were supplied by Algona, apparently so well circulated that they were hard to keep in repair. Every two weeks movies were shown, and Hong noted that "a small orchestra with a piano, two violins, an accordion, guitar and drum play occasionally." Sunday music included operatic material by Wagner and Verdi. The camp's musical diversions, as described by a prisoner, allowed the POWs to forget "all the worries and needs of everyday life."[39]

In March, Red Cross's Dr. Zehnder arrived to consider the POWs' health, accommodations, and general sense of well-being. Assembly-line work, he reported, was generally disliked. Some POWs, according to their spokesman, suffered from infections of the hands due to constant contact with chickens; the camp reportedly had about twenty cases of infected hands. Apart from that and some cases of flu, however, the health of the POWs was generally good, and steps were being taken to make it better. By March, the muddy ground of the camp had been properly drained; the POWs had planted flower boxes, placed benches here and there, and built an arbor. These improvements, the prisoners claimed, gave the camp "a familiar impression of order and cleanliness."[40]

During the summer of 1945, the low estate of the camp's guards became a topic of discussion in the Fairmont *Daily Sentinel*. An editorial deplored the "mistreatment" of guards, and suggested that their duty was among the last tasks that a soldier would want to do. The guards had not been invited to the local Memorial Day services, and had not been asked to help with a "Here's Your Infantry" show that had passed through Fairmont. Appealing to the town and its organizations to pay proper respect, the editorial apologized on behalf of the city: "We hope that before you leave something will happen so that you may carry with you something besides unpleasant memories of the town in which you are so well performing one of war's most disagreeable duties."[41]

Whatever might be said against them, it was clear that the POWs worked hard. A local pea-viner claimed they were the best help he ever had. On his farm, prisoners worked two shifts, the first from 6:00 a.m. until 5:00 p.m., the second until the appropriate amount of acreage was finished for the day, sometimes as late as midnight. The POWs worked fast; occasionally they were advised to slow down to avoid clogging the machinery. After the pea pack, POWs were used to shock the area's oat fields; by the first two weeks of August, 234 POWs were helping on 56 different farms. After oats, they started work on the sweet corn harvest, much briefer than usual because cold weather had shortened the growing season.[42]

With the best small-grain outlook in years in 1945, POWs were used in neighboring Jackson County to the west, where as many as 17 farmers used 95 prisoners. The prisoners, along with 800 Mexican and civilian workers, detasseled corn and shocked a total of more than a thousand acres. The county agent evaluated the POWs' work as "generally good." Blue Earth County farmers were allowed to use prisoners; near the city of Truman just north of Fairmont, the men were said to be "industrious, courteous and careful in their work."

In nearby Watonwan County, four locations were set up to handle the requests for prisoners. The St. James chamber of commerce was responsible for getting its local businessmen into the fields; drivers were provided with gasoline. Local stores closed early to free up additional laborers, and transient workers were available. Authorities in this area stressed that "these prisoners are Germans, but not Nazis, have proved their working worth, are not troublesome and go without guards." County placement officers traveled daily to Fairmont to obtain the number of men needed, sometimes hauling a total of 75 prisoners. Their 3,345 hours of work in Watonwan County was deemed "generally satisfactory." Farmers in western Faribault County employed prisoners as well. In addition to hourly wages the farmers had to pay 45 cents daily for each man, to cover the expense of their housing.[43]

Again, POWs helped in the Fairmont cannery. Although Jamaicans had been recruited for canning, not enough were available. The Winnebago plant, with expanded facilities and faster machines, employed Mexicans, Jamaicans, and prisoners from the base camp at Algona. Not until early October did the camp start reducing its numbers as local people became available for work.[44]

POWs were used at Lanesboro Produce, Fairmont Ice, Jeck Poultry, and several nurseries. The prisoners had to travel three hours each day to one factory; their spokesman once wished the camp could be moved closer to the job. POWs worked for the city of Fairmont, for DeKalb and Pioneer Seed companies detasseling corn, and in the nearby town of Elmore, helping tear down an old school building.[45]

After the camp closed in December, empathy for the POWs'

guards and their duties resurfaced in the Fairmont *Daily Sentinel.* Years of war were blamed for making "patriotic" organizations indifferent to them. They weren't invited to parades or parties, though many of them had been overseas and in battle. The paper had an affirmative recollection of the POWs themselves. The editorialist hoped that the well-behaved prisoners, who had done valuable service for small pay, would carry a favorable view of the American way of life back to Germany, where they would broadcast what they had experienced. The *Sentinel* was glad they had been well fed and housed, and that Fairmont's citizens had learned to see them as human beings just like themselves. "Local history," the paper affirmed, "will not fail to record that during the great war Fairmont had its prisoner of war camp. It was not a disagreeable experience, but let us pray it will never have another."[46]

One employer near Fairmont maintained particularly close contact with a prisoner, one of several POWs who worked at the Elmore Nursery. During the six years following the war, prisoner Heinrich Waldschmidt wrote a total of 17 letters to his former employer, illuminating many of the difficulties the POWs faced at home: the increasing fear of writing letters to relatives in the Russian zone, the uncertainty of employment, and the daily discomforts one had to live with during the early years of rebuilding Germany. Waldschmidt hoped to move to the United States; the nursery owner, Mr. Coupanger, went to the length of hiring a law firm in nearby Blue Earth to handle negotiations with the American Consulate. Coupanger was informed, however, that there was no possibility of his sponsoring the former POW. Decades after Waldschmidt received the disappointing news and contact with his former employer faded, he offered the following reminiscences.[47]

Prisoner Perspective
Heinrich Waldschmidt

In 1947, days after Heinrich Waldschmidt had returned to Germany by way of England, he was in the woods near his home, driving wild game for American officers stationed nearby. One of the Americans called out, "That is the one that laid a doll in his bed and was out at the county fair." The voice was that of his old camp commander in Fairmont, Minnesota, Captain Gaitskill.

Waldschmidt's road to Fairmont began when he joined the German army as a teenager. Stationed in Greece, he participated in the invasion of Crete, and was soon afterwards in North Africa, defending the last German air base there with his tank unit. In early May the unit destroyed its own tanks and surrendered with the rest of the Afrika Korps. Waldschmidt worked briefly in a field hospital that received wounded men from Sicily, but by fall he had passed through New York on his way to Indianola, Nebraska. At the Indianola POW camp he became friends with a sergeant who forwarded a letter to Waldschmidt's uncle, his mother's brother, living in St. Louis, who had immigrated in 1912. Two weeks later he had his uncle's reply, the first letter received by any prisoner in the camp. The uncle even visited him at Indianola, and encouraged Waldschmidt to spend as much time out of camp as possible and get to know the United States and its people.

By April 1944 Waldschmidt had been transferred to Algona, Iowa. He recalls that the camp spokesman there was suspicious of the letters and newspapers that came from Waldschmidt's uncle; the spokesman considered the uncle "an enemy," and Waldschmidt "one that betrays Germany." Soon afterwards, Waldschmidt followed his uncle's advice and volunteered to work just over the state border in Minnesota, at Fairmont.

He enjoyed the Fairmont cannery, but the camp officials and cannery management were concerned that Waldschmidt and others who spoke some English would get too close to the civilian female workers. He was thus one of ten-odd prisoners picked for work at the Elmore Nursery. There he soon became well acquainted with the owner and his family. Waldschmidt and the other POWs helped with all operations of the nursery, including landscaping a new church in nearby Blue Earth and planting trees for an entire week in a local park.

Later in the fall, the Elmore Nursery's POWs were allowed to accompany the owner to northern Minnesota and Canada, to cut Christmas trees.

The relationship achieved a remarkable level of trust; at times when Mr. Coupanger, the owner, and his family were vacationing or out of town, the POWs ran the nursery themselves. Waldschmidt took charge of the money from sales. Once, when the family was on vacation, there were so many sales that Waldschmidt carried thousands of dollars in his pouch. The owner's family often ate lunch with the prisoners. Waldschmidt must have impressed the family with his ability as a storyteller; during the lunch break, the owner's young daughter often came running up to him requesting "a new fairy tale" before he started eating.

Heinrich Waldschmidt with Barbara Ann Coupanger during a reunion in 1995. Waldschmidt's uncle, an American living in St. Louis, suggested how Waldschmidt should spend his time as a prisoner: "I wasn't in the base camp very often. I was always out, that was advice from my uncle. He said, go among the people and then you will learn the most. Don't stay sitting in the camp."[48] *Courtesy of Barbara Coupanger*

Like other POWs who spoke English, Waldschmidt was able to make the most of lax security at the camp. Unloading trash at a landfill, the prisoners found discarded civilian clothing, including shirts, pants, and even shoes. They wore these clothes instead of their PW-marked outfits when they sneaked under the camp fence in the evening, often to attend events that civilian fellow-workers had spoken of. At the county fair they encountered the camp's head guard, apparently with no negative results. They had a complex arrangement with local girls, who drove by the camp in their cars, honked twice, and waited; the prisoners knew they had 15 minutes to sneak under the fence for the rendezvous. When the POWs reentered the camp later in the evening, the guards who noticed them were unconcerned.

Waldschmidt's experiences in Fairmont, particularly the work at the Elmore Nursery, made camp life a rather agreeable adventure. The experience ended when the camp closed in December 1945, requiring him to return to Algona. Shortly afterwards, he was released through Omaha, traveled West to San Francisco, and by March boarded a Liberty Ship bound for England. Arriving in England, he stayed there less than a year, working for a British major and taking part in re-education programs for young German soldiers. In January 1947 he finally arrived home in Germany.

His accidental meeting ten days later with his former commander from Fairmont led to his first post-war employment. Captain Gaitskill was friendly: "If you are interested, come to me on Monday. . . . and then you will work for us. . . . We know each other." Waldschmidt accepted the offer and worked at the nearby army base until 1951. Eventually he worked for a German company that installed heating systems at American Army and Air Force bases; the affiliation lasted 19 years until his retirement.

In hindsight, Waldschmidt says: "It pleased me that we came to America, I in any case with certainty." Waldschmidt still maintains contact with his uncle's family in America. It was his uncle's advice that issued in his unusual experiences as a prisoner in a foreign land, and in fond memories that have lasted a lifetime.

Based on the author's interview with Waldschmidt in Germany on February 12, 1995.

Owatonna
Steele County
March 23, 1944–December 21, 1945

Owatonna was Minnesota's longest-lived camp established for canning and other farm-related work. A prominent local family joined the cannery in bringing war prisoners to Steele County in March 1944, when thirty-five POWs arrived under the jurisdiction of the Concordia, Kansas base camp. Buildings were leased and renovated a mile north of Owatonna, on acreage belonging to the Cashman family, which operated farms and one of the largest nurseries in the northwestern United States.[49]

The camp was compact and easily guarded. The POWs lived in the home of former State Senator Thomas Cashman, an older brother to the current operators of the family nursery. The carctaker's house was assigned to the guards; a large garage served as the prisoners' mess hall. In April, more POWs arrived. The Owatonna Canning Company contracted for a large share of the labor; when neither the cannery nor Cashman Nurseries needed prisoners, they performed other agricultural work. Some workers were also sent to work for the Goodhue Canning Company, where they picked corn in the cannery's fields.[50]

Howard Hong's report in June recorded the development of camp activities. A POW Lutheran pastor held services for the prisoners on alternate Sundays, and a local priest from Owatonna visited every other week. The priest provided an altar cloth and Catholic hymnals; additional hymnals had already been supplied by the Lutheran Commission for POWs. Services were conducted in the mess hall, and twenty to thirty POWs attended. A heavy workload, the summer heat, and the lack of a schoolroom limited the development of classes, but occasional lectures were presented by one of the prisoners, a lawyer in civilian life. Music and poetry were widely enjoyed, and there were plans for a camp orchestra, aided by a violin, a clarinet, and music left by Hong.[51]

Public discontent with the camp was voiced during the summer, amplifying the concerns of a local union, the United Construction Workers of Owatonna. Michael Cashman, one of two Cashman brothers in charge of the nursery, published a response to rumors circulating about the treatment of the prisoners. The rumors, he said, were based on "criticism and unfounded statements." He invoked the rules of the Geneva Convention, and pointed out that the Owatonna POWs enjoyed "ball playing, basketball, swimming and other forms of recreation." There had been no attempts at escape, and "no unruly situations."[52]

A night shift was established at the cannery to make better use of the POWs, and they subsequently worked both shifts. POWs were trained to use the machinery for hoisting and cooking. An American civilian, who claims the prisoners were as good as any other workers at the cannery, recalls in particular that one POW injured himself while playing with the equipment. The POW had saved his money to pay for his transfer to the branch camp in order to join his twin brother, but he developed an infection and was returned to Algona after just five days at Owatonna. In the cannery's fields, prisoners worked without guards, pulling pea vines and pitching them into the viner. For the corn harvest, cannery foremen periodically checked on the eleven-man POW crews responsible for hand-picking the corn. Years later, the head field-man for the cannery remarked that "the prisoners were good guys to work with. We didn't have any problems with them." Besides the cannery, local companies using prisoners were the Owatonna Milk Processing Company, the Illinois Cooperage Company, the Owatonna Tile and Cement Company, and the Owatonna Nursery Company. Some men were also transported to a farm near Hollandale to aid an asparagus farmer, who made the proper negotiations with the military and the Cashmans. The crop was successfully taken in, and the state extension service cited Hollandale's arrangements in its 1944 annual report as a way to avoid serious shortages of farm help.[53]

In September, a visiting military officer reported that the camp's administration and operation was satisfactory. The officer also noticed a large picture of Hitler in the mess hall and had it removed.[54]

In November, when work at the cannery was ending, Howard Hong visited the camp. An English class, developed during the summer, was under way, as well as courses in commercial arithmetic, commercial correspondence, and biology. Hong noted that a local Lutheran minister, lecturing on the history of Minnesota, had been well-received by the POWs. Musical activities continued, including a male chorus. Literary readings and recorded music took place in the evening. Plans for a POW marriage-by-proxy during Christmas were being arranged for a German private who was, in fact, married over the holiday.[55]

Left to right: POW doctor, POW spokesman Hektor, and an officer at the Owatonna camp. The Owatonna spokesman met with both Howard Hong of the YMCA and representatives of the International Committee of the Red Cross when they toured the camp. Hong reported in November 1944 that the POW doctor was a talented pianist who stimulated the camp's music program. The "musical activities," according to Hong, were "most prominent."[56]
Courtesy of Karl Becker

On January 2, 1945, fire destroyed the Cashman residence that housed the POWs. No prisoners were injured since most were not present. Discovered around 2:00 in the afternoon, the fire burned past 9:00 in the evening, fed by nearly 300 gallons of stored fuel. Firemen from Owatonna and the surrounding area confined the blaze to one building, but the supply of water ran out since the camp lay beyond the city water supply. An emergency supply was brought in with trucks from a nearby milk-processing company.[57] A POW's report to the base-camp newspaper presents a satirical view of the catastrophe:

> POW camp Owatonna was destroyed by fire. Because of the extinguishing by the city firemen, which was soooo fast, the house burned down to the foundations. More than 60 POWs homeless; no dead; one slightly injured from salvaging work. Canteen (with beer supply), and washroom saved. Barbed wire still intact. Cause of fire: American construction of the chimney. POW fire extinguishers (pocket format) completely insufficient. Fire welcomed sensation for the population of the area. Prisoners putting up with the stroke of fate with usual stubbornness.[58]

The POWs had their evening meal in a nearby building and spent the night in the city armory. While new accommodations were being arranged, they lived in the town hall, the armory, and a school. Most of the prisoners' property, and that of the guards, was saved. In short order, prisoners not actively working were returned to Algona, and barns and other buildings at the Cashman farm were remodeled to house the remaining POWs. Barracks were eventually built by the U.S. Army just north of the Cashman house. Reportedly they were very cold in the winter. Each of the eight barracks contained six men; additional POWs were quartered in the administration building.[59]

On March 10, the Red Cross's Dr. Zehnder arrived and recorded his evaluation of the new accommodations set up after the fire. Prisoners spoke to him about reimbursement for possessions lost in the disaster, but since no one could prove exactly what had been lost, it was doubtful that the demand could be honored. The fire had destroyed most of the camp's books, but a fresh supply was to arrive soon from Algona.

The POWs seized the opportunity to voice other complaints to Zehnder. They faulted local companies which chose only certain POWs for labor, depriving the rest of potential earnings. Zehnder concluded, however, that the problem would vanish at the peak of the season, since all prisoners would likely be employed. The camp doctor protested that he was not given enough initiative, and that a civilian doctor from town was handling the camp's most serious cases. Apparently in agreement, Zehnder advised the camp commander to arrange an exchange of doctors so the POW physicians could more readily practice their profession.[60]

Security was not a significant issue at Owatonna. One guard patrolled the camp in the evening; head-counts at 6:00 a.m. and 7:30 p.m., including one overall shakedown a day, completed the security measures. Only one recorded incident suggested tension among the POWs themselves. A prisoner made anti-Nazi statements which irritated the POW spokesman, who told the commander that he would "kill him [the fellow prisoner] personally" if he were not removed from the camp. The offending POW was transferred to Howard Lake; the camp is not known to have experienced other such incidents.[61]

In 1945, religious services attracted increasing interest, and a religious study-group was begun. English, commercial studies, and various lectures made up the educational program. Lessons in calculations for craftsmen were provided by one POW, and speeches were given to study groups by POWs with specialized knowledge. Films were shown; music was available evenings and weekends, and helped to fill up the Sunday recreational programs. A small orchestra, with "spirited" solos, provided entertainment, valued by the POWs as "cheering up . . . our old war-torn hearts."[62]

The long life of the camp, together with consistent support from Howard Hong, made it possible for the POWs to develop an impressive array of sporting activities. Soccer games were well attended, often pitting teams of older prisoners, over 30 years of age, against younger teams. At least once the opposing teams joined their strengths to play against a neighboring camp, quite possibly in Faribault. In early March 1945, boxing matches were set up under the direction of a POW private who had been an amateur boxer in Germany. He trained the POWs with punching balls and bags. A well-equipped ring was set up, but boxing had to be discontinued because of a severe insufficiency of calories in the POWs' diet, the consequence of reduced rations. Fistball, table tennis, and chess, in addition to various card games, filled out the prisoners' schedule of diversions.[63]

Nevertheless some prisoners, it appears, needed even more diversion.

POWs at the Owatonna camp. *Courtesy of Karl Becker*

Owatonna POWs just inside the compound fence, where they watched people drive by. *Courtesy of Karl Becker*

One POW walked off the compound grounds by himself in January. Three other prisoners individually left the camp in August and visited the local county fair. After a bed check at 10:30 p.m. revealed their absence, the camp's alarm was sounded, the FBI in St. Paul was notified, and agents left to aid in the search. The first prisoner arrived back at camp on his own volition at 1:30 a.m. wearing civilian clothes. Guards picked up the second prisoner an hour later on his way back to camp; he admitted attending the fair where he rode "the ferris wheel, bought a sandwich, and played a game machine." The search for the third prisoner continued until 4:30 a.m., when he appeared back at camp and turned himself in. All the men had been at the fair and told camp authorities they "had not planned to run away." They reported to FBI officials that "they wanted to have a good time" and had no desire returning to Germany if it meant living in the Russian-occupied zone. No other "escapes" are recorded.[64]

The small-grain harvest brought prisoners into area fields, including some in Waseca County, where they joined POWs from Wells. By contrast with the Wells prisoners, Owatonna POWs brought no midday lunches with them; farmers were required to provide their meals.[65]

In September the Red Cross paid a second visit, unique in the history of the Minnesota camps. Talking this time to Mr. Schnyder, the delegate, the POW doctor once again expressed his desire to treat "more interesting cases." At the time of Schnyder's visit the prisoners had little free time, and all classroom instruction had been canceled because of the heavy workload. Prisoners were apparently starting to show some concern about the postwar situation in Europe. They asked Schnyder whether they would have to return to the Russian-occupied section of Germany, but he was unable to offer any information.

In December 1945 the camp was closed, and the POWs were moved to the base camp at Algona.[66]

Owatonna resident Evelyn Kubat worked at the cannery alongside the POWs in 1944 during the late-evening shift, which usually lasted until 2 a.m. Along with other civilians, she placed canned pumpkin in boxes taken from a conveyor; the POWs hauled these boxes to railroad cars. Communication between the civilian workers and the prisoners was limited, but friendships sprang up. "We got acquainted with a few of them," Kubat says; occasionally, if a prisoner "couldn't work that night, he'd send a note along with one of the other fellows to give to us." Over the years Kubat kept two of those notes. One prisoner wrote:

> Evelyn! Last time, I was very sorry, so cannot have
> say you good bye, as I wanted to do it. Perhaps
> I work once more Monday night, when the others have
> their free day. For the case I cannot do so, I shall keep
> you in best remembrance for ever. My instantaneous dead
> life hier thwarts all my plans and it is senseless to meditate
> and to build castles in the air. But what I have told to you
> was the plain untarnished truth and my conviction.
> The feeling to have made acquaintance of one person very
> congenious, makes me happy and I have a good
> knowledge of human nature. From this country I get
> only unagreeable experiences. This is a beautiful exception.
>
> I congratulate you very much for the future.
>
> And now you know: speech is silver, silence is golden!!!

The prisoners and their civilian co-workers also exchanged pictures. Preparing for a trip to Germany in 1985, Kubat wrote to an address on the back of one of her photos, hoping to make contact with her POW friend after 40 years' separation. The happy result was that Karl Becker visited with her during her travels in Germany, and ultimately traveled back to Minnesota. His "Prisoner Perspective" appears below.[67]

Prisoner Perspective
Karl Becker

Karl Becker's landing at the Twin Cities airport in Minnesota, in 1994, fulfilled his life-long wish to revisit the camp where he had been a prisoner exactly 50 years earlier. He came to stay with an American former co-worker, in Owatonna, a town he would never have seen if he had not been captured in Tunisia in May 1943, when the entire Afrika Korps surrendered to the English Eighth Army.

Becker passed through a number of POW camps in Africa, finally arriving at Casablanca, where he put in four weeks' work with American soldiers and civilians, building a new POW camp. After its completion he crossed the Atlantic to Norfolk, Virginia, in a 60-vessel convoy of Liberty Ships, and traveled overland to Concordia, Kansas, where he spent about a year working in the hospital kitchen. With radios and war reports, Concordia POWs kept themselves informed about the war, often using little flags to mark front lines on maps. Becker particularly remembers Concordia for an uncomfortable incident involving a fellow prisoner, who chased a soccer ball between the warning fence and the outside fence, and was shot for doing so.[68]

Concordia embodied all the merits and demerits of any base camp, yet Becker wanted to experience something different. He volunteered to go to Owatonna, where more varied work, and possibly more diversion, was said to be available. There he worked at the Owatonna Canning Company, on farms, in the nearby town of Kenyon installing water connections, at a milk cannery and a potato-processing factory, and in the construction of wooden barrels. He spent most of his time, however, at Cashman Nurseries, with other prisoners and 40 Americans.

In the fall of 1944, Becker and his companions harvested young trees and bound the bottoms for transport, after which a crane loaded the trees into waiting railroad cars or storage. Guards, who initially accompanied the prisoners to the work site, later let them work alone. Camp life was generally placid. After Senator Cashman's house burned, the POWs occupied small barracks, quite cold during the winter. Camp security was loose; one prisoner often went out in the evenings with two girls, and the camp doctor took his place in case of a head count. The prisoners befriended a local German shepherd dog; after they had trained him, Becker laughingly recalls, the dog would obey only German commands.

Becker, left, next to American Evelyn Kubat, who worked in the canning factory with Becker. This photo was taken during his return visit to Owatonna in 1994. Becker, like many of the prisoners at Owatonna, worked a variety of jobs while at the camp. This diversified work routine was appealing to many of the prisoners who were originally in larger base camps outside of Minnesota. *Courtesy of Owatonna People's Press*

Karl Becker, left, before he was stationed in North Africa. *Courtesy of Karl Becker*

On Sunday afternoons the POWs were allowed to go swimming at a local gravel pit. Each of the prisoners had his own radio next to his bed, obtained by an exchange of cigarettes with American workers. One POW hoarded as many cigarettes as possible; when the camp closed he was the proud owner of a stash of 1,600. Each prisoner received a cake on his birthday, baked by the camp baker. Becker purchased two watches, one for his father and one for himself, from a catalog circulated among the prisoners.

After Owatonna, Becker spent time in Fort Crook, Nebraska, working in the prisoners' mess hall. Shortly afterwards he left the U.S., arrived in Le Havre after a nine-day voyage, and learned that he would be staying in France. The French forced him to work an entire year in a coal mine. He attempted escape with two other German prisoners; the other two were successful, but Becker was captured by a French soldier disguised as a German prisoner. He finally arrived home on April 17, 1947, and was able to start working at once at the foundry that had employed him before the war. He worked there until his retirement in 1981.

Becker remembers a few disagreeable incidents—Americans driving by the Owatonna camp, shouting "Germany surrenders, Germany surrenders," for example—but on the whole, he says, he was treated very well. Because he was captured early in the war like others in the African campaign, the conflict quickly faded into the distance for him and had few effects on his life in Owatonna.

Based on the author's interview with Becker in Owatonna, Minnesota, on August 9, 1994.

> **St. Charles**
> **Winona County**
>
> **June 1944–October 1944**
> **April 18, 1945–October 10, 1945**

Whitewater State Park, six miles north of St. Charles, Minnesota, was established in 1919 to "protect the tranquil beauty and natural value of the upper Whitewater valley." German prisoners were able to enjoy the beauty of the place, starting in 1944. The POWs were enchanted by their camp's surroundings, framed by a steep cliff whose white-gray color helped create "a romantic sight." The camp had previously been used by the Works Progress Administration and the CCC. Its fourteen buildings included nine barracks for the POWs and one for the officers. A blacksmith shop, a mess hall, an office, and a latrine were located in other buildings. Floodlights and barbed wire completed the scene.[69]

Preparing for the POWs, the county agent conferred with the Lakeside Canning Company and obtained all the necessary papers. A fair amount of negotiation was involved. It was established that the prisoners were truly needed due to labor shortages and that they would not interfere with the recreational facilities at the state park. The application for the prisoners to work at the cannery was approved and procedures were set in place for their use on area farms. The St. Charles *Press* characterized the first POW arrivals: "stoical, self-centered, and seem to be of the opinion that the people of the United States are misinformed as to the real Nazi program of 'civilizing' the entire world."[70]

The POWs were available for shocking and threshing work shortly after their arrival in late June. They were assembled in groups of ten for work, a minimum of five hours and a maximum of eight hours daily. If a farmer could not use his POW detail for five hours continuously, he was to share it with other farmers.[71]

Area firms besides the Lakeside Canning Company were interested in POW labor in 1944. St. Mary's Hospital in Rochester hoped to use about twenty prisoners in its laundry facilities, but a local CIO union circulated a resolution claiming that "such an arrangement would be resented by hospital employees and the people of Rochester and clearly would not add to the prestige of the community." The WMC determined it wasn't feasible; transportation was given as the reason, unavailable at the Owatonna and St. Charles camps. The idea was not forwarded to the appropriate authorities and the issue was dropped. A local restaurant association also suggested the possibility of obtaining prisoners for work at Reid Murdoch and Company in Rochester.[72]

The POWs at Whitewater fit into a well-developed labor program. The two draft boards in Winona County during the war worked closely with the county agent to provide workers for farm work. Trade centers set up in neighboring communities conducted successful recruitment activities. POW assignments to farmers were handled through the county agent's office and the cannery. A farm-help assistant had been hired to help the county agent combat the labor shortage by placing men where they were needed most. Meetings were organized at different locations throughout the county. Prisoners were allowed to work 20 miles from camp, and farmers needing them were required to travel to the camp themselves to obtain the men. St. Charles prisoners worked at least 3,644 man-hours on Winona County farms in 1944. The POWs supplemented a large number of individual citizens and farm couples, as well as boys recruited from Owatonna and other cities. Cool weather in July and August aided the harvest, and shocking crews were successfully recruited, one including the county agent himself.[73]

A storm of controversy was generated by the following verse in the St. Charles *Press*, August 3, 1944:

Your Old Magazines Will Help the Servicemen

When you read your magazine
Did you toss it aside today?
Or did you think of that service man
In a kindly sort of way?

When you cleaned out that closet
Of footballs, basketball and such,
Did you think of a boy in service

Who could use them very much?
Now, please don't think we're nagging,
For we think the army's swell;

But to activate a prison camp
Is a hard task, let me tell!
Would you let us use your radio?
For we'll tell you again:
One radio is insufficient
For one hundred and fifty men.

We boys at the Whitewater camp
Would appreciate and thank
You for things you could leave us
At the First National Bank.

THANK YOU.[74]

Squeezed in at the eleventh hour, this ambiguous doggerel produced a commotion among St. Charles citizens. The "servicemen" in the verse were the U.S. guards stationed at the Whitewater camp, but the piece was misinterpreted by some as soliciting newspapers and magazines for the prisoners. The following week, an outraged reader wrote that the only service the prisoners had performed was to "kill good American boys," and questioned whether others enjoyed sharing the title of servicemen "with these destroyers of world peace, educated in Hitler's school of murder and intolerance." The writer believed that the prisoners would "slit every throat in the community if it better served their purpose or that of their Fuchrer," and that "if they had their way they would be dividing the wealth and comforts of America among their self-styled 'Master Race.'" She concluded, "Let us give them some reasonable amount of recreation, but don't give them a status of Servicemen. And don't give them the idea that America is the nation of silly asses that they always thought it was."[75]

In 1945, German POWs arrived at Whitewater two months earlier than in 1944. The group had come from northern Minnesota and was destined for farm work until the pea harvest, when a larger group of POWs was expected. Available jobs included fencing, manure hauling, and logging. Many prisoners, capable of running farm machinery, worked up to ten hours daily. Officials warned that if the POWs were not used to the fullest advantage they would be moved to another camp, because labor shortages were evident elsewhere. The demand for Whitewater POWs was actually slight in the spring of 1945 because of frequent rains, and many farmers declined to use prisoners at all because of the time needed to transport them.[76]

Other work was available, however. A number of farmers interested in having timber removed were granted prisoners for the purpose. The county agent recorded that one group of prisoners chose to strike for a short time, protesting "that they were not being given enough food to do heavy work." While under contract for agricultural work, one area resident employing prisoners on his turkey farm had two prisoners paint a house in town. The POWs were accused by nearby residents of painting a swastika on the home before covering it. As a result, a local trade council filed a complaint with the War Manpower Commission. The employer was informed that his POWs were to be used only for farming-related work under contract with the Lakeside Canning Company. Prisoners worked at the area soil conservation tree nursery, and also on the loading dock at the Reid Murdoch

Canning Company, the first use of POWs in Rochester. A POW detail, brought in buses to a nearby Altura turkey factory, came back to camp singing at the end of the week, having received beer and whisky from their employer as a token of his satisfaction with their work. When they had time to spare, prisoners cared for the grounds and facilities at Whitewater State Park, possibly as a result of a military report on the camp's operations protesting that "there was no excuse for prisoners being idle . . . grass needed cutting, roads in bad condition, kitchens and other buildings very dirty."[77]

As in 1944, a coordinated attack was made on Winona County's labor shortage in 1945. Seven Bahamians were recruited, but only two stayed until the threshing season. Twenty-two parolees from state penal institutions were also helpful on Winona County farms. The pace of work intensified as time progressed, and county farmers hired people who were able to work only a few hours each day. While the POWs were busy with the pea harvest, shocking crews became a problem when the county's grain fields all ripened simultaneously. Women and mixed crews were recruited; one crew was made up of women workers from the county courthouse. Pictures of various groups were published in the local papers to increase public interest in the recruiting effort. Fortunately 75 prisoners employed at the Reid Murdoch cannery in Rochester finished working there before the end of the grain harvest; the county agent immediately allocated them for farm work.[78]

Before completing their work at Reid Murdoch, a staff writer for the Minneapolis *Sunday Tribune* had the opportunity to work amongst the prisoners. He reported that "it gives you a funny feeling to work beside German prisoners of war. . . . [and] that's the way it affected most workers." During lunch break, he quoted civilian workers saying: "I'll bet those damn Jerries are eating better than we are right now." Another complained that the prisoners had "nice easy work," and that Germans didn't "treat our boys that good!" Assigned to a clean-up crew, this reporter was able to get a "close-up view" of the Germans; they didn't speak much and cannery bosses had to direct "work mostly by gestures."

A single guard was assigned to watch the prisoners at Reid Murdoch, unloading peas as they arrived at the plant. Asked whether they would run away, the guard replied, "'They got it too nice where they are.' . . . [and] tapping the carbine, 'they wouldn't get very far.'" The conversation turned to a crowd of people from Rochester who had driven to the factory to watch the prisoners. "I see they've come to see my pee-wees," the guard said. "It's okay as long as they keep their distance."[79]

Busy since May, St. Charles POWs performed almost every farm job in Winona County, and were particularly helpful with haying, harvesting, and filling silos. In Wabasha County to the north, they "proved very helpful." In Olmsted County to the west, there was "considerable difficulty" in obtaining the prisoners and securing their transportation. Eventually a local school superintendent organized the transportation, and 35 POWs were available to farmers, who "were well satisfied with the work done." When the harvest was over, a group of twenty prisoners was left behind to dismantle the camp, and most of the others went to Crookston. Although no reports from Howard Hong are available, the local press generally portrayed a normal camp where few problems arose. Occasional infractions were punished by a bread and water diet, and sometimes by incarceration at the St. Charles City Hall. At least one POW found a way to exit the camp safely on Sundays; on three occasions he met an American woman and eventually contracted a venereal disease.[80]

The POWs had their own office and library at the camp, enjoyed access to both a football and a soccer field, and maintained a garden. Newspapers and radios were universally available. The prisoners special-ordered items for their hobbies, including tools, musical instruments, and paints. Music was enjoyed, often performed by a small band of POWs which tried practicing every night for its Sunday concerts, when much American music was played. The POWs made their own cigarette machines to roll their own cigarettes. Their daily fare was monotonous; the main dish was usually soup, and the usual whole meat was mutton, varied with oxtails, salt pork, kidneys, hearts, or livers. Powdered eggs and potatoes were also provided.[81]

In time, camp commander Captain Jack I. Elson was able to claim that the "swaggering, insolent died [sic] in-the-wool Nazis, the troublemakers, have been pretty well weeded out"; the remaining POWs were a cross-section of the German armed forces: students, farmers, businessmen, carpenters. On V-E day, a "tenseness" was noted among the prisoners. Those captured early in the war "were slow to believe" the news of their army's defeat, but later began "to accept the eventual and total defeat of their army and navy" as other POWs were brought from Europe. Ernst Kohleick, a student and a "recent" POW who arrived from Europe in 1945, offered the following reminiscences.[82]

Prisoner Perspective
Ernst Kohleick

Four days after Germany surrendered on May 8, 1945, Ernst Kohleick docked in the United States against the backdrop of New York's skyline. Just 19 years old, he had begun duty in Denmark as part of the occupation army. In 1945 he was sent to the front near Marburg-on-Lahn, Germany; after three days he was captured by Americans, on March 29. Kohleick was sent through Belgium to Compiègne near Paris, but since the camp was overflowing with recently captured prisoners he was moved along to Bolbec. His ship stopped in Southhampton on April 27 after leaving Le Havre, and arrived in New York on May 12. Part of the convoy of over 100 ships, quite possibly the last to leave Europe, returned after having traveled halfway across the Atlantic.

After New York, Kohleick disembarked in Boston and eventually arrived in Algona on May 16. On the next day, all the new arrivals were personally greeted by the commander, Col. Arthur Lobdell. A month's stay in Algona gave Kohleick the chance to learn about the United States; he was transferred to St. Charles at the end of June. His own home in Germany had been destroyed in 1943, and the undisturbed landscape of Whitewater State Park was in stark contrast to the wreckage he had seen in Europe. When Kohleick's group of younger POWs arrived, some only 15 and 16 years old, the Afrika Korps veterans already at St. Charles were quick to realize the desperate situation of Germany.

July 10 was the first workday at the Lakeside Canning Company in Plainview. When Kohleick's group of POWs left camp for the cannery around 5 p.m. each day, they saw civilians walking with their families in undisturbed surroundings, everything apparently intact, a reminder of peaceful times the POWs themselves had once known. Kohleick worked the night shift, starting at 6 p.m., usually from 9 to 12 hours depending on the day's harvest. Many prisoners worked on conveyor belts, loading cans of peas and corn into large vats in which the cans were cooked. The POWs had limited contact with the cannery's civilian workers, but at times one of the Americans would bring a little bag of chocolate for the prisoners, most often without anything said. It was a simple yet important gesture of empathy.

After all the day's peas or corn had been canned, the machines were cleaned in preparation for the next daytime crew. Arriving back at camp to sleep during the day, the POWs were fed breakfast by their native Austrian cook, who often included Austrian items in his menu. When the POWs helped local farmers during lull periods at the cannery, they were often invited to the family table like "a child in the house," in Kohleick's phrase. The prisoners were made welcome, not treated like criminals or inferior beings. The farmers' generosity reflected the reduced-ration policy that came into existence after the end of the war; many farmers supplemented the meals Kohleick brought to the fields.

On October 5 Kohleick was sent to Hollandale to cut cabbage and harvest other vegetables. The POWs slept in tents, on regular beds. Kohleick became well acquainted with a farm family near Hollandale, and the family even made efforts through a relative in the military to determine whether his parents were still living. Before the inquiry could bring a response, he was sent back to Algona, October 22, for about a month. At Algona he started taking courses, including one in American history taught by some of the American personnel at Algona. Colonel Lobdell praised the prisoners for their classwork. Kohleick took courses related to medicine, including anatomy, and shortly before his return to Europe he was tested in English. He left Algona on November 21, arrived in Boston two days later, and left for France. Because he was able to prove that he had been ill during the war, he was released early into civilian life, January 17, 1946. On arriving in his hometown he learned that both his parents had survived the war.

Shortly before becoming a soldier in 1944, Kohleick had completed his requirements for university study. After the war he was admitted to the University of Cologne; during his first semester he helped rebuild a dormitory in which he eventually lived as a student himself. He began the study of Latin and English during the winter semester of 1948-1949. In 1958 he passed his second state exam and began teaching Latin and English in various high schools. An assistant principal by 1975, he was eventually promoted to a principalship, from which he retired in 1990.

With his family, Kohleick returned to Minnesota in 1976, visiting Whitewater State Park and various people whom he had met as a prisoner. The Plainview cannery showed its appreciation of its former worker by offering him a case of canned vegetables. Kohleick's first trip to America, however, made the greater impact of the two: a young prisoner's first taste of a mature democracy, a political system completely

Ernst Kohleick, right, with his family during their trip to the U.S. in 1976. On the left is Jean Nienoord, a U.S. civilian who worked with Kohleick during the war. *Courtesy of Ernst Kohleick*

Ernst Kohleick near his home in Germany, 1995. *Author's photo*

different from the one he had known. Democracy, with its attendant freedoms and its effect on individual people, constituted an important lesson for the young Kohleick.

His first systematic exposure to English was also important, enabling him to read newspapers, magazines, and brochures, to converse with American people, and to learn about the new land and its way of life. Thus, Kohleick's American experience shaped his future and manifested itself in his work as an English teacher.

Based on the author's interview with Kohleick in Germany on February 24, 1995.

Chapter 6

Logging Camps

"We don't want these Heil Hitler guys around"
Midwest Labor, February 11, 1944, p. 1.

An estimated 22,000 prisoners worked for the U.S. logging and pulpwood industries during World War II, some of them in four northern Minnesota camps. Although official goals for lumber production, including paper and pulpwood, were in decline after early 1943, POW labor for Minnesota logging operations was discussed beginning in May. Pulpwood was an important commodity, used not only for paper but also for explosives and shipping containers. Minnesota lumber inventories were low in 1943 compared to the previous year. As autumn neared, the labor shortage in the pulpwood industry had become critical, a shortage attributable to low wages and unappealing work. Efforts to attract workers from other industries proved insufficient, and by September, approval had been granted for use of POW labor in the pulpwood industry.[1]

By November 1943, between 3,500 and 4,000 workers were needed by Minnesota timber operators, who started applying for POWs after an October discussion between unions and producers. Well-attended meetings in Bemidji and Duluth provided lumber operators with detailed information about POW use. The examples of the Olivia and Princeton camps earlier in the year were spoken of at one of these meetings, but it was emphasized that the successful use of prisoners in lumber regions had yet to be proven. Preparations were underway for one camp, near Park Rapids, scheduled to supply POWs to the Park Rapids Saw Mill Company among other employers. In early December, at least 500 POWs were certified for use in northern Minnesota, and some were already expected in mid-December. In the meanwhile, however, negotiations with several operators had been suspended because of union opposition. At this point, it was reported that work at certain mills and plants would perhaps be "seriously curtailed through lack of the raw material."[2]

Although the most widespread union hostility to POW labor in the U.S. lumber industry was in the Pacific Northwest, concerted opposition made the establishment of northern Minnesota's camps anything but harmonious. Ilmar Koivunen, an organizer of the International Woodworkers of America (IWA), threatened to strike all Minnesota lumber workers if POWs were used, and claimed that the War Manpower Commission's program for labor shortages was defective. According to Koivunen, working conditions were the principal offenses: amenities such as bathing facilities and electricity, sought after by lumberjacks for years, were being provided for the "fascist criminals." Nevertheless, because the IWA was unable to fulfill the demand for workers in the northern woods, the War Department ordered that prisoners be used despite union objections. The IWA and the WMC agreed that POWs would not be supplied to operators with union contracts, unless the union agreed; prisoners were thus never used in the more heavily unionized parts of the state.[3]

Opposition to the use of prisoners was a continuing theme in state CIO newspapers, especially when the POWs arrived in the woods in early 1944. The union was particularly bitter about the private producer who would "get his camp fully equipped as a gift from the government," and it viewed the local representative of the WMC, Frank M. Rarig Jr., as "the worst kind of a scallywag in ignoring the wishes of the people of northern Minnesota." Koivunen once escorted Irene Paull, a labor activist and a regular columnist for Minnesota's official CIO newspaper, through the camp near Remer. She described the residents of the area as "average Americans who do not know the enemy and all his works."[4]

Organizations sympathetic to the IWA expressed their own concerns about the use of POW labor. The Argo-Wassa Civilian Defense Council, for example, questioned the POWs' productivity, suggested that they might "set the countryside on fire," and warned that people would fear "NAZI beasts roaming the woods." The inexperience of the POWs as woodsmen was another concern; still another was that the dangerous nature of the work would violate the Geneva Convention. Lumberjacks were convinced that the use of POWs was "an attempt on the part of timber operators to force us lumberjacks out of business or something like that." One representative of state, county, and municipal workers claimed that hiring POWs was a "threat to the American way of life." Mayor Edward Hatch of Duluth reported to a union newspaper that "it would be a bad influence on the men in the woods to have Nazi war prisoners come in here and work."[5]

After the POWs arrived and demonstrated their usefulness, the furor

This cartoon appeared in a 1944 issue of the *Midwest Labor*, a union news-paper published in Duluth. An accompanying article stated: "The Timber Worker's Union urges the workers and unions of Minnesota to demand of Rarig that he immediately withdraw the prisoners from the Minnesota woods. The pulp trust, with the help of Rarig, has got its foot through the door. Close the door before it is too late!" *Courtesy of Midwest Labor, February 11, 1944*

Ilmar Koivunen, right, and Sgt. Norman Rasmussen at a timber convention on January 15, 1945. *Courtesy of Minnesota Historical Society*

largely subsided. At least one setback occurred in October 1944 when CIO unions were successful in preventing the use of prisoner labor from one camp; the operators were unable to fill their contracts, and the POWs were "idle" in the camp. The Deer River *News* reported that the importance of harvesting the timber "does not seem to make any difference to the unions. They rule the roost and their own welfare seems to be the only consideration." The article concludes, "How these German prisoners of war must laugh at a government that permits such conditions!" Ilmar Koivunen reappeared at least once, in 1945, when he approached the Minnesota State Board of Health to propose a law requiring the board's licensing and supervision of lumber camps. He showed pictures of the POWs, claiming that they "have pool tables, ping pong tables, single bunks, clean linens and other recreational facilities and live like kings. . . . We get our beer from the swamp, while they get their beer from bottles." Despite these objections, however, northern Minnesota sustained four separate POW camps during the last two years of the war.[6]

The Remer, Bena, and Deer River camps all began as branch camps of Concordia, Kansas, and passed to the jurisdiction of Algona on June 8, 1944. All four were located at old CCC campsites in forested regions of Itasca and Cass counties. A seven-foot barbed wire fence surrounded each camp, and all were set up for year-round use, with athletic fields, well-stocked canteens, and carpentry shops. All but the camp near Grand Rapids were in service for more than a year. Guard training was emphasized; Bena, for example, had classes four evenings a week. A military report from Bena suggested that "the isolated nature of this work, at hand, makes it most important that lectures and training in military subjects and physical subjects as well as moral and social subjects be stressed."

The young, able-bodied POWs selected for these camps helped at least eight operators cut and haul lumber, primarily pulpwood, in a wide radius around each camp; security was proportionally loose, and just a single guard was sometimes sent along with the prisoners. Meals were available to the prisoners at work sites. At Deer River, for example, the meal included coffee, sandwiches, sausage, cheese, and eggs. Contrary to the unions' accusations, charges were levied on the contractors for unemployment insurance, social security, and tax and compensation insurance. Allowances were made, on the other hand, for the rental, maintenance, loss, and breakage of tools, since the contractors provided these items to the POWs. Overall, the cost of prisoner use to the lumber industry was high.[7]

Some of the problems that arose at the logging camps were noted by Captain D. L. Schwieger, an inspector with the U.S. military. He considered fraternization between prisoners and American personnel too high, and recommended to the commanding officer that it be "be eliminated in that it was due to cause a large amount of unfavorable publicity." It was also reported that some German officers were placing "undue pressure . . . upon the German POW enlisted men."[8]

In northern Minnesota, the POWs found themselves in a recreational paradise. The seemingly boundless out-of-doors and the lure of wonderful fishing eventually occasioned some tension with local citizens. The wilderness also offered isolation; official opinion considered it an escape deterrent, but in fact it gave opportunity for the most significant attempted escape in all the Minnesota camps.

Hans Welker, a prisoner at the camp near Bena during the escape, immigrated to Minnesota after the war. He now lives in California and offers the final Prisoner Perspective of the book.

Remer
Cass County
January 31, 1944–January 1945

On January 31, 1944, a group of U.S. soldiers arrived with 37 prisoners and started nine days' work to prepare former CCC camp F-46, about two miles northeast of Remer. Military reports detail the extensive work that was necessary. Water lines that were frozen, broken, or in disrepair could be reached only by laborious digging. The excavations through six feet of frozen ground required surface fires, maintained for 48 hours before the digging could begin. With temperatures ranging from 0 to -35 degrees Fahrenheit at night, the workers were given "arctic-type" clothing, and kept up bonfires close to their work areas. Struggling to maintain their good spirits, they once decided "to compete even in the raising of fantastic beards and mustaches." On February 7, 1944, when the camp was ready, 238 POWs arrived.[9]

Certain Remer citizens were initially frightened by the prisoners' presence so close to town, but eventually the locals became accustomed to their "guests" and often drove out to watch the trucks that took them to their logging destinations. Some Remer people even visited the camp on Sundays. On one occasion, a local French-speaking family drove into the camp and asked permission to talk with one of the prisoners who spoke French. A suspicious guard stopped the conversation when he decided it had lasted too long, and searched the trunk of the family's car before it left the camp.[10]

Covering ten acres, the Remer camp had 27 buildings, including a machine shop, a pump house, a tool warehouse, and other utility structures. The eight sleeping-barracks, occupied by 30 to 32 men each, were cleaned each day by POW orderlies, chosen by a rotating clock labeled with all the prisoners' names. The orderlies were responsible for obtaining firewood and water. Each prisoner had his own bed and a stand for personal things. Among the camp's facilities were a canteen, a barber shop, and a homemade altar constructed from pine boards and small birch trees. Birch saplings were also used to make partitions for the sleeping quarters; a military inspector warned against this possible fire hazard a short time later. Military inspectors deemed the initial sanitary situation "hardly adequate," with an

Remer first-aid wagon with guards and POWs. In a report on Remer in 1944, Hong comments that "the countryside is not only healthful but very attractive as well, because of both the climate and the wooded countryside."[11] *Courtesy of Gerald Delin*

Prisoners at Remer. On the right is a German sergeant who spoke good English. The German POW spokesman at Remer also spoke English; he had been in the United States prior to the war and had visited Duluth.[12] *Courtesy of Gerald Delin*

Prisoners loading logs, January 1945. A military report in July 1944 indicated that the contractors "were quite satisfied with the prisoner of war labor."[13] *Courtesy of Gerald Delin*

Trucks used to transport POWs to and from work sites. Herman Delin, job foreman and supervisor for the prisoners, stands next to two guards. Government trucks transported prisoners at all the northern Minnesota camps. A government inspecting officer noted that their maintenance was under prisoner supervision and that the "condition of the vehicles was outstanding."[14] *Courtesy of Beverly Buck and Gerald Delin*

unacceptable water supply and sewage control "sadly in need of re-pair." Consequently, a new well was drilled, and a latrine was built for the American personnel.[15]

Americans and POWs were segregated in the mess hall, where the food was good "but not always sufficiently varied." Undoubtedly there was plenty to eat; a local citizen commented years later that he was permitted to remove the camp's daily garbage to feed his pigs. The same citizen recorded a mean-spirited trick played on him by the POWs. Once he had trouble finding his dog, who came to camp with him; hours later he learned that the prisoners had buried the animal alive, leaving him just enough room above ground to breathe.[16]

Beginning with a tract of woods 17 miles southwest of camp, the prisoners did logging work for Herman Delin, whose contract for pulpwood had recently brought him to Pine River from southern Min-nesota. A detailed article in the Duluth News-Tribune sheds light on the prisoners' daily routine. For winter work, they were issued items such as woolen underwear, heavy socks, gloves, and logger's boots. They rose at 6:30 and ate breakfast. Beginning at 7:30, eight to ten trucks were warmed up before the POWs left in them at 8:00. A "chow wagon" brought them sandwiches and coffee in the woods. They were back in camp for supper by 5:30 p.m., and retired at 10:30. Five prisoners protested the rigors of their life with a slowdown and were sent back to Concordia. An early POW trick was to cut logs less than the required size and stack them to give the appearance that the workers had cut their quotas. The prisoners dropped the practice after they were confronted with it.[17]

Soon after the camp opened, a rural-industries supervisor for the timber industry visited the Remer compound and described the fol-lowing experience in a written report:

> There are three German officers in this camp—two lieutenants and one captain. One of the lieutenants, who has been appointed the Transportation Officer, took Lt. Fan-ning, Mr. Moore and me to the place where the pulpwood cutting was in progress. He was a very amiable sort of fel-low, but showed the true Nazi characteristic of giving a ci-vilian the part the military didn't want. In other words, farmers with teams straddled the edge of the road in the ditch while he blew his horn and roared down the road. I had a feeling his pace was a little too fast for the footing,

and eventually we went into a dandy skid. He pulled the car out of this one all right by some dexterous maneuvering but did not profit by the experience, and a little later the car went into another skid which ended up in the ditch. Luckily a large truck was nearby loaded with pulpwood, which pulled us back on the road. This little experience seemed to humble our speed-driving Nazi officer enough so that the rest of the trip gave us an opportunity to at least count the lakes as we went by.[18]

Within a week of the report, there was an accident on a road near Grand Rapids, when a civilian motorist struck two guards on leave. They both received fractured legs and were treated at the county hospital. The driver, under the influence of alcohol, was charged accordingly.[19]

The POWs were generally well-behaved and enjoyed the Remer area, but they reportedly never did more than an acceptable minimum of work. Army officials pointed out early in the fall of 1944 that poor supervision by both civilians and the camp administration was a factor in low pulpwood production. According to one civilian supervisor, the POWs started out well in the morning, but when they had some wood cut they were apt to build a fire and "fool around the rest of the day." Many showed their inexperience; they often felled a tree into a stand of trees rather than a cleared area, making cutting and clearing more difficult. A daily round trip for the prisoners was as long as 34 miles, and even reached 62 miles when certain routes were impassable because of spring thaws, which at times even halted the work. Muddy roads were a recurring problem; tow cars were seen "hauling equipment out of the mud, back onto icy surfaces, or out of snowdrifts."[20]

The camp's homemade altar was used on Sundays by a POW Protestant pastor from the Deer River camp and a priest from Collegeville, who celebrated Mass for 40 to 50 men. A local Remer priest also said mass, hearing confessions for 15 minutes before the liturgy. A German doctor, using books and journals supplied by a civilian physician, was in charge of the camp dispensary, and treated both Americans and prisoners for various ailments such as cuts and sore throats. In a small room devoted to education, music classes were offered, including individual instruction in guitar, accordion, and violin. Some instruments were sent by the YMCA for the camp. Besides beginning and advanced English, subjects such as mathematics, philosophy, and

Remer post headquarters, fall 1945. The Remer camp had an athletic field of about five acres, used for soccer and baseball. In addition, prisoners had access to boxing gloves, ice skates, baseball equipment, and soccer balls.[21] *Courtesy of Werner Schmiedeberg*

POWs lined up before returning to camp in Remer. During the day, guards stationed themselves on each end of the work detail while other guards patrolled the center.[22] *Courtesy of Gerald Delin*

Herman Delin on left end of the pulpwood pile with prisoners. *Courtesy of Gerald Delin*

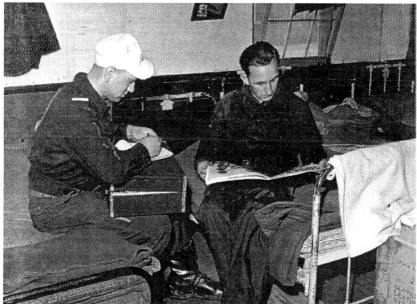

Prisoners shown reading at the Remer Camp, February 1944. Military records show that Remer prisoners were avid letter writers. In April 1944 alone, they received more than 1,450 pieces of mail and sent out over 1,400.[23] *Courtesy of Minneapolis Star & Tribune, Minnesota Historical Society*

forestry were available. German language and literature were to be added later.[24]

A tennis court planned for the camp eventually became a fist-ball court. A soccer field was also being used when Howard Hong visited in June 1944. Ping-pong was played, and billiards were to be available when cues arrived. A painting and wood-carving competition was welcomed by the camp commander and the prisoners' spokesman. The spokesman suggested that one prisoner be left out of the competition because he already had "some renown in Germany" as a portrait painter. The camp's natural surroundings multiplied the POWs' recreational options. Collections of natural specimens and a tame deer fed from a nippled Pepsi-Cola bottle were noted by Hong. In the Remer camp Hong observed a certain "contentment and resignation" not apparent in larger camps.[25]

The facility closed in January 1945, and the prisoners were sent to help establish a new camp near Grand Rapids in nearby Itasca County.

> ## Bena
> ## Cass County
>
> ## February 7, 1944–June 1944
> ## October 1944–October 1945

A quarter-mile from the town of Bena, the Cass County camp had a 2,000-foot frontage on Lake Winnibigoshish. An advance group of POWs from Remer was sent to put it in order. Although recent occupancy had had left the former CCC camp in good condition, necessary renovations were estimated at $2,425 including plumbing and electrical work. The POWs themselves claimed that bringing the camp up to standard required "massive remedies." The snow-covered woods presented a stark contrast to their warm surroundings in Kansas. Unlike at the Deer River camp, the first large group of these men arrived "very quietly, and with very little excitement."[26]

The Deer River *News* visited the camp a week and a half after it opened and wrote in response to popular misapprehensions: "a great many rumors, unfounded and without verification, could be heard in this community. Reports of no guarding, escaped prisoners and other suppositions, were repeated as facts." The paper sketched the POWs' daily activities. The typical regimen required rising at 6:00 a.m., with breakfast at 6:45. The prisoners were sent into the woods by 7:30. In their opinion, to be transported in open trucks in such a cold climate was "punishment" in itself. They had lunch and a "substantial meal" in the evening, before they were required to retire at 10 p.m. According to the *News*, a "feature of the camp" was its own "Canine Corps" under a dog sergeant, six well-trained dogs including a Chesapeake and a mastiff. One was described as "an attack dog" that "seemed very vicious," such that anyone prowling around the camp was assured of "a warm reception." Security was maintained by guards patrolling the perimeter of the camp 24 hours a day.[27]

After the camp's jurisdiction was transferred from Concordia to Algona, Howard Hong visited it in June 1944. He took particular note of the surroundings: the camp stood just three hundred yards behind a tourist camp and close to the shore of the lake. A monk from St. Cloud had come to say Mass; a Protestant POW pastor from the Deer River camp came every other week to hold services. French, English, chemistry, mathematics, music, and history courses were available for the prisoners; their library had about 200 books. A stage had been installed in the recreational hall for performances by some of the camp's musicians, and a bandstand was planned for outdoor performances. In one corner of the hall, the POWs set up an "oasis," a bar where beverages in colored bottles attested how the prisoners "put drinks away in the old days."[28]

The two most popular sports were soccer and swimming; the nearby lake, two minutes from camp, was considered "within bounds." The POWs also constructed 15 boats for their own use. A visiting military inspector reported 100 prisoners fishing, boating, and canoeing among civilians, also fishing, and some conversing with the prisoners. One POW, a boxing trainer before the war, taught the sport to as many as twenty other POWs. Boxing gloves, jumping ropes, and a punching ball were available for the undertaking. A sports festival was being planned, and medals were to be awarded. A proposed painting and wood-carving contest between the three northern camps was well received by the POWs. Their workshop was suited to the purpose, 1,200 square feet full of wood and tools.[29]

Responding to the question what they were most proud of in their camp, the POWs answered, "the landscaping inside the camp. We have planted hundreds of trees, shrubs, and flowers. And we shall have a good vegetable garden in a few weeks."[30]

Bena has the distinction of producing the most involved attempted escape from a Minnesota camp. According to the Grand Rapids *Herald-Review*, two POWs simply "walked out into the woods." It was later established, however, that after careful planning they had dug their way under the fence on Saturday night after bedcheck. The paper was confident that the men likely would not be gone long, since "they will be driven out by hunger."

Trains in the area were guarded; automobiles were searched at Cass Lake twenty-some miles to the west. The Itasca County Sheriff searched the city of Grand Rapids, and promising clues were followed up at Effie and Bear River the following day. Meanwhile, the escaping prisoners, Heinz Schymalla and Walter Mai, had managed to paddle away in one of the many rowboats Bena POWs had built earlier in the year. The POWs had hoped to travel down the Mississippi to New Orleans and catch a ship for Europe, but after five days on the river they mistakenly rowed into Jay Gould Lake.

A resort owner spotted the escapees pulling ashore. He approached them, thinking they might be interested in one of his cabins, but at once suspected that they were the two escaped POWs because of their "aloofness and inability to speak readily." He returned home and called the sheriff. Apprehensive, the POWs abandoned their boat, only to encounter two local lawmen looking for them a short time later. The prisoners surrendered. Mai was quoted by the *Itasca County Independent* as saying, "you think America is fine, but it is not as good as the Fatherland."

The prisoners were brought to the county jail in Grand Rapids and then escorted to Algona. After a hearing for each of them, Col. Lobdell sentenced them to "30 days in confinement with 14 continuous days on bread and water." The FBI agent later wrote to the local sheriff: "It is gratifying to work with such splendid officers and to receive the wholehearted cooperation which you and your men gave us."

A second, less dramatic escape was attempted in April 1945; two POWs, aged 19 and 21, who wanted to avoid separation, slipped away the day prior to a transfer. They were captured six miles south of camp the next day, brought by the FBI to Algona, and placed in solitary confinement.[31]

In May, a proclamation was placed on a bulletin board that "organized resistance of the German armed forces" had ended and that the POWs were "released from any obligation entered into with a government which no longer exists."[32]

There was little activity at the camp in September 1945, when the Red Cross's Mr. Schnyder paid a visit. With the majority of the men working out of Ortonville, only forty prisoners remained at Bena. Opportunity for activities other than work was limited, Schnyder found. Fewer movies were being shown, and classroom instruction had temporarily ceased since the teachers were not at the camp. Swimming in the nearby lake had been suspended because too many tourists were there during the summer months. Nevertheless, the forty prisoners were enjoying "a relatively high amount of freedom." Schnyder reported that many were concerned because their mail had stopped arriving. Their spokesman inquired whether the prisoners would be able to return to any occupation zone when they were sent back to Europe. The camp closed the following month.[33]

Prisoner Perspective
Hans Welker

Hans Welker was captured in North Africa and sent out of Oran on a Liberty Ship. He arrived in Concordia, Kansas, in August 1943. There, German POW officers wielded considerable authority over the prisoners, requiring them to rise early and leading them around with wooden rifles for exercise. Like others interned at Concordia, Welker remembers how high tensions were when a German POW was shot for chasing a soccer ball. The dead man's fellow prisoners marched around in protest, and their officers called the Americans "gangsters."

Welker was transferred to Bena in February 1944. Life in the camp was hardly fun, but not entirely boring; radio newscasts and mail from home varied the monotony. The prisoners played some ping-pong, but chess was the predominant recreation, and the POWs were able to buy chessmen in their canteen. There was no high-wire fence as at Concordia and Algona; prisoners slipped through Bena's inadequate fence and sometimes went out with local girls. Daytime encounters were the eventual result, and a POW officer at Bena thought it necessary to caution the prisoners about visits with locals. As Welker recalls, the dramatic escape-attempt of two POWs in November 1944 was known only to a few other prisoners.

The discovery of German concentration camps in Europe changed the atmosphere at Bena. The prisoners were required to watch films of the liberated camps. Soon afterwards, camp authorities did away with all privileges and the "nice" things at the Bena canteen, including candy and cigarettes. The quantity of food served in camp was so much reduced that contractors complained about the POWs' defective performance—limbs left on logs, for example. After the complaints, the camp's rations improved, but were never up to their wartime standard.

Welker was in a group of prisoners transferred to Ortonville from Bena during the summer canning season. The POWs first spent time in the fields, harvesting wheat and barley; afterwards they worked in sweet corn canning. Not much diversion was available at Ortonville. The POWs went roller skating, a leisure activity organized by a local German immigrant, but after a prisoner's correspondence mentioned skating privileges more than once, they were canceled.

Hans Welker in 1944. The photo was taken while Welker was temporarily stationed at the Ortonville camp, established to furnish labor for the Big Stone Canning Company nearby. *Courtesy of Hans Welker*

Hans Welker with his wife in California, 1997. *Courtesy of Hans Welker*

After a short stay in Grand Forks, North Dakota, picking sugar beets and potatoes, Welker returned to Bena and Deer River, and then to the base camp. He was at Algona only briefly before his repatriation out of Fort Crook, Nebraska. Brought to Oakland, California, and shipped out on a transport vessel coming from Japan, Welker traveled through the Panama Canal and then to England, where he stayed for a year, working at American airfields. Released in May 1947, he returned to Germany.

In 1953 Welker returned to the United States because he liked it better than his homeland. He headed for Bena and stayed in the area for a total of five years. On his arrival he revisited the camp where he had been interned, but fireplaces were all that remained. At Bena, Welker was employed by one of the contractors he had worked for as a POW. Because of diminishing employment possibilities in Minnesota, he moved to California in 1958 and continued to work with wood, making roof-trusses and braces for pre-cut homes for 23 years. Meanwhile he and his wife became U.S. citizens and raised three sons.

Based on the author's interview with Welker on October 8, 1994.

Deer River (Cut Foot Sioux)
Itasca County

April 5, 1944–December 26, 1945

The Deer River *News* for March 23, 1944, announced that a POW camp was to be set up just south of Squaw Lake, at old CCC camp 707. The facility, 23 miles north of Deer River, was also called camp Cut Foot Sioux; the two names were used for it interchangeably. The camp opened on April 5, and 131 prisoners arrived the following day. The *News* suggested that, but for lack of a band, "it might have been a Fourth of July celebration," because of all the citizens who came to greet the incoming train. Inquisitive locals noticed that the POWs had a dog with them, as well as a number of musical instruments in their luggage. The POWs themselves described their arrival as "literally a jump into the most beautiful area of Minnesota."[34]

The camp, electrified by its own little power station, included four barracks, a kitchen with a dining room, and a washroom with showers. Its administration building contained a recreation room equipped with a piano, a theater, and a canteen with a house bar. Additionally there were two sports areas, a public house with a music pavilion, an entertainment room, and a classroom. American and German officers were housed together in the same building outside the enclosure; a U.S. military inspector suggested that the German officers be housed inside the camp.[35]

As the summer approached, the POWs and their guards became interested in the recreational opportunities offered by the Itasca County forest. There were "run-ins" between local wardens and camp guards who were shooting ducks and other game. The guards obligingly inquired whether their prisoners could get fishing licenses, but the possibility was "seriously frowned upon by people in this section." No court action grew out of the illegal hunting, but the Army assured the local authorities that the guards would be properly punished. As to the POWs, it was officially concluded that since they were not under state law, they were simply excluded from hunting and fishing privileges.[36]

Even though a guard checked all vehicles entering and leaving during the day, and guards on evening duty were to be "especially watchful for any suspicious actions by the POWs," security at the camp was apparently lax during the early months of its existence. It was not surrounded by wire at first. A local newspaper account, written years later, explains that no fence was erected because the wartime shortage of steel delayed the delivery of proper fencing for several months. The camp had no perimeter guard during the day, and the gate stood open. A visiting American officer noticed this irregularity in the fall of 1944, and remarked that "the most outstanding feature of this camp is [the] lack of orthodox security measures." He concluded, however, that the dense forests and the camp's "remoteness from civilization" provided sufficient security.[37]

The POWs apparently agreed. Writing to relatives in Germany, one was satisfied that "deserting is quite impossible anyhow, as too many wolves and Indians ill-disposed to white people are running around here." Another Deer River prisoner reported:

> In the thick woods live Indians, wolves, bears, stags and porcupines. The redskins still have their old customs, medicine men, almost no civilization. When they drink, which is prohibited, they get crazy and dig for the hatchet, swing the tomahawk and go to war. A short time before we arrived they captured a wolf, according to authentic (American) reports. Our hosts are taking good care of us, and have warned us several times.[38]

By May 1945, Deer River citizens were agitated about the conduct of the camp. Another hunting-and-fishing incident was partly to blame; a local businessman and the game warden had found two POWs fishing on a small lake a mile from camp, unguarded and out of season. The Deer River *News* described the prisoners as "big huskies, fat and sleek and well-fed, quite arrogant and cocksure." Commanding officer Lt. Schmiedeberg called the game warden and asked him not to publicize the arrest of the prisoners, but the game warden said "he was not taking orders from the army." The news was out, and the freedom granted to the prisoners angered locals, who noted that American POWs in Germany were not able to "roam over the countryside and fish and hunt."[39]

Meanwhile, telegrams had been sent to congressmen and others, questioning the administration of the POW camp. In short order, Lt. Schmiedeberg left on another assignment, another commander arrived

POWs from Deer River carrying tools, March 1945. They report: "From the camp group that is now 179 men strong, there are more than 80% daily that go with the ax and the saw into the forest."[40] *Courtesy of Minneapolis Tribune–Roy Swan, Minnesota Historical Society*

Loading logs near Deer River, March 1945. The prisoners reported in their base camp newspaper that "with exception of the hunting season from November 13–25, our camp is in continual eight-hour operation." These logs were sawn to the proper length and stacked for shipping. The majority of the prisoners in the northern camps were there to cut pulpwood; a government inspector once estimated that each prisoner was cutting eight-tenths of a cord of pulpwood per day.[41] *Courtesy of Minneapolis Tribune–Roy Swan, Minnesota Historical Society*

Werner Schmiedeberg posing with the camp dog at the door of the Deer River headquarters, January 1945. The faded sign above the door still had CCC markings from the 1930s. *Courtesy of Werner Schmiedeberg*

Deer River entrance. *Courtesy of Werner Schmiedeberg*

from Algona, and the two POWs who had been caught fishing were put in the Itasca County jail at Grand Rapids, on a bread and water diet for a week. Schmiedeberg ordered that the two men be given a week's hard labor including digging ditches. The military stressed that it was difficult to watch "all the prisoners every hour of the day." Apparently, according to the Deer River *News*, the POWs "slipped away for a few hours fishing when no one was looking." Shortly after the incident, Algona's Colonel Lobdell contacted the publisher of the *News* about proper reporting procedures. Responding in a letter, the publisher wrote: "I confess considerable ignorance about how to treat news matters of that nature." After discussing the situation with two Army officers, he concluded "that future news reports, if any, will be treated with due consideration to army requirements."[42]

Back in camp, the POWs made good use of the accommodations they had helped to build. A table-tennis tournament with 46 players went on for two months in January and February 1945. The camp's "primeval forest stage Cut Foot Sioux" presented a comedy in March. The prisoners were particularly attentive to the POW who portrayed a woman in the play, a "spitting image performance." New and old masters were presented in the theater room on Easter Sunday, when the POWs heard the music of such composers as Strauss, Brahms, and Dvořák. As summer arrived, there was no time for theater productions, but an orchestra with eleven musicians had been assembled and record concerts had become common. Several academic classes including German literature and two levels of English were available to the prisoners.[43]

On September 14, Mr. Schnyder of the Red Cross arrived. Two days earlier, at Algona, he had been briefed about the work of the camps in northern Minnesota. Col. Lobdell had explained that POW labor accounted for three-quarters of the lumber harvested during the previous year in the Chippewa National Forest, and that shipping crates and paper were the two main products made from the cut wood.[44]

Schnyder reported favorably on accommodations for the 135 prisoners and compared the region's climate to that of central Europe. "This camp with its trees and flower beds," wrote Schnyder, "seems like one of the most beautiful CCC camps we have seen." The POW doctor gave Schnyder his opinion that the prisoners were not receiving enough calories. The doctor had already raised the question with a Washington official who had recently toured the camp, and had been

Lunchroom at Deer River camp, March 1945. Prisoners described that "in order to do their timber craft, the rest of the comrades make sure that the old wood choppers find a livable warm home, water and electricity when they come home." This mess hall was used for classes and lectures as well.[45]
Courtesy of Minneapolis Tribune–Roy Swan, Minnesota Historical Society

able to gain some improvements for the prisoners, who in his opinion would have begun fainting while at work. Camp spokesman Hans Schulte inquired, on behalf of the camp doctor, whether he would be able to keep his collection of professional books after captivity. Spokesman Schulte also asked Schnyder whether a group of prisoners would be paid for work missed due to a road mishap. U.S. Captain Gunnar Norgaard touring with the ICRC officials reported that he would look into the matter.[46]

By December 20, 1945, only the Deer River prisoners remained in the lumber-producing area of Minnesota. Plans for dismantling the facility were apparently carried out during the next week: all military equipment was to be sent out by truck, except a large bulldozer to be shipped by rail. Shortly before the camp closed, the Deer River *News* reported that the prisoners had not been so cooperative at first, but in time did settle into a routine that produced a lot of timber. Without the prisoners, it appears logging in the Deer River area would have languished, since civilian labor was "almost entirely unavailable." The camp passed into history on December 26, 1945.[47]

> ## Grand Rapids
> ## Itasca County
>
> ## January 1945–April 1945

Little information is available on the Grand Rapids camp, which ran for only four months at the end of the war. It was set up when the Remer camp closed because of a lack of new logging contracts. Men transferred from Remer in January 1945 helped established the camp, 22 miles north of Grand Rapids, to fulfill contracts near Day Lake. The CCC site had been unused for the previous two years, but the necessary equipment had already been delivered before the POWs' arrival.[48]

Former Grand Rapids commander Werner Schmiedeberg recalls that the installation of fence posts around the compound was a "particularly big problem," because the bits in the worker's jackhammer broke as they pounded through the permafrost. The solution was provided by a forge operator from a nearby taconite mine; he tempered a large piece of steel into a bit that proved equal to the task.[49]

When the camp was in operation, Col. Arthur Lobdell came from Algona to clear up certain "misapprehensions" about the use of prisoners in the area. Eventually, prisoners worked at various locations within a 30-mile radius of the Grand Rapids facility.[50]

Entrance to Grand Rapids camp, February 1945. Camp buildings are noticeable in the background. *Courtesy of Werner Schmiedeberg*

Grand Rapids commander Werner Schmiedeberg wearing his muskrat hat, January 1945; he purchased it at a local store. Schmiedeberg was responsible for setting up the facilities at Grand Rapids. After the camp closed in April, Schmiedeberg received his final assignment as a camp commander at Wells.[51] *Courtesy of Werner Schmiedeberg*

Epilogue

The only prisoner-of-war camps in Minnesota's history closed over 50 years ago. Their story is occasionally dramatic but hardly earth-shaking: there was a war, soldiers were captured, they became prisoners, and they worked in America. In the story's simplicity, however, is an enduring lesson about the way history works: the POWs and the Americans who interacted with them, adding their distinctive thread to the fabric of the state's past, were ordinary people doing ordinary things.

Economically, the use of prisoners in Minnesota was a success, particularly in agriculture. Three camps in the northwestern part of the state, for example, along with two others in nearby Grafton and Grand Forks, North Dakota, supplied over 750 POWs in the fall of 1945, saving approximately 34 percent of the area's sugar beet crop, valued at $1,407,600. One county agent claimed that most of the sugar beets and potatoes could not have been harvested without prisoner labor.[1]

POWs were indispensable in communities with canneries, where their total numbers peaked at more than two thousand. The Minnesota Canners Association has estimated that prisoners were instrumental in harvesting and processing 63 percent of the state's corn and pea production in 1944. In 1945 they saved roughly 65 percent of the pea crop, valued at over $9.8 million. At some canneries, POWs constituted the entire labor supply for certain operations. Records show, for example, that 100 percent of the area pea crop canned by the Reid Murdoch Company in Rochester, the Faribault Canning Company, and the Cool Spring Canning Company could not have been processed without prisoner labor.[2]

Prisoners were helpful to farms and businesses, particularly during lull periods at the canneries. In 1944 they worked on hundreds of farms in at least ten Minnesota counties, and in twice as many counties in 1945. More than twenty small businesses in Minnesota used prisoners. In some cases, the POWs may have been more than marginally helpful; it seems likely that the Ochs Brick and Tile Company in Springfield, for example, would have closed during the war if prisoners had not been available. Even as loggers in northern Minnesota, the POWs worked well enough to justify total earnings in the tens of thousands of dollars.[3]

No evidence suggests that the wartime use of prisoners for agricultural and other work in Minnesota displaced any local labor. Occasional union protests were usually of small effect except in East Grand Forks, Rochester, and Mankato. Although union workers and leaders in northern Minnesota were vigorously opposed to the use of POW labor, their protests were largely without impact. In retrospect, then, POWs were essentially just hired workers, whose use depended on nothing more complicated than community attitudes and the shortage of labor.[4]

Time has dramatically changed the farms and farm-related industries in which prisoners were once employed. The Odegard farm north of Princeton was sold to new owners in the 1960s. Henry Peterson's truck farm in Moorhead has changed ownership and is now much smaller than Peterson's operation. Because of changes in the size of local farming operations, the vegetable farms near Hollandale have evolved into fields of soybeans, sugar beets, and potatoes. Mechanization, beginning in the 1950s, has permanently altered harvesting practices for potatoes and sugar beets near the Red River in northwest Minnesota, where sugar beets have grown into more than a billion-dollar-yearly industry.[5]

Minnesota's canning industry has also changed considerably, but its presence is still important to many of the state's small communities. Several canneries where POWs worked are in operation; the Montgomery cannery, for example, which used the most POWs of any camp in Minnesota during the war, is now Cenaca Foods Inc.[6]

Many of the small business establishments where POWs worked are no longer in existence, but some remain. The Ochs Brick and Tile Company in Springfield, which employed New Ulm POWs, produces a decorative brick now distributed nationwide. The Rogers Brothers Seed Company, with facilities in Olivia during the war, has merged with another Minnesota seed company. The Cashman family, which helped establish the Owatonna branch camp, now operates nurseries in North Dakota and Montana.

In the north, lumbering persists, but changes in the industry have essentially eliminated the manual labor that once defined it. The camps themselves have been variously affected by the past fifty years. Some buildings survive, including several on local fairgrounds. The modified CCC camps in northern Minnesota, on the other hand, are evidenced only by old foundations and chimneys. Before its demise,

One building at the former POW camp south of New Ulm. At least one former prisoner has visited the old campsite since the war. Herbert Richter, a young POW cook at the camp, moved permanently to Minnesota after the war, first settling in Bemidji. He visited New Ulm several times and had hoped to retire there, but he settled in Kenosha, Wisconsin, instead.[7] *Author's photo*

Entrance to the Peterson farm near Moorhead in 1995. *Author's photo*

Barracks used to house prisoners next to the cannery in Faribault, shown here before their demolition in 1990. *Courtesy of Faribault Daily News*

Crookston prisoners were housed in this winter sports arena, photographed in 1996. *Author's photo*

the camp near Remer was maintained for sight-seeing tours, but the buildings were sold in the 1950s and trees were planted in their place. The camp's guard-house went to a local family for one dollar, to serve as a child's playhouse. Its only tangible reminder is a nearby road, cleared and used by the Remer prisoners to haul lumber to the railway. Today it is appropriately called "Prisoner of War Road." The old CCC camp near St. Charles was extensively damaged by a tornado in 1953; the surviving buildings were eventually razed to make room for a campground. New Ulm is the only campsite left essentially untouched. The wooded setting has doubtless changed, but the buildings, still in good condition, are used by Boy Scouts and other camping groups during the summer months.[8]

Werner Schmiedeberg, commanding officer at three Minnesota facilities, capped his career as a machinist by becoming a partner in the firm Machine Specialties in 1967. He retired to Florida in 1982, after more than forty years in the industry.[9]

Howard Hong, still working on Kierkegaard's manuscripts, winters in Northfield and spends his summers on Lake Superior's north shore. With his wife he travels periodically to Denmark, where the couple are finishing their translations of Kierkegaard's manuscripts into English, a projected total of 25 volumes. Over the years, Hong has maintained particularly close contact with two prisoners, Viktor Zwettler, the Algona camp engraver, and Alex Funke, the Algona camp pastor. Hong and his wife are godparents to a child of Funke's. Zwettler's daughter, who presently lives in Massachusetts, stayed at Hong's residence while studying at St. Olaf College.

Not only has Hong maintained contact with former prisoners, but his connection to the Algona camp is still tangible. Some of Algona's buildings were moved to St. Olaf after the war to accommodate students back from military service. The single Algona structure remaining at the college, used today for classes and office space, was an officers' building where Hong stayed when he visited the camp. An Algona washroom, removed from the St. Olaf campus years ago, was taken to Hong's home for use as a shed for lumber from his tree farm.[10]

Farms change owners, businesses close, and buildings vanish, but Minnesota's POWs and those whose paths they crossed have left an indestructible legacy. Surely it is not unrealistic to believe that the camps' good effects were more than merely economic. For the young men imprisoned in them, Minnesota was, surprisingly, a safe haven in a world at war. As citizens of a dictatorship, they had been instructed that they were members of a Master Race, and that the people of other nations were their enemies. As prisoners of a democracy, many of them discovered that they themselves, like their "enemies," were just people.

St. Paul, Minnesota
December 1999

Postscript

This book grew from a seed planted around 1985, when an elderly neighbor in Olivia, Minnesota, showed me a photograph of Italian POWs who had worked on her husband's farm in 1943. I had just finished mowing her lawn, and while I drank a glass of lemonade she fondly recalled the well-behaved Italians. Her stories intrigued me, and she offered me the photograph as a memento of our conversation. For me, the picture became a lasting reminder of former prisoners in Olivia, and the beginning of a historical journey.

In August 1990 I went to Germany as an exchange student, during my junior year at the University of St. Thomas in St. Paul, Minnesota. Thinking back to the photograph in Olivia, I wondered what had happened to the former German POWs in my hometown during the war. In the hope of locating at least one of these people, I began a search for information about them. Meanwhile, I was given some names and addresses left by German POWs in a neighbor's 1944 autograph book. Some were written in the antique German script; two were in Russian, with addresses near Kiev. Some of the POWs included poems and trivia; others just signed their names. One inscribed his entry, "for the remembrance of Olivia, and the nice people." Another, eager for a response, wrote, "We hope that you will write a small letter after the war."

Searching for current addresses, I mailed letters to people with the prisoners' surnames in their hometowns. In these dozens of letters I introduced myself and explained my interest in locating a former prisoner who had once worked in Olivia.

Having turned up very few leads, I began to feel that my quest was perhaps futile. Then I received a letter from Alfred Neber; one of my inquiries had finally reached a former prisoner. Neber had no recollection of leaving his address behind nearly fifty years earlier, but he recognized his handwriting on the copy I included with my letter. After additional exchanges and a short train trip to his home, we met for an afternoon to discuss his experiences as a former prisoner.

My successful search for Neber stimulated my desire to know more. Soon after my return to the United States I learned that the POW camp in my hometown was just one of a large network; by a natural extension of my interest I researched the 21 camp locations in

Minnesota and their base camp in Algona, Iowa. For four years I contacted archives, wrote letters, and visited various people who could supply information.

Although the majority of war-prisoners in Minnesota were German, I made an earnest effort to locate Italian ex-prisoners so I could add their observations to my picture of the POW experience. The few I found, however, were reluctant to offer information. Some concluded that I was seeking former Axis collaborators; they declined to acknowledge any wartime contact with Americans and were eager to deny any collaborationist behavior.

In 1994 I returned to Germany as a graduate student, and had the opportunity to visit many of the prisoners with whom I had been in contact by mail. After my return to the United States, I decided to offer this account of an intriguing moment in Minnesota's past.

I still have the old photo I started with, my neighbor's picture of POWs waiting with mess kits for their noon meal. That photo, the initial inspiration for my project, is the frontispiece with which this narrative begins.

My purpose in *Swords into Plowshares* has been to bring together the surviving pieces of information about Minnesota's POW camps, and to make them accessible to the widest possible audience. They will not support the symmetrical account, with tidy conclusions, that I would have preferred to offer. An ideal history might resemble Allan Powell's splendid treatment of the Utah camps, based on a plentiful array of official records. Unfortunately no such riches are available to us; Minnesota's camps were, after all, mere branches of base camps in other states, survived by little more than tantalizing clues.

Some of my readers will perhaps regret the absence of detailed analysis from these pages. But my concern, in addition to serving the interests of historians, has been to tell a story that lay readers can follow. Thus, beyond the minimum of interpretation that a coherent narrative requires, I have left to others the task of sifting and weighing the evidence and building theses upon it. Meanwhile, for whatever use the scholar or the layman may wish to make of it, the material itself is readily accessible here.

For brevity's sake, I have skipped lightly over the larger context in which Minnesota's "POW experience" took place: the major military events of World War II, the social and political currents of the era, the national and local impact of Selective Service, the mobilization of civilian life in such institutions as rationing. My own introductory chapter is meant to provide a simple context for the camp histories that follow. Anything more ambitious would merely echo what is readily available elsewhere.

The local histories themselves are, necessarily, of unequal weight; we know much more about New Ulm, for example, than about Hollandale or Grand Rapids. I would have preferred to write uniformly detailed subchapters, but the surviving evidence is as it is, and scholarly guesswork, no matter how sophisticated, cannot close the gaps. It has been suggested to me that the narrative's unevenness might be smoothed by its presentation according to certain broad themes, rather than camp-by-camp. My conclusion, however, is that ready access to local detail is best served by the present arrangement.

It would have been pleasant to base my work on many authoritative eyewitness testimonies. But the truth is that I am lucky to have located Howard Hong and Werner Schmiedeberg, apparently the only "official" survivors of the Minnesota compounds.

Finally, readers of my book will find that some questions remain unanswered. Why, for example, did the "enemies" suddenly dropped into the state cause so little apparent consternation? Given the violent sentiments attending World War I and its aftermath, why were Minnesota citizens and German soldiers generally so cordial to one another? Unfortunately, the answers to such questions must be speculative; evidence alone will not supply the "balance" that scholarship yearns for.

In all these perplexities, it seems useful to remember the words of Bruce Catton: *

> History after all is the story of people: a statement that might seem too obvious to be worth making if it were not for the fact that history so often is presented in terms of vast incomprehensible forces moving far under the surface, carrying human beings along, helpless, and making them conform to a pattern whose true shape they never see. The pattern does exist, often enough, and it is important to trace it. Yet it is good to remember that it is the people who make the pattern, not the other way around.

* *American Heritage* 6, no. 1.

Appendixes

Alphabetical Lists of Camp Algona's Branch Camps by State

MINNESOTA	Camp No.	IOWA	Camp No.
Ada	31	Charles City	17
Bena	4	Clinton	19
Bird Island	15	Eldora	13
Crookston	30	Muscatine	23
Deer River	6	Onawa	25
Fairmont	2	Shenandoah	20
Faribault	9	Storm Lake	26
Grand Rapids	18	Tabor	21
Hollandale	16	Toledo	27
Howard Lake	12	Waverly	14
Montgomery	8		
Moorhead	1	NORTH DAKOTA	
New Ulm	7		
Olivia	28	Grafton	33
Ortonville	11	Grand Forks	32
Owatonna	5		
Remer	3	SOUTH DAKOTA	
Saint Charles	10		
Warren	34	Sioux Falls	29
Wells	24	Yankton	22

Abbreviations and Definitions

The following abbreviations, acronyms, and institutional names appear in the text:

AFL	American Federation of Labor
Afrika Korps	The elite German army formation in North Africa
Bethel	A constituent organization of the von Bodelschwingh Institut
CCC	Civilian Conservation Corps
CIO	Congress of Industrial Organizations
County Agent	The director of a county extension office
D-Day	June 6, 1944. The first day of the Normandy Invasion.
Extension Office	One of a state-wide organization of agricultural offices, providing agricultural services under direction from the state
FHCC	Farm Help Coordinating Committee
Flak	Contraction from the German word *Flugzeugabwehrkanone*, meaning anti-aircraft gun
Geneva Convention	Convention pertaining to wounded and war prisoners originally signed in Geneva, Switzerland, in 1864. Two conventions signed in July 1929 deal in particular with prisoners of war and with wounded and sick soldiers.
ICRC	International Committee of the Red Cross
IRC	International Red Cross
ISS	International Student Services
IWA	International Woodworker's Association
Liberty Ship	Class of U.S. cargo ships during World War II
Nazi	Contraction from the German word *Nationalsozialist*, meaning National Socialist. A member of Hitler's political party.

PMG	Provost Marshal General. Head of the U.S. army's military police and the officer responsible for the direction of all POW affairs.
POW	Prisoner of War
PW or P.W.	Description used during the war for a prisoner of war, synonymous with POW. This was stenciled onto prisoners' uniforms.
SS	SS abbreviates the German word *Schutzstaffel*, the elite guard of the Nazi party.
U-Boot	Contraction of the German word *Unterseeboot*, meaning submarine
USES	United States Employment Service
V-E Day	May 8, 1945. The day of victory for the Allied forces in Europe during World War II.
von Bodelschwingh Institut	Large organization of hospitals and other organizations, located near Bielefeld, Germany, and under direction of the German Lutheran church
War Department	The department of the federal government that supervised the U.S. Army, including the Army Air Force, during World War II.
War Prisoners Aid	YMCA program which provided recreational materials for prisoners of war
WMC	War Manpower Commission
WPA	Works Progress Administration
YMCA	Young Men's Christian Association

Notes

Chapter One: POWs in America

1. Arnold Krammer, *Nazi Prisoners of War in America* (New York: Stein and Day Publishers, 1979), p. xiv; George G. Lewis and John Mewha, *History of Prisoner of War Utilization by the United States Army, 1776–1945* (Washington, D.C.: Department of the Army, 1955), 83–86, 90–91; Jack Fincher, "By Convention, the Enemy Within Never Did Without," *Smithsonian*, June 1995, 132.
2. Graham H. Stuart, "War Prisoners and Internees in the United States," *American Foreign Service Journal*, 21 (October 1944): 530; John Brown Mason, "German Prisoners of War in the United States," *American Journal of International Law* 39 (1945): 199; Cummins E. Speakman Jr., "Reeducation of German Prisoners of War in the United States during World War II." (Thesis, University of Virginia, June 1948), 8–9; Krammer, *Nazi Prisoners of War in America*, 4, 15, 17; Ronald H. Baily, *Prisoners of War* (Chicago: Time-Life Books, 1981), 144, 158.
3. Maxwell S. McKnight, "The Employment of Prisoners of War in the United States," *International Labour Review* (Montreal) 50 (July 1944): 48; Krammer, *Nazi Prisoners of War in America*, 26–27, 153; Lewis and Mewha, *Prisoner of War Utilization*, 86; Sidney B. Fay, "German Prisoners of War," *Current History* 8 (March 1945): 196; U.S. Congress, House, Committee on Military Affairs, "Investigations of the National War Effort," H.R. 1992, 12 June 1945, pp. 18–19, as cited in Krammer, *Nazi Prisoners of War in America*, 257.
4. "Our Growing Prison Camps: How U.S. Treats War Captives," *National Week*, 28 May 1943, 23, 24; Krammer, *Nazi Prisoners of War in America*, 50–64, 240; McKnight, "Employment of Prisoners of War," 50, 52; Fay, "German Prisoners of War," 195; Baily, *Prisoners of War*, 168; Fincher, "By Convention," 131.
5. Baily, *Prisoners of War*, 156, 159; Krammer, *Nazi Prisoners of War in America*, 79, 88–89; McKnight, "Employment of Prisoners of War," 48; Lewis and Mewha, *Prisoner of War Utilization*, 126.
6. McKnight, "Employment of Prisoners of War," 49, 55; Krammer, *Nazi Prisoners of War in America*, 88; Lewis and Mewha, *Prisoner of War Utilization*, 125.
7. Lewis and Mewha, *Prisoner of War Utilization*, 101; Walter W. Wilcox, *The Farmer in the Second World War* (Ames, Iowa: Iowa State College Press, 1947), 83, 95.
8. McKnight, "Employment of Prisoners of War," 58; Lewis and Mewha, *Prisoner of War Utilization*, 126, 133–35; Baily, *Prisoners of War*, 148-49, 160. A detailed account of a war-prisoner camp established for logging can

be found in Allen V. Koop, *Stark Decency: German Prisoners of War in a New England Village* (Hanover, NH: University Press of New England, 1988); Krammer, *Nazi Prisoners of War in America*, xiv, 88–91; Kathy Roe Coker, "World War II Prisoners of War in Georgia: German Memories of Camp Gordon, 1943–1945," *Georgia Historical Quarterly* 76 (winter 1992), 849; Fincher, "By Convention," 136. A concise example of German POW employment in state agricultural industries can be found in Duane Ernest Miller, "Barbed-Wire Farm Laborers: Michigan's Prisoner of War Experience during World War II," *Michigan History* 73 (September/October 1989), 12–17; the Michigan Extension Service governed the use of prisoners on Michigan farms.

9. McKnight, "Employment of Prisoners of War," 51, 60, 62; Lewis and Mewha, *Prisoner of War Utilization*, 77.

10. Baily, *Prisoners of War*, 160; Lewis and Mewha, *Prisoner of War Utilization*, 79, 88, 93, 171–72; "Convention Relative to the Treatment of Prisoners of War. Geneva, 27 July 1929," Article 31. Detailed information pertaining to the use of prisoners in accordance with the Geneva Convention can be found in "The Conditions of Employment of Prisoners of War: The Geneva Convention of 1929 and Its Application," *International Labour Review* (Montreal), 47 (February 1943), 169–96; "Our Growing Prison Camps," 23; McKnight, "Employment of Prisoners of War," 54–56; Fincher, "By Convention," 135; Krammer, *Nazi Prisoners of War in America*, 80, 97, 98. Although Allied prisoners were released after Italy's surrender, the status of the Italian prisoners was not entirely clear; this is discussed in Louis E. Keefer, *Italian Prisoners of War in America, 1942–1946: Captives or Allies?* (New York: Praeger Publishers, 1992), xvi.

11. Krammer, *Nazi Prisoners of War in America*, 115, 189–227, 248; Fincher, "By Convention," 133, 135, 140–42; Speakman, "Re-education of German Prisoners," 21–41. The official name of the Intellectual Diversion Program was the Special Projects Division. This can be found in Ron Robin, *The Barbed-Wire College: Reeducating German POWs in the United States during World War II* (Princeton: Princeton University Press, 1995), 8; Henry W. Ehrmann, "An Experiment in Political Education: The Prisoner-of-War Schools in the United States," *Social Research* 14 (September 1947), 304–320.

12. McKnight, "Employment of Prisoners of War," 48; Fincher, "By Convention," 127; Baily, *Prisoners of War*, 159, 160; Krammer, *Nazi Prisoners of War in America*, 115–17, 136, 145–46.

13. Fincher, "By Convention," 140; Fay, "German Prisoners of War," 196–97; Baily, *Prisoners of War*, 164–65. Conflicts arose in certain camps, many because of differences in political opinions among the prisoners; an example can be found in Thomas R. Buecker, "Nazi Influence at the Fort Robinson Prisoner of War Camp during World War II," *Nebraska History* 73 (spring 1992), 32–41; Krammer, *Nazi Prisoners of War in America*, 40; *Minneapolis*

Star Tribune, 6 December 1990, sec. A, p. 2; Allan Kent Powell, *Splinters of a Nation: German Prisoners of War in Utah* (Salt Lake City: University of Utah Press, 1989), 225.

14. Lewis and Mewha, *Prisoner of War Utilization*, 172; John E. Manley, "Administration and Relationships of War Prisoners Aid of the YMCA in the United States during World War II," World Alliance File #18, Kautz Family YMCA Archives, St. Paul, Minnesota, 56; Krammer, *Nazi Prisoners of War in America*, 229, 244.

15. Krammer, *Nazi Prisoners of War in America*, 238–39, 243, 249.

16. Ibid., 259–61, 266. For examples of return visits from former prisoners, see *Chicago Tribune*, 5 June 1996, p. 1, and *Detroit News and Free Press*, 26 November 1992, sec. A, p. 17.

Chapter Two: Minnesota's POW Camps

1. Edward J. Pluth, "Prisoner of War Employment in Minnesota during World War II," *Minnesota History* 44 (winter 1975), 291; Wilcox, *The Farmer in the Second World War*, 84; *Minneapolis Morning Tribune*, 10 October 1942, p. 1; Kelly Zwagerman, "A Study of German Prisoner of War Labor in Faribault, Minnesota during World War II." (Graduate research paper, Mankato State University, December 1989), 10, 11; *Minneapolis Morning Tribune*, 14 July 1942, p. 11; *Minneapolis Morning Tribune*, 22 July 1942, p. 9.

2. "Advisory Group Selected to Aid Farm Help Chief," 26 February 1943, Minnesota Farm Help Coordinating Committee Newsletter, HD 1775f.M6A 5 1943, Minnesota State Historical Society, St. Paul, MN, 1; "Minnesota Set to Begin Drive for Farm Help," 28 February 1943, Minnesota Farm Help Coordinating Committee Newsletter, HD 1775f.M6A 5 1943, Minnesota State Historical Society, St. Paul, MN, 1–3; "Farm Help Plan Based on Local Administration," 14 March 1943, Minnesota Farm Help Coordinating Committee Newsletter, HD 1775f.M6A 5 1943, Minnesota State Historical Society, St. Paul, MN, 1–3.

3. "Farm Labor Conference at Morris," 7 March 1943, Minnesota Farm Help Coordinating Committee Newsletter, HD 1775f.M6A 5 1943, Minnesota State Historical Society, St. Paul, MN, 2; "Mankato Meet Lays Foundation Farm Help Drive," 7 March 1943, Minnesota Farm Help Coordinating Committee Newsletter, HD 1775f.M6A 5 1943, Minnesota State Historical Society, St. Paul, MN, 1; "State Set to Mobilize its Farm Workers," 10 April 1943, Minnesota Farm Help Coordinating Committee Newsletter, HD 1775f.M6A 5 1943, Minnesota State Historical Society, St. Paul, MN, 1; Pluth, "Prisoner of War Employment," 291–92; *Minneapolis Morning Tribune*, 22 June 1943, p. 20; *Minneapolis Sunday Tribune*, 13 June 1943, Minnesota section, p. 5; "State Can Get War Prisoners for Farm Work," 23 June 1943, Minnesota Farm Help Coordinating Committee Newsletter, HD 1775f.M6A 5, Minnesota State Historical Society, St. Paul, MN, 1–2.

4. *Minneapolis Morning Tribune*, 2 July 1943, p. 9; "Report on the Minnesota Farm Labor Program, 1943," 1943, Agriculture Extension Service, University of Minnesota Archives, Minneapolis, Minnesota, 9–10; Pluth, "Prisoner of War Employment," 292–94; "Our Growing Prison Camps," 23.

5. *Minneapolis Morning Tribune*, 28 February 1944, p. 16; Pluth, "Prisoner of War Employment," 296; "Cooperative Agreement between Agricultural Extension Service of the University of Minnesota and War Manpower Commission for Furnishing Facilities and Services," 1944, File "R," Farm Labor Program WWII, University of Minnesota Archives, Minneapolis, MN, appendix A.

6. *Cass County Pioneer*, 9 June 1944, p. 5; Pluth, "Prisoner of War Employment," 297; *Mankato Free Press*, 6 June 1944, p. 7; *Tägliche Volkszeitung-Tribüne*, 7 June 1944, p. 6; "Report on the Minnesota Farm Labor Program, 1944," 1944, Agriculture Extension Service, University of Minnesota Archives, Minneapolis, Minnesota, 8, 9.

7. Pluth, "Prisoner of War Employment," 297; "Report on the Farm Labor Program, 1944," 9–10; "Report on the Minnesota Farm Labor Program, 1945," 1945, Agriculture Extension Service, University of Minnesota Archives, Minneapolis, Minnesota, 1–2.

8. Patrick G. O'Brien, Thomas D. Isern, and R. Daniel Lumley, "Stalag Sunflower: German Prisoners of War in Kansas," *Kansas History* 7 (autumn 1984), 183–86; Karl Becker to Simmons, 1 January 1994; Hans Welker, interview by author, phone interview, Olivia, Minnesota, 8 October 1994; Krammer, *Nazi Prisoners of War in America*, 36. Security was also a high priority at Concordia; this is discussed in Penny Clark, "Farm Work and Friendship: The German Prisoner of War Camp at Lake Wabaunsee," Emporia State Research Studies (Emporia) 36 (winter 1988), 7. A thorough discussion of Camp Concordia can be found in Lowell A. May, *Camp Concordia: German POWs in the Midwest* (Manhattan, Kansas: Sunflower University Press, 1995), 30–31, and in Kurt C. Teufel, ed., "The History of Camp Concordia from Site Survey to Inactivation," 1945, Federal Records Center, Kansas City, Missouri; "Records of the Office of the Provost Marshal General," Schwieger Report, 3 July 1944, Record Group 389, National Archives, Washington, D.C. (hereafter cited as Schwieger Report, 3 July 1944), 2.

9. George H. Lobdell, "Minnesota's 1944 PW Escape: Down the Mississippi in the Lili Marlene #10," *Minnesota History* 54 (fall 1994), 113, 116; "Standard Operating Procedure for Prisoner of War Branch Camps," Prisoner of War Camp, Algona, Iowa, circa July 1944, A. T. Lobdell Manuscript Collection, 2, 4; George H. Lobdell to Simmons, 26 July 1995.

10. George H. Lobdell to Simmons, 26 July 1995; "Standard Operating Procedure," 2; Harvey Fleshner to Simmons, 7 December 1995.

11. Roy W. Schultz, interview by Mark Peihl, phone interview, 27 February 1991, Clay County Historical Society, Moorhead, MN; Zwagerman, "Prisoner

of War Labor in Faribault," 21; *Minneapolis Star Tribune*, 7 December 1987, sec. A, p. 1.

12. "Records of the Office of the Provost Marshal General," Dawson Report, 29 September 1944, Record Group 389, National Archives, Washington, D.C. (hereafter cited as Dawson Report), 5, 7; *New Ulm Daily Journal*, 25 July 1945, p. 1.

13. Schwieger Report, 3 July 1944, 3; Krammer, *Nazi Prisoners of War in America*, 6, 149.

14. Werner Schmiedeberg to Simmons, 18 August 1996.

15. Andre Vulliet, "Preliminary Report of the War Prisoners Aid Young Men's Christian Associations during World War II," 1946, World Alliance File #18, Kautz Family YMCA Archives, St. Paul, Minnesota, 9, 10, 73.

16. Ibid., 10.

17. Manley, "Administration and Relationships," 45–46. Other YMCA field secretaries included Andre Vulliet, a Swiss who eventually worked for the War Prisoners Aid in Geneva after the war; Danish architecture student Helge Westerman; Spaniard Louis Hortal; and German language student from Ireland, Sidney Ievers. Other workers included Swedes Gustav Almquist and Sture Persson. This is shown in Manley, "Administration and Relationships," 45–46, and in Howard Hong, interview by author, tape recording, Northfield, MN, 3 May 1994, and in Howard Hong, interview by author, tape recording, Hovland, MN, 10 September 1995 (hereafter cited as Hong Interviews); Vulliet, "Preliminary Report," 15.

18. Charles Howard Hopkins, *John R. Mott 1865–1955* (Grand Rapids: William B. Eerdmans Publishing Company, 1979), 692, 695; Charles Howard Hopkins, *History of the YMCA in North America* (New York: Association Press, 1951), 713; Hong Interviews; *Manitou Messenger*, 14 May 1943, p. 2; *Northfield Independent*, 6 May 1943, p. 1; *Northfield News*, 6 May 1943, p. 1.

19. Hopkins, *John R. Mott 1865–1955*, 692; Manley, "Administration and Relationships," 45–46; Hong Interviews.

20. Hong Interviews; Darias Davis was a direct assistant to Tracy Strong.

21. Ibid.; John Douglas Mullen, *Kierkegaard's Philosophy: Self-Deception and Cowardice in the Present Age* (New York: Times Mirror, 1981), 149. Further explanations of Kierkegaard's "Works of Love" can be found in Gregor Malantschuk, *Kierkegaard's Thought* (Princeton: Princeton University Press, 1971), 323–25, and M. Holmes Hartshorne, *Kierkegaard, Godly Deceiver: The Nature and Meaning of His Pseudonymous Writings* (New York: Columbia University Press, 1990), 28, 46–52. Hong registered as a conscientious objector during the war and eventually received a 4F classification for hay fever from the draft board; this is shown in Howard Hong to Simmons, 25 September 1998.

22. Vulliet, "Preliminary Report," 19.

23. Hong Interviews.

24. Ibid.; Manley, "Administration and Relationships," 46; *Manitou Messenger*,

27 April 1945, p. 1; *Manitou Messenger*, 11 May 1945, p. 2.

25. Hong Interviews; Erich Maschke, ed., *Zur Geschichte der deutschen Kriegsgefangenen des Zweiten Weltkrieges* (To the History of the German Prisoners of War in World War Two), vol. 15, *Die Deutschen Kriegsgefangenen des Zweiten Weltkrieges: Eine Zusammenfassung* (German Prisoners of War of World War Two: A Summary) by Erich Maschke (Munich: Verlag Ernst und Werner Gieseking, 1974), 48, 52. The Maschke Commission was formally known as the "Scientific Commission for the History of the German Prisoners of War." It took nearly 16 years to complete its task, which resulted in a series of 22 books, considered to be the authoritative study of the German POWs in World War II; this can be found in Günter Bischof and Stephen Ambrose, eds., *Eisenhower and the German POWs: Facts against Falsehood: Some Reflections on the Maschke Commission*, by Rolf Steininger (Baton Rouge: Louisiana State University Press, 1992), 171, 177. More information about the Maschke Commission can be found in Erich Maschke, ed., *Zur Geschichte der deutschen Kriegsgefangenen des Zweiten Weltkrieges* (To the History of the German Prisoners of War of World War Two), vol. 15, *Die Deutschen Kriegsgefangenen des Zweiten Weltkrieges: Eine Zusammenfassung* (German Prisoners of War of World War Two: A Summary) by Erich Maschke (Munich: Verlag Ernst und Werner Gieseking, 1974).

26. Hong Interviews.

27. Ibid.; "Records of the Office of the Provost Marshal General," YMCA visit from Hong, 17, 18 October and 3 November 1944, Record Group 389, National Archives, Washington, D.C.; Erich Maschke, ed., *Zur Geschichte der deutschen Kriegsgefangenen des Zweiten Weltkrieges* (To the History of the German Prisoners of War of World War Two), vol. 10, *Die deutschen Kriegsgefangenen in amerikanischer Hand: USA* (German Prisoners of War in American Captivity: USA) by Hermann Jung (Munich: Verlag Ernst und Werner Gieseking, 1972), 109.

28. Hopkins, *John R. Mott 1865–1955*, 695.

29. Alex Funke, interview by author, tape recording, Bielefeld, Germany, 21 February 1995.

30. Hong Interviews. The original quotation on page 20, ". . . Algona PW camp" was modernized by the author to ". . . Algona POW camp."

31. Ibid.; *Manitou Messenger*, 16 November 1945, p. 3; *Manitou Messenger*, 1 February 1946, p. 3.

32. *Lagerzeitung* (Algona German POW base camp newspaper), 23 January 1946, p. 16.

33. Friedhelm Henkel, interview by author, tape recording, Hatzbach, Germany, 12 February 1995; Henkel appears on the Algona records as Friedrich Wilhelm. He later combined his given names to Friedhelm.

34. Alex Funke, interview by author, tape recording, Bielefeld, Germany, 21 February 1995.

35. Hong Interviews.

36. Vulliet, "Preliminary Report," 61–62.
37. Ibid., 61; Manley, "Administration and Relationships," 56; Hopkins, *History of the YMCA*, 713–14.
38. *Drahtpost* (Algona German POW base camp newspaper), 28 January 1945, p. 20; *Drahtpost* (Algona German POW base camp newspaper), 11 February 1945, p. 12; Friedhelm Henkel, interview by author, tape recording, Hatzbach, Germany, 12 February 1995.
39. Howard Hong, interview by author, tape recording, Northfield, MN, 3 May 1994.
40. Erich Maschke, ed., *Zur Geschichte der deutschen Kriegsgefangenen des Zweiten Weltkrieges* (To the History of the German Prisoners of War of World War Two), vol. 14, *Geist und Kultur der deutschen Kriegsgefangenen im Westen* (Spiritual and Cultural Activities of German Prisoners of War in the West) by Kurt W. Böhme (Munich: Verlag Ernst und Werner Gieseking, 1968), 2; Edward J. Pluth, "The Administration and Operation of German Prisoner of War Camps in the United States during World War II." (Ph.D. diss., Ball State University, 1970), 214, 216; Pluth indicates that the National Catholic Welfare Council (NCWC) was another organization providing services to prisoners; Erich Maschke, ed., *Zur Geschichte der deutschen Kriegsgefangenen des Zweiten Weltkrieges* (To the History of the German Prisoners of War of World War Two), vol. 15, *Hilfen für die deutschen Kriegsgefangenen* (Help for the German Prisoners of War) by Kurt W. Böhme (Munich: Verlag Ernst und Werner Gieseking, 1974), 377.
41. James Avery Joyce, *Red Cross International and the Strategy of Peace* (New York: Oceana Publications, 1959), 110–12; Maschke, ed., *Hilfen für die deutschen Kriegsgefangenen*, 377; International Committee of the Red Cross, *Inter Arma Caritas: The Work of the International Committee of the Red Cross during the Second World War* (Geneva: International Committee of the Red Cross, 1947), 40–42; Erich Maschke, ed., *Zur Geschichte der deutschen Kriegsgefangenen des Zweiten Weltkrieges* (To the History of the German Prisoners of War of World War Two), vol. 15, *Berichte der IKRK-Delegierten über ihre Lagerbesuche* (Reports of the ICRC Delegates about Their Camp Visits) by Kurt W. Böhme (Munich: Verlag Ernst und Werner Gieseking, 1974), 89; "Convention Relative to the Treatment of Prisoners of War. Geneva, 27 July 1929," Article 88; Max Huber, *Das Internationale Rote Kreuz: Idee und Wirklichkeit* (The International Red Cross: Idea and Reality) (Zurich: Max Niehans Verlag, 1951), 69.
42. Erich Maschke, ed., *Berichte der IKRK-Delegierten*, 88–90, 93, 94; International Committee of the Red Cross, *Inter Arma Caritas*, 41. For more information about the delegates chosen, see Max Huber, *Das Internationale Rote Kreuz: Idee und Wirklichkeit* (The International Red Cross: Idea and Reality) (Zurich: Max Niehans Verlag, 1951).
43. Joyce, *Red Cross International*, 134; Maschke, ed., *Berichte der IKRK-Delegierten*, 90, 99, 101; International Committee of the Red Cross, *Inter*

Arma Caritas, 42; Pluth, "Administration and Operation," 213; International Committee of the Red Cross, *The International Committee of the Red Cross and the Second World War: General Introduction* (Geneva: 1998) accessed 7 April 1998 [http://www.icrc.ch/unicc/icrcnews], 3; Maschke, ed., *Eine Zusammenfassung*, 52.

44. Maschke, ed., *Berichte der IKRK-Delegierten*, 95, 97, 101.

45. "ICRC visit from Zehnder at Algona," 8 March 1945; "ICRC visit from Zehnder at Fairmont," 9 March 1945; "ICRC visit from Zehnder at New Ulm," 9 March 1945; "ICRC visit from Zehnder at Owatonna," 10 March 1945; "ICRC visit from Zehnder at Clarinda," 15, 16 March 1945, Politisches Archiv des Auswärtigen Amts, Bonn, Germany.

46. "ICRC visit from Schnyder at Algona," 12 September 1945; "ICRC visit from Schnyder at Owatonna," 13 September 1945; "ICRC visit from Schnyder at Montgomery," 13 September 1945; "ICRC visit from Schnyder at Faribault," 13 September 1945; "ICRC visit from Schnyder at Deer River," 14 September 1945; "ICRC visit from Schnyder at Bena," 14 September 1945, Politisches Archiv des Auswärtigen Amts, Bonn, Germany.

47. Records indicate that the number of prisoners in Minnesota's camps reached 2,998 in September 1945; "POW Labor Reports," 15, 28 September 1945, A. T. Lobdell Manuscript Collection. An old CCC camp near Savage, Minnesota, housed thousands of Japanese-Americans during the war. The camp was established in San Francisco in 1941 to translate a variety of Japanese-language war documents. For security reasons the camp was moved to Savage in 1942, and it remained in operation until 1944 when it was moved to Fort Snelling; this is shown in *Unsung Heroes, Military Intelligence Service: Past, Present, Future* (MIS-Northwest Association, 1996).

48. George H. Lobdell to Simmons, 26 July 1995; Werner Schmiedeberg to Simmons, 18 August 1996.

49. *Mankato Free Press*, 15 July 1944, p. 7.

50. *Blue Earth Post*, 23 March 1944, p. 9.

51. Ibid., p. 9.

52. Pluth, "Prisoner of War Employment," 293, 298, 302–3; *East Grand Forks Weekly Record*, 6 August 1943, p. 1; *Minneapolis Morning Tribune*, 4 August 1943, p. 1; *Minneapolis Morning Tribune*, 6 August 1943, p. 16; *Minneapolis Star Journal*, 7 August 1943, p. 7; *Minneapolis Star Journal*, 13 August 1943, p. 9.

Chapter Three: Farm-Labor Camps

1. "Cooperative Agreement between Agricultural Extension Service of the University of Minnesota and War Manpower Commission for Furnishing Facilities and Services," 1944, File "R," Farm Labor Program WWII, University of Minnesota Archives, Minneapolis, MN, appendix A; "Report on the Minnesota Farm Labor Program, 1944," 2–7; "Lyon County Annual Report

1945," 1945, Lyon County Extension Office, 51; "Jackson County Annual Report 1943," 1943, Jackson County Extension Office, 45; "Report on the Minnesota Farm Labor Program, 1945," 1, 4, 8.

2. *Princeton Union*, 5 August 1943, p. 1; Henry Peterson and Paul Horn, interview by Gloria Thompson, 11 January 1973, Moorhead, Minnesota, tape recording, Northwest Minnesota Historical Center, Moorhead; "Records of the Office of the Provost Marshal General," YMCA visit from Hong, 4 August 1944, Record Group 389, National Archives, Washington, D.C.; Georges Denzene and Beverly J. Jackson, *The Hollandale Story: 1918–1950* (Freeborn County Historical Society, 1989), 1–3.

3. *Minneapolis Star Journal,* 20 July 1943, p. 11; *Princeton Union*, 29 July 1943, p. 1; *Minneapolis Morning Tribune*, 24 July 1943, p. 5; *Minneapolis Star Journal*, 5 August 1943, p. 2; "Potatoes, Peat and Prisoners of War," *Isanti County Traveler*, summer 1995, 12.

4. *Princeton Union*, 29 July 1943, p. 1; Robert Odegard, interview by author, Roseville, MN, tape recording, 13 April 1994 (hereafter cited as Odegard Interview). Robert Odegard is the son of Odin Odegard and worked with the prisoners in 1943. The Odegard family also owned and operated a 1,000-acre dairy farm. "Potatoes, Peat and Prisoners of War," *Isanti County Traveler*, summer 1995, 12; *St. Paul Dispatch*, 7 September 1943, p. 13; *Tägliche Volkszeitung-Tribüne*, 9 September 1943, p. 6; *Princeton Union*, 9 September 1943, p. 1; *Princeton Union*, 2 September 1943, p. 1.

5. "Potatoes, Peat and Prisoners of War," *Isanti County Traveler*, summer 1995, p. 12; "Mille Lacs County Annual Report 1943," 1943, Mille Lacs County Extension Office, 20, 21; Odegard Interview.

6. *Minneapolis Star Journal*, 9 September 1943, p. 1.

7. "Mille Lacs County Annual Report 1943," 20, 21; *Princeton Union*, 7 October 1943, p. 1; Odegard Interview.

8. *Redwood Falls Gazette*, 9 September 1943, p. 1; *Minneapolis Star Journal*, 9 September 1943, p. 1.

9. *Minneapolis Star Journal*, 9 September 1943, p. 1; *Princeton Union*, 23 September 1943, p. 1; *Princeton Union*, 9 September 1943, p. 1.

10. *Minneapolis Morning Tribune*, 24 July 1943, p. 5; *Tägliche Volkszeitung-Tribüne*, 4 November 1943, p. 6; *Princeton Union*, 4 November 1943, p. 1; Odegard Interview.

11. *Princeton Union*, 4 November 1943, p. 1.

12. Paul Horn, interview by Gloria Thompson, 11 January 1973, Moorhead, Minnesota, tape recording, Northwest Minnesota Historical Center, Moorhead (hereafter cited as Horn Interview).

13. *Moorhead Daily News*, 23 May 1944, p. 1.

14. *Moorhead Daily News*, 29 May 1944, p. 1; *Moorhead Daily News*, 31 May 1944, p. 1; Horn Interview; Mark Peihl, "POWs Work at Moorhead Truck Farm," *Clay County Historical Society Newsletter*, March/April 1991, 16; "Records of the Office of the Provost Marshal General," YMCA visit from

Hong, 4 August 1944, Record Group 389, National Archives, Washington, D.C.

15. "Records of the Office of the Provost Marshal General," YMCA visit from Hong, 4 August 1944, Record Group 389, National Archives, Washington, D.C.

16. *Kossuth County Advance*, 29 June 1944, p. 1.

17. Arthur T. Lobdell to V. Tobler, 1 July 1944.

18. "Clay County Annual Report 1944," 1944, Clay County Extension Office, 12; Florence Drury, interview by Mark Peihl, tape recording, 25 February 1991, Clay County Historical Society, Moorhead (hereafter cited as Drury Interview). Florence Drury was a lifetime resident of Moorhead who worked as a bookkeeper on the Peterson farm. She had daily contact with the prisoners. "Records of the Office of the Provost Marshal General," YMCA visit from Hong, 4 August 1944, Record Group 389, National Archives, Washington, D.C.

19. *Moorhead Daily Times*, 26 June 1944, p. 1; *Minneapolis Morning Tribune*, 26 June 1944, p. 16; *St. Paul Dispatch*, 26 June 1944, p. 11; *Mankato Free Press*, 26 June 1944, p. 1; *Barnsville Record-Review*, 29 June 1944, p. 1; *Kossuth County Advance*, 29 June 1944, p. 1; George H. Lobdell to Simmons, 24 August 1998. Franz Hummer's remains were exhumed when the Algona camp closed. Algona commander Col. Lobdell assumed they were returned to Germany.

20. "Records of the Office of the Provost Marshal General," YMCA visit from Hong, 4 August 1944, Record Group 389, National Archives, Washington, D.C.

21. "The Rotary Wheel," 23 August 1944, Fargo Rotary Club Newsletter, 1.

22. "Moorhead Investigation File, 1944 and 1945," A. T. Lobdell Manuscript Collection.

23. "Records of the Office of the Provost Marshal General," YMCA visit from Hong, 4 August 1944, Record Group 389, National Archives, Washington, D.C.; "Records of the Office of the Provost Marshal General," Weekly Reports on Prisoners of War, 16–23 November 1944, Record Group 389, National Archives, Washington, D.C.; *The Country Press*, 2 February 1945, p. 1; *Moorhead Daily News*, 18 July 1945, p. 3.

24. "Moorhead Investigation File, 1944 and 1945," A. T. Lobdell Manuscript Collection.

25. "Clay County Annual Report 1944," 12; "Clay County Annual Report 1945," 1945, Clay County Extension Office, 21.

26. Hermann Massing to Simmons, 11 August 1993.

27. Cordelia Bloch to Simmons, 26 April 1995; Cordelia Bloch, "When I Was in Prison You Visited Me: Teenage Experience Leads to Prison Visitation Ministry," *Journey*, Quarterly publication of Franciscan Sisters of Little Falls, Minnesota (winter 1986), 5.

28. Drury Interview; Henry Peterson, interview by Gloria Thompson, 11 January

1973, Moorhead, Minnesota, tape recording, Northwest Minnesota Historical Center, Moorhead.

29. Horn Interview; Drury Interview.

30. Alois Sauer to Peterson, 1 September 1948.

31. Harvey Fleshner to Simmons, 7 December 1995.

32. Alois Sauer to Peterson, 1 September 1948; Unknown to Peterson, 14 November 1947; Joachim Müller to Peterson, 12 December 1947.

33. Folrath Georgiwold to Peterson, 22 May 1948; Franz Wdowig to Peterson, 8 September 1948; Horst Mueller to Peterson, 1 September 1947; 4 March 1948.

34. Denzene and Jackson, *The Hollandale Story: 1918–1950* (Freeborn County Historical Society, 1989), 1–3; *Minneapolis Sunday Tribune*, 6 June 1943, Minnesota section, p. 5; *Minneapolis Sunday Tribune*, 13 June 1943, Minnesota section, p. 6; *Albert Lea Evening Tribune*, 6 November 1945, p. 7; "POW Labor Report," 28 September 1945, A. T. Lobdell Manuscript Collection.

35. Ernst Kohleick, interview by author, tape recording, Wuppertal, Germany, 24 February 1995; *Albert Lea Evening Tribune*, 13 August 1995, p. 9C; *Ah La Ha Sa* (Albert Lea High School paper), 16 November 1944, p. 1; *Albert Lea Evening Tribune*, 6 November 1945, p. 7.

36. Ernst Kohleick, interview by author, tape recording, Wuppertal, Germany, 24 February 1995.

37. *Albert Lea Evening Tribune*, 6 November 1945, p. 7.

38. *Albert Lea Tribune*, 13 August 1995, p. 9C; *Albert Lea Tribune*, 10 March 1996, p. 2C; Shirley Hamer to Simmons, 4 March 1996.

39. "Norman County Annual Report 1944," 1944, Norman County Extension Office, 23–25; "Norman County Annual Report 1945," 1945, Norman County Extension Office.

40. *Norman County Index*, 18 October 1945, p. 1; *Norman County Index*, 11 October 1945, p. 1; *East Grand Forks Weekly Record*, 21 September 1945, p. 1; "Norman County Annual Report 1945," 1945, Norman County Extension Office.

41. *Norman County Index*, 18 October 1945, p. 1; "Norman County Annual Report 1945," 1945, Norman County Extension Office; *Norman County Index*, 11 October 1945, p. 1; "West Polk County Annual Report 1945," 1945, West Polk County Extension Office, 11.

42. "West Polk County Annual Report 1944," 1944, West Polk County Extension Office, 22–24.

43. "West Polk County Annual Report 1945," 9–11; *Crookston Daily Times*, 3 October 1945, p. 2; *Crookston Daily Times*, 4 October 1945, p. 2; *Crookston Daily Times*, 5 October 1945, p. 2; *East Grand Forks Weekly Record*, 21 September 1945, p. 1; *East Grand Forks Weekly Record*, 5 October 1945, p. 1.

44. *Crookston Daily Times*, 4 October 1945, p. 2; *Crookston Daily Times*, 5 October 1945, p. 2; "West Polk County Annual Report 1945," 11; *Crookston Daily Times*, 3 October 1945, p. 2; *Crookston Daily Times*, 12 October 1945,

p. 2; *Crookston Daily Times*, 11 October 1945, p. 1; *Crookston Daily Times*, 6 October 1945, p. 5; *Crookston Daily Times*, 8 October 1945, p. 2.
45. Hans Kratzheller to Simmons, 10 April 1996.
46. Ibid.
47. *Crookston Daily Times*, 9 October 1945, p. 2; *Crookston Daily Times*, 10 October 1945, p. 2; *Crookston Daily Times*, 11 October 1945, p. 1; *Crookston Daily Times*, 10 November 1945, p. 2; "West Polk County Annual Report 1945," 11.
48. "Marshall County Annual Report 1944," 1944, Marshall County Extension Office, 34–36; *Red Lake Falls Gazette*, 11 October 1945, p. 1.
49. "Marshall County Annual Report 1944," 34–38.
50. "Marshall County Annual Report 1945," 1945, Marshall County Extension Office, 31–32, 34; *Warren Sheaf*, 17 January 1945, p. 1.
51. *Warren Sheaf*, 3 October 1945, p. 1; "Marshall County Annual Report 1945," 33.
52. *Warren Sheaf*, 10 October 1945, p. 1.
53. "Marshall County Annual Report 1945," 32, 33, 36–37; *Warren Sheaf*, 21 November 1945, p. 1; *Warren Sheaf*, 24 October 1945, p. 1; *Warren Sheaf*, 31 October 1945, p. 1; *Warren Sheaf*, 7 November 1945, p. 1.

Chapter Four: Camps Established for Canneries

1. "Report on the Minnesota Farm Labor Program, 1945," 4.
2. *Wells Mirror*, 22 March 1945, p. 1; *Montgomery Messenger*, 29 June 1945, p. 1; *Montgomery Messenger*, 19 October 1945, p. 1; *Montgomery: From "The Big Woods" to the Kolacky Capital, 1856–1976* (Montgomery's Bicentennial Committee, 1976), 68.
3. "Big Stone County Annual Report 1944," 1944, Big Stone County Extension Office, 28, 31.
4. *Ortonville Independent*, 6 July 1944, p. 1; "Big Stone County Annual Report 1944," 31; Loren Clark, interview by LaDona Conrads, 30 December 1973, Moorhead, Minnesota, Interview S262, tape recording, Northwest Minnesota Historical Center Collections, Livingston Lord Library, Moorhead State University, Moorhead, MN (hereafter cited as Clark Interview). Loren Clark was born and raised in Big Stone County and started working for the Big Stone Cannery in the 1930s; he was the plant superintendent when the prisoners were employed. *Clinton Advocate*, 5 July 1944, p. 1; *Beardsley News*, 6 July 1944, p. 1; *Lagerzeitung* (Algona German POW base camp newspaper), 9 August 1945, p. 16; "Records of the Office of the Provost Marshal General," Officers in Branch Camps, Record Group 389, National Archives, Washington, D.C.
5. *Ortonville Independent*, 13 July 1944, p. 1; *Ortonville Independent*, 20 July 1944, p. 1; *Clinton Advocate*, 12 July 1944, p. 1; *Graceville Enterprise*, 18 July 1944, p. 1; "Big Stone County Annual Report 1944," 32, 33.

6. "Big Stone County Annual Report 1944," 6, 32–35; *Ortonville Independent*, 10 August 1944, p. 1; *Ortonville Independent*, 31 August 1944, p. 1; *Ortonville Independent*, 5 October 1944, p. 1; *Clinton Advocate*, 30 August 1944, p. 1; *Graceville Enterprise*, 15 August 1944, p. 1.

7. "Big Stone County Annual Report 1945," 1945, Big Stone County Extension Office, 10–12; *Ortonville Independent*, 12 July 1945, p. 1; "Records of the Office of the Provost Marshal General," Officers in Branch Camps, Record Group 389, National Archives, Washington, D.C.

8. "Big Stone County Annual Report 1945," 11, 12; *Ortonville Independent*, 26 July 1945, p. 1.

9. "Big Stone County Annual Report 1945," 12; *Clinton Advocate*, 8 August 1945, p. 1; *Beardsley News*, 12 July 1945, p. 1; *Beardsley News*, 26 July 1945, p. 1.

10. "Big Stone County Annual Report 1945," 12.

11. Hans Welker to Simmons, 2 January 1996.

12. "Big Stone County Annual Report 1945," 12–15.

13. *Clinton Advocate*, 26 September 1945, p. 1; *Clinton Advocate*, 3 October 1945, p. 1; *Clinton Advocate*, 17 October 1945, p. 1; "Big Stone County Annual Report 1945," 2, 12–15, 17.

14. Clark Interview; Edgar Johnson interview by Brenda Moerer, 9 February 1974, Moorhead, Minnesota, Interview S259, tape recording, Northwest Minnesota Historical Center Collections, Livingston Lord Library, Moorhead State University, Moorhead, MN. Edgar Johnson was an area farmer who employed prisoners from the Ortonville camp.

15. "Wright County Annual Report 1944," 1944, Wright County Extension Office, 55; "Wright County Annual Report 1945," 1945, Wright County Extension Office, 30–31; *Howard Lake Herald*, 3 August 1944, p. 1; *Howard Lake Herald*, 10 August 1944, p. 1; *Cokato Enterprise*, 3 August 1944, p. 1; George H. Lobdell to Simmons, 31 July 1999.

16. "Records of the Office of the Provost Marshal General," Lt. Colonel A. T. Lobdell to Commanding General, 7th Service Command, 26 August 1944, Box 2745, Record Group 389, National Archives, Washington, D.C.; George H. Lobdell to Simmons, 31 July 1999; Jim Robins, "Minnesota's POW Camps," *Minneapolis St. Paul Magazine*, January 1986, 75; *Minneapolis Star Tribune*, 7 December 1987, sec. A, p. 1.

17. "Records of the Office of the Provost Marshal General," YMCA visit from Hong, 12 August 1944, Record Group 389, National Archives, Washington, D.C.; Myron Heuer to Simmons, 12 September 1994; *Howard Lake Herald*, 14 September 1944, p. 1.

18. Myron Heuer to Simmons, 16 July 1994; *Olivia Times Journal*, 14 September 1944, p. 3; *Madison Lake Times*, 14 September 1944, p. 1; Robins, "Minnesota's POW Camps," 75; *Minneapolis Star Tribune*, 7 December 1987, sec. A, p. 1.

19. *Cokato's First Century, 1878–1978* (Cokato Centennial Committee 1979), 71; Myron Heuer to Simmons, 14 August 1994.

20. George Rauenhorst, interview by author, personal discussion, Olivia, Minnesota, 13 June 1992; *Olivia Times Journal*, 23 September 1943, p. 3; *Olivia Times Journal*, 12 August 1943, p. 1; *Olivia Times Journal*, 19 August 1943, p. 1; *Olivia Times Journal*, 26 August 1943, p. 1; *Redwood Falls Gazette*, 31 August 1943, p. 1; *Olivia Times Journal*, 7 September 1943, p. 1.

21. *Olivia Times Journal*, 9 September 1943, p. 1; *Olivia Times Journal*, 23 September 1943, p. 1; *Redwood Falls Gazette*, 12 October 1943, p. 1; Eileen Rockvam to Simmons, 7 July 1994; *Olivia Times Journal*, 28 October 1943, p. 6.

22. Eileen Rockvam to Simmons, 19 July 1994.

23. *Olivia Times Journal*, 9 September 1943, p. 1; *Minneapolis Star Journal*, 15 September 1943, p. 18; *Olivia Times Journal*, 16 September 1943, p. 1; Mrs. Immanuel Lenz, interview by author, tape recording, Olivia, Minnesota, 30 December 1989; *Olivia Times Journal*, 28 October 1943, p. 6; Lawrence Stadther, interview by author, personal discussion, Olivia, Minnesota, summer 1995; *Olivia Times Journal*, 16 September 1943, p. 1.

24. *Olivia Times Journal*, 16 September 1943, p. 1; *Redwood Falls Gazette*, 12 October 1943, p. 1.

25. "Renville County Annual Report 1943," 1943, Renville County Extension Office, 9; *Olivia Times Journal*, 28 October 1943, pp. 1, 6; *Olivia Times Journal*, 23 September 1943, p. 3.

26. "Renville County Annual Report 1945," 1945, Renville County Extension Office, 37, 38; Frank D. Svoboda, *Looking Back: A History of Agriculture in Renville County, Minnesota* (Renville County Historical Society, 1976), 66; *Redwood Falls Gazette*, 28 August 1945, p. 1; *Olivia Times Journal*, 9 August 1945, p. 1; *Olivia Times Journal*, 23 August 1945, p. 1; *Olivia Times Journal*, 6 September 1945, p. 1; *Olivia Times Journal*, 15 November 1945, p. 1; "Records of the Office of the Provost Marshal General," Semi-Monthly Reports on Prisoners of War, 16 October 1945, Record Group 389, National Archives, Washington, D.C.

27. *Olivia Times Journal*, 20 July 1944, p. 1; *Olivia Times Journal*, 31 August 1944, p. 1; *Bird Island Union*, 31 August 1944, p. 1; *Olivia Times Journal*, 21 September 1944, p. 1; *Bird Island Union*, 21 September 1944, p. 1; "Records of the Office of the Provost Marshal General," Weekly Reports on Prisoners of War, 1 November 1944, Record Group 389, National Archives, Washington, D.C.; Winifred Murray, interview by author, tape recording, 27 March 1990; *Mankato Free Press*, 8 September 1944, p. 4.

28. *Olivia Times Journal*, 21 September 1944, p. 1; Eileen Rockvam to Simmons, 7 July 1994; "Renville County Annual Report 1944," 1944, Renville County Extension Office, 12.

29. *Olivia Times Journal*, 5 October 1944, p. 1; Mrs. Immanuel Lenz, interview by author, tape recording, Olivia, Minnesota, 30 December 1989. Mrs. Lenz accompanied her husband when he visited the POWs, and attended at least one of his services for them. More detailed information pertaining to the work of Missouri Synod pastors can be found in Steven Victor Dahms,

"The Work of the Lutheran Church–Missouri Synod and Its Pastors and Congregations Among German Prisoners of War in the United States During World War II." (Thesis, University of Wisconsin–Oshkosh, May 1989), 1–38.
30. "Records of the Office of the Provost Marshal General," YMCA visit by Hong, 12 August 1944, Record Group 389, National Archives, Washington, D.C.; "George Taylor Address Book," 1943, Dorothy Steinbeisser, Olivia, MN; Klaus Thaner to Simmons, 25 February 1991.
31. Alfred Neber, interview by author, tape recording, Kindenheim, Germany, 20 July 1991.
32. Ibid.
33. *Wells Mirror*, 18 May 1944, p. 1; *Le Sueur News-Herald*, 7 March 1945, p. 3; *Faribault County Register*, 30 May 1944, p. 1; *Blue Earth Post*, 18 May 1944, p. 1; "Faribault County Annual Report 1945," 1945, Faribault County Extension Office, 41–42; *Wells Centennial Steering Committee 1869–1969*, p. 4; Carlienne Frisch, "German Prisoners in Minnesota Were 'Good Workers,'" *Land Magazine*, 18 June 1981, 32–33; *Wells Mirror*, 22 March 1945, p. 1.
34. *Wells Mirror*, 22 March 1945, p. 1; *Lagerzeitung* (Algona German POW base camp newspaper), 30 September 1945, p. 16; Werner Schmiedeberg to Simmons, 18 August 1996.
35. *Wells Mirror*, 14 June 1945, p. 1; *Wells Mirror*, 5 July 1945, p. 1; *Wells Mirror*, 19 July 1945, p. 1; *Wells Mirror*, 1 August 1945, p. 1; "Faribault County Annual Report 1945," 42.
36. Harold Matz, interview by Norma Matz, June 1994, Wells, MN, tape recording, Faribault County Historical Society. Harold Matz was a farmer in Faribault County who spoke German and whose father employed prisoners. Werner Schmiedeberg to Simmons, 18 August 1996.
37. "Faribault County Annual Report 1945," 42; *Mankato Free Press*, 6 August 1945, p. 7; *Waseca Herald*, 9 August 1945, p. 1; *Fairmont Daily Sentinel*, 12 December 1945, p. 1.
38. "Records of the Office of the Provost Marshal General," YMCA visit from Hong, 10 August 1945, Record Group 389, National Archives, Washington, D.C. The word "problem" in this passage was originally spelled "probelm," and "PW Fund" was modernized to "POW Fund."
39. *Lagerzeitung* (Algona German POW base camp newspaper), 30 September 1945, p. 16.
40. Werner Schmiedeberg to Simmons, 18 August 1996. The plant foreman at Wells also remembers the prisoners having several pets with them; this is shown in Carlienne Frisch, "German Prisoners in Minnesota Were 'Good Workers,'" *Land Magazine*, 18 June 1981, 33.
41. Frisch, "German Prisoners in Minnesota Were 'Good Workers,'" 33; *Albert Lea Evening Tribune*, 13 October 1945, p. 5; *Fairmont Daily Sentinel*, 12 December 1945, p. 1; Werner Schmiedeberg to Simmons, 18 August 1996.
42. *Montgomery Messenger*, 16 June 1944, p. 1; *Mankato Free Press*, 17 June

1944, p. 5; *Montgomery Messenger*, 23 June 1944, p. 1; "Records of the Office of the Provost Marshal General," Officers in Branch Camps, Record Group 389, National Archives, Washington, D.C.; *Fairmont Daily Sentinel*, 21 June 1944, p. 2; *St. Paul Pioneer Press*, 22 June 1944, p. 1.

43. *Fairmont Daily Sentinel*, 21 June 1944, p. 2; *Kossuth County Advance*, 22 June 1944, p. 1; *Tägliche Volkszeitung-Tribüne*, 25 June 1944, p. 7; *Mankato Free Press*, 21 June 1944, p. 1; *Austin Daily Herald*, 22 June 1944, p. 13; *St. Paul Dispatch*, 24 June 1944, p. 5.

44. *Montgomery Messenger*, 30 June 1944, p. 1; *Mankato Free Press*, 30 June 1944, p. 5.

45. "Records of the Office of the Provost Marshal General," YMCA visit from Hong, 24 July 1944, Record Group 389, National Archives, Washington, D.C.

46. *Jordon Independent*, 15 June 1944, p. 1; *Montgomery Messenger*, 16 June 1944, p. 1; *Montgomery Messenger*, 4 August 1944, p. 1; *Montgomery Messenger*, 8 September 1944, p. 1; *Mankato Free Press*, 11 August 1944, p. 5; *Mankato Free Press*, 30 June 1944, p. 5; "Le Sueur County Annual Report 1944," 1944, Le Sueur County Extension Office, 12; *Montgomery Messenger*, 13 October 1944, p. 1; *Mankato Free Press*, 28 September 1944, p. 11. There was a meeting held in Scott county in April 1944 that discussed the option of establishing a POW camp at a CCC camp in Jordon. An official from the Minnesota Extension Service at the meeting indicated that a requirement was to have work available so the prisoners could work in a group of at least ten. Since farmer's needs were only for individual prisoners, the proposal was withdrawn. This is shown in "Scott County Annual Report 1944," 1944, Scott County Extension Office, 45–46.

47. *Montgomery Messenger*, 15 June 1945, p. 1; *Montgomery Messenger*, 8 June 1945, p. 1; *Mankato Free Press*, 13 June 1945, p. 20; *Montgomery Messenger*, 29 June 1945, p. 1; *Montgomery: From "The Big Woods" to the Kolacky Capital, 1856–1976* (Montgomery's Bicentennial Committee, 1976), 68; *Montgomery Messenger*, 19 October 1945, p. 1; *Mankato Free Press*, 5 July 1945, p. 9; "Records of the Office of the Provost Marshal General," Officers in Branch Camps, Record Group 389, National Archives, Washington, D.C.; "Records of the Office of the Provost Marshal General," Semi-Monthly Reports on Prisoners of War, 1 August 1945, Record Group 389, National Archives, Washington, D.C.; *Montgomery Messenger*, 13 July 1945, p. 1; *Jordon Independent*, 26 July 1945, p. 1.

48. "Le Sueur County Annual Report 1945," 1945, Le Sueur County Extension Office, 27; *Montgomery Messenger*, 3 August 1945, p. 1; *Le Center Leader*, 2 August 1945, p. 1; *Le Center Leader*, 19 July 1945, p. 1.

49. George H. Lobdell to Simmons, 29 February 1996.

50. "ICRC visit from Mr. Schnyder at Faribault," 13 September 1945, Politisches Archiv des Auswärtigen Amts, Bonn, Germany.

51. Hans Kratzheller to Simmons, 10 April 1996; Hans Kratzheller to Simmons, 9 September 1995; *Montgomery Messenger*, 12 October 1945, p. 1.

52. *Faribault Daily News Republican and Pilot*, 8 April 1944, p. 1; *Faribault Daily News Republican and Pilot*, 13 April 1944, p. 9.

53. *Faribault Daily News Republican and Pilot*, 24 May 1944, p. 1; "Faribault City Council Minutes," 23 May 1944, p. 1; *Faribault Daily News Republican and Pilot*, 16 March 1944, p. 3; Pluth, "Prisoner of War Employment," 300; *Faribault Daily News Republican and Pilot*, 6 June 1944, p. 5; *Faribault Daily News Republican and Pilot*, 20 June 1944, p. 1.

54. Zwagerman, "Prisoner of War Labor in Faribault," 21; *Dakota County Tribune*, 30 June 1944, p. 1; *Kenyon Leader*, 25 August 1944, p. 1.

55. "Records of the Office of the Provost Marshal General," YMCA visit from Hong, 9 August 1944, Record Group 389, National Archives, Washington, D.C.

56. George H. Lobdell, "Minnesota's 1944 PW Escape: Down the Mississippi in the Lili Marlene #10," *Minnesota History* 54 (fall 1994), 122; *Faribault Daily News Republican and Pilot*, 2 November 1944, p. 14.

57. *Drahtpost* (Algona German POW base camp newspaper), 3 June 1945, p. 10; "Records of the Office of the Provost Marshal General," YMCA visit from Hong, 22 May 1945, Record Group 389, National Archives, Washington, D.C.; "Records of the Office of the Provost Marshal General," YMCA visit from Hong, 9 August 1945, Record Group 389, National Archives, Washington, D.C.

58. Zwagerman, "Prisoner of War Labor in Faribault," 21–24; "ICRC visit from Mr. Schnyder at Faribault," 13 September 1945, Politisches Archiv des Auswärtigen Amts, Bonn, Germany; *Faribault Daily News Republican and Pilot*, 4 September 1945, p. 1; *Faribault Journal*, 6 September 1945, p. 1; *Mankato Free Press*, 4 September 1945, p. 6; *Dakota County Tribune*, 7 September 1945, p. 1.

59. *Dakota County Tribune*, 27 July 1945, p. 1; *Cannon Falls Beacon*, 10 August 1945, p. 3; *Cannon Falls Beacon*, 5 October 1945, p. 3; *Cannon Falls Beacon*, 12 October 1945, p. 3; *Dakota County Tribune*, 12 October 1945, p. 3; *Cannon Falls Beacon*, 5 October 1945, p. 3; *Goodhue County Tribune*, 16 August 1945, p. 1.

60. *Dakota County Tribune*, 16 November 1945, p. 1; *Dakota County Tribune*, 2 November 1945, p. 1; *Dakota County Tribune*, 7 December 1945, p. 1.

61. "Scott County Annual Report 1945," 1945, Scott County Extension Office, 48–49.

62. "ICRC visit from Mr. Schnyder at Faribault," 13 September 1945, Politisches Archiv des Auswärtigen Amts, Bonn, Germany.

63. "ICRC visit from Mr. Schnyder at Algona," 12 September 1945, Politisches Archiv des Auswärtigen Amts, Bonn, Germany.

Chapter Five: Camps Established for Multiple Industries

1. "Brown County Annual Report 1943," 1943, Brown County Extension

Office, 30; *New Ulm Daily Journal*, 10 May 1944, p. 1; *Sleepy Eye Herald-Dispatch*, 25 May 1944, p. 1; *Sleepy Eye Herald-Dispatch*, 1 June 1944, p. 1; *Sleepy Eye Herald-Dispatch*, 8 June 1944, p. 1; *Sleepy Eye Herald-Dispatch*, 15 June 1944, p. 1; *New Ulm Review*, 1 June 1944, p. 1; *New Ulm Review*, 8 June 1944, p. 1; *Springfield Advance-Press*, 8 June 1944, p. 2.

2. *New Ulm Daily Journal*, 7 June 1944, p. 1; "Records of the Office of the Provost Marshal General," Officers in Branch Camps, Record Group 389, National Archives, Washington, D.C.; *New Ulm Daily Journal*, 9 June 1944, p. 1; *New Ulm Daily Journal*, 15 June 1944, p. 8.

3. *New Ulm Daily Journal*, 9 June 1944, p. 1; "Historical Notes," 3 December 1981, 165–66; *Walnut Grove Tribune*, 15 June 1944, p. 1; *Springfield Advance-Press*, 6 July 1944, p. 1; "Records of the Office of the Provost Marshal General," Special Use Permit, 19 June 1944, Record Group 389, National Archives, Washington, D.C.

4. *Drahtpost* (Algona German POW base camp newspaper), 14 January 1945, pp. 14, 15.

5. "Records of the Office of the Provost Marshal General," YMCA visit from Hong, 24 July 1944, Record Group 389, National Archives, Washington, D.C.; *New Ulm Daily Journal*, 9 June 1944, p. 1; *Drahtpost* (Algona German POW base camp newspaper), 14 January 1945, pp. 14, 15.

6. Charles Crouch, interview by author, tape recording, Sleepy Eye, Minnesota, 19 April 1994. Charles Crouch worked for more than 40 years at the Sleepy Eye cannery and was the warehouse foreman during World War II.

7. Frisch, "German Prisoners in Minnesota Were 'Good Workers,'" 32–33.

8. *New Ulm Daily Journal*, 2 October 1944, p. 1; *Springfield Advance-Press*, 5 October 1944, p. 1; *Springfield Advance-Press*, 26 June 1991, sec. 2, p. 1; Pluth, "Prisoner of War Employment," 300–1; *Springfield Advance-Press*, 6 July 1944, p. 1.

9. *Sleepy Eye Herald-Dispatch*, 5 October 1944, p. 1; "World War II POW Camps," *WCCO Dimension*, 10 February 1991. Transcript available at WCCO Television, Minneapolis, Minnesota; Frisch, "German Prisoners in Minnesota Were 'Good Workers,'" 32; *New Ulm Daily Journal*, 30 June 1945, p. 1; *Springfield Advance-Press*, 5 July 1945, p. 1; *Sleepy Eye Herald-Dispatch*, 14 June 1945, p. 1. Records indicate the prisoners also worked at a business named Stork Bros. in February 1945. This is shown in "Records of the Office of the Provost Marshal General," Algona Branch Camps, February 1945, Record Group 389, National Archives, Washington, D.C.; *Drahtpost* (Algona German POW base camp newspaper), 14 January 1945, pp. 14, 15.

10. Frisch, "German Prisoners in Minnesota Were 'Good Workers,'" 33; *Drahtpost* (Algona German POW base camp newspaper), 14 January 1945, p. 14.

11. "World War II POW Camps," *WCCO Dimension*, 10 February 1991. Transcript available at WCCO Television, Minneapolis, Minnesota; Frisch, "German Prisoners in Minnesota Were 'Good Workers,'" 32.

12. *Drahtpost* (Algona German POW base camp newspaper), 24 December 1944, p. 21; "ICRC visit from Dr. Zehnder at New Ulm," 9 March 1945, Politisches Archiv des Auswärtigen Amts, Bonn, Germany.

13. *Sleepy Eye Herald-Dispatch*, 26 July 1945, p. 1; *New Ulm Daily Journal*, 25 July 1945, p. 1.

14. *New Ulm Daily Journal*, 30 June 1945, p. 1; *Springfield Advance-Press*, 5 July 1945, p. 1; "ICRC visit from Dr. Zehnder at New Ulm," 9 March 1945, Politisches Archiv des Auswärtigen Amts, Bonn, Germany; "Brown County Annual Report 1945," 1945, Brown County Extension Office, 17–19; *Gaylord Hub*, 27 July 1945, p. 1; *Springfield Advance-Press*, 11 October 1945, p. 1.

15. *Sleepy Eye Herald-Dispatch*, 2 August 1945, p. 1; *Sleepy Eye Herald-Dispatch*, 19 July 1945, p. 1; *New Ulm Daily Journal*, 27 July 1945, p. 1; *New Ulm Daily Journal*, 2 August 1945, p. 4; *Springfield Advance-Press*, 26 July 1945, p. 1; "Brown County Annual Report 1945," 18–21; *Springfield Advance-Press*, 2 August 1945, p. 1; *Cottonwood Current*, 17 August 1945, p. 1; *Redwood Falls Gazette*, 2 August 1945, p. 1; *Redwood Falls Gazette*, 16 August 1945, p. 1; *Redwood Falls Gazette*, 9 August 1945, p. 1.

16. *Wabasso Standard*, 26 July 1945, p. 1; *Sanborn Sentinel*, 25 July 1945, p. 1; *Walnut Grove Tribune*, 26 July 1945, p. 1; *Walnut Grove Tribune*, 2 August 1945, p. 1; *Morgan Messenger*, 26 July 1945, p. 1; *Morgan Messenger*, 2 August 1945, p. 1; *Morgan Messenger*, 9 August 1945, p. 1; *Redwood Falls Gazette*, 16 August 1945, p. 1; *Redwood Falls Gazette*, 7 August 1945, p. 1; *Redwood Falls Gazette*, 9 August 1945, p. 1.

17. Muriel Jeske to Simmons, 25 January 1994.

18. *Drahtpost* (Algona German POW base camp newspaper), 14 January 1945, pp. 14–15.

19. *Cottonwood Current*, 17 August 1945, p. 1; "Lyon County Annual Report 1945," 1945, Lyon County Extension Office, 52.

20. *Gaylord Hub*, 20 July 1945, p. 1; *Gaylord Hub*, 10 August 1945, p. 1; *Winthrop News*, 19 July 1945, p. 1; *Winthrop News*, 2 August 1945, p. 1; *Winthrop News*, 9 August 1945, p. 1; *Mankato Free Press*, 6 August 1945, p. 7.

21. *St. Peter Herald*, 17 August 1945, p. 1; *Mankato Free Press*, 17 August 1945, p. 4; *New Ulm Daily Journal*, 24 August 1945, p. 1; *Sleepy Eye Herald-Dispatch*, 9 August 1945, p. 1; "Brown County Annual Report 1945," 19.

22. "District Court of the United States No. 1108," 1946, National Archives–Central Plains Region, R7, U5, S8, Box 29, 1108-2, Kansas City, Mo.; *Sleepy Eye Herald-Dispatch*, 24 January 1946, p. 1; *Springfield Advance-Press*,

24 January 1946, p. 1. Different spellings are given for Lichtenberg in the court transcripts. Lichtenberg is the spelling in both newspaper articles.

23. *Mankato Free Press*, 28 August 1945, p. 11.

24. *New Ulm Review*, 24 January 1945, p. 1; "Records of the Office of the Provost Marshal General," Semi-Monthly Reports on Prisoners of War, 15 December 1945, 1 January 1946, Record Group 389, National Archives, Washington, D.C.

25. *Fairmont Daily Sentinel*, 27 May 1944, p. 1; *Mankato Free Press*, 5 June 1944, p. 1; *Fairmont Daily Sentinel*, 29 May 1944, p. 1; *Fairmont Daily Sentinel*, 25 May 1944, p. 1.

26. *Fairmont Daily Sentinel*, 5 June 1944, p. 1; *Fairmont Daily Sentinel*, 7 June 1944, p. 1.

27. *Mankato Free Press*, 22 June 1944, p. 16; *Winnebago Times*, 9 March 1944, p. 1.

28. George H. Lobdell to Simmons, 2 September 1998.

29. *Fairmont Daily Sentinel*, 15 June 1944, p. 1.

30. *Fairmont Daily Sentinel*, 14 August 1944, p. 1.

31. *Fairmont Daily Sentinel*, 7 September 1944, p. 1; Lobdell, "PW Escape," 122.

32. *Fairmont Daily Sentinel*, 20 July 1944, p. 4; *Fairmont Daily Sentinel*, 3 August 1944, p. 1; *Fairmont Daily Sentinel*, 12 December 1945, p. 1.

33. "Records of the Office of the Provost Marshal General," Algona Branch Camps, July, August 1944, Record Group 389, National Archives, Washington, D.C.; "Records of the Office of the Provost Marshal General," Officers in Branch Camps, Record Group 389, National Archives, Washington, D.C.; *Fairmont Daily Sentinel*, 12 December 1945, p. 1; *Lagerzeitung* (Algona German POW base camp newspaper), 21 July 1945, p. 15; *Fairmont Daily Sentinel*, 5 September 1944, p. 1; *Fairmont Daily Sentinel*, 6 September 1944, p. 1.

34. Lobdell, "PW Escape," 122; *Fairmont Daily Sentinel*, 28 September 1944, p. 1; *Fairmont Daily Sentinel*, 30 November 1944, p. 3.

35. *Fairmont Daily Sentinel*, 12 December 1945, p. 1; "ICRC visit from Dr. Zehnder at Fairmont," 9 March 1945, Politisches Archiv des Auswärtigen Amts, Bonn, Germany.

36. *Lagerzeitung* (Algona German POW base camp newspaper), 21 July 1945, p. 15.

37. Ibid.

38. *Fairmont Daily Sentinel*, 7 September 1944, p. 1; *Winnebago Times*, 10 August 1944, p. 1; *Winnebago Times*, 14 September 1944, p. 1; *Fairmont Daily Sentinel*, 5 September 1944, p. 1; *Mankato Free Press*, 28 September 1944, p. 11; *Fairmont Daily Sentinel*, 6 September 1945, p. 1; *Fairmont Daily Sentinel*, 29 November 1944, p. 1.

39. "Records of the Office of the Provost Marshal General," YMCA report from Hong, 28 January 1945, Record Group 389, National Archives, Washington, D.C.; *Lagerzeitung* (Algona German POW base camp newspaper), 30 August 1945, pp. 15, 16.

40. "ICRC visit from Dr. Zehnder at Fairmont," 9 March 1945, Politisches Archiv des Auswärtigen Amts, Bonn, Germany; *Lagerzeitung* (Algona German POW base camp newspaper), 21 July 1945, p. 15.

41. *Fairmont Daily Sentinel,* 9 July 1945, p. 6.

42. *Fairmont Daily Sentinel,* 12 July 1945, p. 1; *Fairmont Daily Sentinel,* 1 August 1945, p. 1; *Fairmont Daily Sentinel,* 21 July 1945, p. 1; *Blue Earth County Enterprise,* 9 August 1945, p. 1; *Fairmont Daily Sentinel,* 14 August 1945, p. 1; *Fairmont Daily Sentinel,* 4 September 1945, p. 1.

43. *Jackson County Pilot,* 9 August 1945, p. 1; *Truman Tribune,* 16 August 1945, p. 1; *Blue Earth County Enterprise,* 26 July 1945, p. 1; *Blue Earth County Enterprise,* 2 August 1945, p. 1; *St. James Courier,* 31 July 1945, p. 1; *Mankato Free Press,* 6 August 1945, p. 7; *Mankato Free Press,* 7 August 1945, p. 11; *Watonwan County Plaindealer,* 26 July 1945, p. 1; *Watonwan County Plaindealer,* 9 August 1945, p. 1; *Winnebago Times,* 19 July 1945, p. 1; "Watonwan County Annual Report 1945," 1945, Watonwan County Extension Office, 31; "Jackson County Annual Report 1945," 1945, Jackson County Extension Office, 63.

44. *Fairmont Daily Sentinel,* 4 September 1945, p. 1; *Fairmont Daily Sentinel,* 17 August 1945, p. 1; *Fairmont Daily Sentinel,* 12 December 1945, p. 1; *Winnebago Times,* 5 April 1945, p. 1; *Winnebago Times,* 31 May 1945, p. 1; *Winnebago Times,* 21 June 1945, p. 1; *Winnebago Times,* 9 August 1945, p. 1.

45. *Fairmont Daily Sentinel,* 12 December 1945, p. 1; "Records of the Office of the Provost Marshal General," Algona Branch Camps, January, March, May, 1945, Record Group 389, National Archives, Washington, D.C.; "ICRC visit from Dr. Zehnder at Fairmont," 9 March 1945, Politisches Archiv des Auswärtigen Amts, Bonn, Germany; *Fairmont Daily Sentinel,* 14 August 1945, p. 1; *Fairmont Daily Sentinel,* 23 August 1958, p. 2; Mildred Coupanger, interview by author, personal discussion, Elmore, Minnesota, 20 October 1995.

46. *Fairmont Daily Sentinel,* 15 December 1945, p. 6.

47. Heinrich Waldschmidt to Coupanger, 20 November, 23 November 1946; 21 February, 4 April, 10 August, 3 November, 24 December 1947; 8 March, 26 April, 1 November 1948; 8 March, 25 November 1949; 5 April, 6 June 1950; 15 October, 15 November 1951; 8 February 1952.

48. Heinrich Waldschmidt, interview by author, tape recording, Hatzbach, Germany, 12 February 1995.

49. Kurt C. Teufel, ed., "The History of Camp Concordia from Site Survey to Inactivation," 1945, Chapter 3, sec. F.; *Owatonna Daily People's Press,* 25 March 1944, p. 6; *St. Paul Dispatch,* 15 December 1933, p. 1; *History of Rice and Steele Counties Minnesota,* vol. 2 (Chicago: H.C. Cooper and Co., 1910), 1231, 1232; *Tägliche Volkszeitung-Tribüne,* 29 March 1944, p. 6.

50. Teufel, ed., "Site Survey to Inactivation," Chapter 3, sec. F; *Minneapolis Morning Tribune,* 1 October 1963, p. 19; *Kenyon Leader,* 25 August 1944, p. 1.

51. "Records of the Office of the Provost Marshal General," YMCA visit from Hong, 26 June 1944, Record Group 389, National Archives, Washington, D.C.

52. *Owatonna Daily People's Press*, 25 July 1944, p. 6; Pluth, "Prisoner of War Employment," 299–300; *Minneapolis Morning Tribune*, 25 March 1944, p. 1. James Cashman was the second brother and operator at the nursery.

53. Lorenzo Bakko, interview by author, tape recording, Owatonna, Minnesota, 3 May 1994. Lorenzo Bakko worked at the Owatonna Canning Company for 40 years and eventually became its president before he retired. Lorenzo Bakko to Simmons, 12 April 1994; *Owatonna Peoples Press*, 13 October 1985, sec. A, p. 3; *Minneapolis Star Tribune*, 1 January 1986, sec. B, p. 4; "Records of the Office of the Provost Marshal General," Algona Branch Camps, March 1945, Record Group 389, National Archives, Washington, D.C. These records show that prisoners were employed by Bordon; whether or not this is one of the companies indicated by the *Owatonna Daily People's Press* is not clear. *Owatonna Daily People's Press*, 21 December 1945, p. 8; "Report on the Minnesota Farm Labor Program, 1944," 12.

54. Dawson Report, 6.

55. "Records of the Office of the Provost Marshal General," YMCA visit from Hong, 21 November 1944, Record Group 389, National Archives, Washington, D.C.; *Drahtpost* (Algona German POW base camp newspaper), 24 December 1944, p. 26.

56. "Records of the Office of the Provost Marshal General," YMCA visit from Hong, 21 November 1945, Record Group 389, National Archives, Washington, D.C.

57. *Owatonna Daily People's Press*, 3 January 1945, p. 1; *Steele County Photo News*, 4 January 1945, p. 10; "ICRC visit from Dr. Zehnder at Owatonna," 10 March 1945, Politisches Archiv des Auswärtigen Amts, Bonn, Germany; Karl Becker to Simmons, 1 January 1994; *Mankato Free Press*, 3 January 1945, p. 9.

58. *Drahtpost* (Algona German POW base camp newspaper), 14 January 1945, p. 14. The original text used the German word *Spritzen* (sprayers) instead of *Löscher* (extinguishers) for the description of the fire extinguisher. The author chose to use "POW fire extinguishers" instead of "POW fire sprayers." The phrase "60 P.W.s" was modernized to "60 POWs."

59. *Owatonna Daily People's Press*, 3 January 1945, p. 1; *Steele County Photo News*, 4 January 1945, p. 10; *Owatonna Daily People's Press*, 13 October 1985, sec. A, p. 1; "ICRC visit from Dr. Zehnder at Fairmont," 9 March 1945, Politisches Archiv des Auswärtigen Amts, Bonn, Germany; Karl Becker to Simmons, 1 January 1994.

60. "ICRC visit from Dr. Zehnder at Fairmont, 9 March 1945," Politisches Archiv des Auswärtigen Amts, Bonn, Germany.

61. *Owatonna Daily People's Press*, 13 October 1985, sec. A, p. 2.

62. "Records of the Office of the Provost Marshal General," YMCA visit from

Hong, 9 August 1945, Record Group 389, National Archives, Washington, D.C.; *Drahtpost* (Algona German POW base camp newspaper), 1 January 1945, p. 17; *Drahtpost* (Algona German POW base camp newspaper), 1 July 1945, p. 11.

63. *Drahtpost* (Algona German POW base camp newspaper), 3 March 1945, p. 10; *Drahtpost* (Algona German POW base camp newspaper), 1 July 1945, p. 11. The English word "fistball" is a direct translation of the German word "Faustball," a game similar to volleyball.

64. Lobdell, "PW Escape," 122; *Minneapolis Daily Times*, 16 August 1945, p. 1; *Minneapolis Star Journal*, 16 August 1945, p. 15; *St. Paul Dispatch*, 16 August 1945, p. 1; *Owatonna Daily People's Press*, 17 August 1945, p. 8.

65. *Waseca Herald*, 9 August 1945, p. 1.

66. "ICRC visit from Mr. Schnyder at Owatonna," 13 September 1945, Politisches Archiv des Auswärtigen Amts, Bonn, Germany; *Owatonna Daily People's Press*, 21 December 1945, p. 8.

67. Evelyn Kubat, interview by author, tape recording, Owatonna, Minnesota, 3 May 1994; *Minneapolis Star Tribune*, 7 December 1987, sec. A, p. 1; *Minneapolis Star Tribune*, 1 January 1986, sec. B, p. 3; *Owatonna Daily People's Press*, 13 October 1985, sec. A, p. 1; Evelyn Kubat to Simmons, 28 January 1993; Evelyn Kubat to Simmons, 26 April 1994.

68. The incident Becker recalls is well documented. Former prisoner Hans Welker in the Bena camp history below recalls the unfortunate event as well. Concordia prisoner Adolf Huebner was shot and killed while chasing a soccer ball that had rolled beyond the warning fence. Tension was high in the camp, and prisoners marched and sang songs inside the compound. More information can be found about the shooting in Lowell A. May, *Camp Concordia: German POWs in the Midwest* (Manhattan, Kansas: Sunflower University Press, 1995), 30–31.

69. R. Newell Searle, *Whitewater: The Valley of Promise* (Minnesota State Heritage Series, #2, 1977), 28; *Drahtpost* (Algona German POW base camp newspaper), 1 July 1945, p. 11; Elroy Preuhs "Algona Prisoner of War Camp No. 10 Whitewater State Park," 1976, Whitewater State Park Archives, St. Charles, Minnesota, 1–3.

70. "Winona County Annual Report 1944," 1944, Winona County Extension Office, 43–44; *St. Charles Press*, 29 June 1944, p. 1.

71. *St. Charles Press*, 13 July 1944, p. 1; *Plainview News*, 14 July 1944, p. 1; "Wabasha County Annual Report 1944," 1944, Wabasha County Extension Office, 44.

72. *Rochester Post-Bulletin*, 21 September 1944, p. 9; *Rochester Post-Bulletin*, 22 September 1944, p. 5.

73. "Winona County Annual Report 1944," 39–44; *Lewiston Journal*, 21 July 1944, p. 1; *Lewiston Journal*, 14 July 1944, p. 1; *Mankato Free Press*, 13 July 1944, p. 1.

74. *St. Charles Press*, 3 August 1944, p. 1.

75. *St. Charles Press*, 10 August 1944, p. 1.
76. *St. Charles Press*, 3 May 1945, p. 1; "Winona County Annual Report 1945," 1945, Winona County Extension Office, 44.
77. "Winona County Annual Report 1945," 44–45; *Winona Republican-Herald*, 9 June 1945, p. 3; *Mankato Free Press*, 9 June 1944, p. 6; *Winona Sunday News*, 9 February 1992, p. 1; *Rochester Post-Bulletin*, 17 July 1945, p. 8; "Records of the Office of the Provost Marshal General," Schwieger Report, 24 June 1945, Record Group 389, National Archives, Washington, D.C. (hereafter cited as Schwieger Report, 24 June 1945), 4.
78. *Plainview News*, 20 April 1945, p. 1; "Winona County Annual Report 1945," 43–50; *Lewiston Journal*, 3 August 1945, p. 1.
79. *Minneapolis Sunday Tribune*, 5 August 1945, Minnesota section, p. 1.
80. "Winona County Annual Report 1945," 45; *St. Charles Press*, 11 October 1945, p. 1; "Wabasha County Annual Report 1945," 1945, Wabasha County Extension Office, 33; "Olmsted County Annual Report 1945," 1945, Olmsted County Extension Office, 8; *Winona Sunday News*, 9 February 1992, p. 1; *Rochester Post-Bulletin*, 17 July 1945, p. 8; Lobdell, "PW Escape," 122.
81. *Rochester Post-Bulletin*, 17 July 1945, p. 8.
82. Ibid., 8; "Records of the Office of the Provost Marshal General," Officers in Branch Camps, Record Group 389, National Archives, Washington, D.C.; *Drahtpost* (Algona German POW base camp newspaper), 30 September 1945, p. 16.

Chapter Six: Logging Camps

1. Krammer, *Nazi Prisoners of War in America*, 93, 105; *Duluth Herald*, 11 November 1943, p. 1; Pluth, "Prisoner of War Employment," 294–95; Lewis and Mewha, *Prisoner of War Utilization*, 132; *Bemidji Sentinel*, 24 December 1943, p. 1.
2. Pluth, "Prisoner of War Employment," 295; "Timber Producers Association Bulletin, #79," 1 December 1943, HD 9750.T58, Minnesota State Historical Society, St. Paul, Minnesota, p. 1; *Bemidji Sentinel*, 12 November 1943, p. 1; *Duluth Herald*, 8 November 1943, p. 1; *Duluth Herald*, 11 November 1943, p. 1; *Duluth Herald*, 8 November 1943, p. 1; *Park Rapids Enterprise*, 25 November 1943, p. 1; *Bemidji Sentinel*, 3 December 1943, p. 1; *Deer River News*, 9 December 1943, p. 1; *Bemidji Sentinel*, 24 December 1943, p. 1.
3. Lewis and Mewha, *Prisoner of War Utilization*, 134; Pluth, "Prisoner of War Employment," 295–96; Robins, "Minnesota's POW Camps," 72; Ilmar Koivunen, interview by Irene Paull, tape recording, August 1968, Cass Bay, Oregon, OH20, Minnesota State Historical Society, St. Paul, Minnesota; *Midwest Labor*, 19 November 1943, p. 1. The *Midwest Labor* was a weekly CIO publication, which evolved into a statewide CIO newspaper; this is shown in *Radicalism in MN, 1900–1960: A Survey of Selected Sources/20th-*

Century Radicalism in Minnesota Project, Carl Ross, project director (St. Paul: Minnesota Historical Society Press, 1994), 20–21.

4. *Midwest Labor*, 4 February 1944, p. 1; *Midwest Labor*, 11 February 1944, p. 1; *Minnesota Labor*, 17 March 1944, p. 3. The *Minnesota Labor* succeeded the *Midwest Labor* in 1944. The paper focused on the activities of unions and was the official publication of the CIO in Minnesota; this is shown in *Radicalism in MN, 1900–1960: A Survey of Selected Sources/20th-Century Radicalism in Minnesota Project*, Carl Ross, project director (St. Paul: Minnesota Historical Society Press, 1994), 20–21.

5. *Midwest Labor*, 17 December 1943, pp. 1–2; *Midwest Labor*, 11 February 1944, p. 4; *Midwest Labor*, 31 December 1943, p. 3; *Midwest Labor*, 10 December 1943, p. 1.

6. *Deer River News*, 12 October 1944, p. 1; *Grand Rapids Herald-Review*, 18 October 1944, p. 1; *Minneapolis Morning Tribune*, 8 March 1945, p. 11. The word "laugh" in the second quotation was spelled "laff" in the original.

7. Schwieger Report, 3 July 1944, 1–5; "Records of the Office of the Provost Marshal General," Branch Camp #402, Bena, Report of Logging Operations, 22 May 1944, Record Group 389, National Archives, Washington, D.C. The following employers used Bena POWs: Goss and Richmond Lumber Co., Melvin Mettler, and Andrew Giffen. Remer POWs were used by the Delin Agency. Deer River POWs were hired by Max Logging Co. Inc., Toivo Hovi, Victor Terho, and Jake Reigel. This is shown in "Records of the Office of the Provost Marshal General," Branch Camp #404, Deer River, Report of Logging Operations, 20 May 1944, Record Group 389, National Archives, Washington, D.C. "ICRC visit from Schnyder at Deer River," 14 September 1945, Politisches Archiv des Auswärtigen Amts, Bonn, Germany; Gerald Delin to Simmons, 17 May 1995; Gerald Delin to Simmons, 11 August 1995; Krammer, *Nazi Prisoners of War in America*, 105–6; "Records of the Office of the Provost Marshal General," Branch Camp #402, Bena, 1944, Record Group 389, National Archives, Washington, D.C.

8. Schwieger Report, 3 July 1944, 3, 5.

9. Teufel, ed., "Site Survey to Inactivation," Chapter 3, sec. F.

10. Anthony Blais, interview by Beverly Buck, personal discussion, summer 1970.

11. "Records of the Office of the Provost Marshal General," YMCA visit from Hong, 12 June 1944, Record Group 389, National Archives, Washington, D.C.

12. Ibid.

13. Schwieger Report, 3 July 1944, 4.

14. Ibid., 3.

15. *Duluth News-Tribune*, 16 April 1944, Cosmopolitan section, pp. 1, 6–7; "Records of the Office of the Provost Marshal General," YMCA visit from Hong, 12 June 1944, Record Group 389, National Archives, Washington, D.C.; Schwieger Report, 3 July 1944, 4; Teufel, ed., "Site Survey to Inactivation," Chapter 3, sec. F.

16. Teufel, ed., "Site Survey to Inactivation," Chapter 3, sec. F; Harold Myers, interview by Beverly Buck, personal discussion, summer 1970; "Records of the Office of the Provost Marshal General," YMCA visit from Hong, 12 June 1944, Record Group 389, National Archives, Washington, D.C.

17. *Duluth News-Tribune*, 16 April 1944, Cosmopolitan section, pp. 1, 6–7; Gerald Delin to Simmons, 1 September 1995; Mahlon Swentkosfke, interview by Beverly Buck, personal discussion, summer 1970.

18. "War Manpower Commission Records," visit by Irving S. Anderson to Remer, 25 February 1944, Record Group 211, National Archives, Washington, D.C.

19. *Itasca County Independent*, 2 March 1944, p. 1.

20. Carl Carlson to Beverly Buck, March 1970; Elmer Spartz, interview by Beverly Buck, personal discussion, summer 1970; Dawson Report, p. 6; Teufel, ed., "Site Survey to Inactivation," Chapter 3 sec. F. The original word "icey" was replaced with "icy." *Minneapolis Sunday Tribune*, 6 February 1944, Sports section, pp. 1, 6; Mrs. Walter Myers, interview by Beverly Buck, personal discussion, summer 1970.

21. "Records of the Office of the Provost Marshal General," Minnesota Branch Camp #401, Remer, 1944, Record Group 389, National Archives, Washington, D.C.

22. "Records of the Office of the Provost Marshal General," Minnesota Branch Camp #401, Remer, Current Work Detail Lists, 1944, Record Group 389, National Archives, Washington, D.C.

23. "Records of the Office of the Provost Marshal General," Minnesota Branch Camp #401, Remer, Report on P.O.W. Mail for April 1944, Record Group 389, National Archives, Washington, D.C.

24. *Duluth News-Tribune*, 16 April 1944, Cosmopolitan section, pp. 1, 6; "Records of the Office of the Provost Marshal General," YMCA visit from Hong, 12 June 1944, Record Group 389, National Archives, Washington, D.C.

25. "Records of the Office of the Provost Marshal General," YMCA visit from Hong, 12 June 1944, Record Group 389, National Archives, Washington, D.C.

26. Teufel, ed., "Site Survey to Inactivation," Chapter 3, sec. F; *Drahtpost* (Algona German POW base camp newspaper), 3 December 1944, pp. 1–16; *Deer River News*, 17 February 1944, p. 1.

27. *Deer River News*, 17 February 1944, p. 1; *Drahtpost* (Algona German POW base camp newspaper), 3 December 1944, pp. 1–16; "Records of the Office of the Provost Marshal General," Branch Camp #402, Bena, 1944, Record Group 389, National Archives, Washington, D.C.

28. "Records of the Office of the Provost Marshal General," YMCA visit from Hong, 12, 13 June 1944, Record Group 389, National Archives, Washington, D.C.; *Drahtpost* (Algona German POW base camp newspaper), 3 December 1944, pp. 1–16; "Records of the Office of the Provost Marshal General,"

Branch Camp #402, Bena, 1944, Record Group 389, National Archives, Washington, D.C.

29. Schwieger Report, 3 July 1944, 4–5; "Records of the Office of the Provost Marshal General," YMCA visit from Hong, 12, 13 June 1944, Record Group 389, National Archives, Washington, D.C.; *Drahtpost* (Algona German POW base camp newspaper), 11 February 1945, p. 13; "Records of the Office of the Provost Marshal General," Branch Camp #402, Bena, 1944, Record Group 389, National Archives, Washington, D.C.

30. "Records of the Office of the Provost Marshal General," YMCA visit from Hong, 12, 13 June 1944, Record Group 389, National Archives, Washington, D.C.

31. Lobdell, "PW Escape," 113–23; *Grand Rapids Herald-Review*, 1 November 1944, p. 1; *Grand Rapids Herald-Review*, 8 November 1944, p. 1; *Itasca County Independent*, 2 November 1944, p. 1; *Itasca County Independent*, 9 November 1944, p. 1; *Grand Rapids Herald-Review*, 2 May 1945, p. 1.

32. *Mankato Free Press*, 9 May 1945, p. 3.

33. "ICRC visit from Schnyder at Bena," 14 September 1945, Politisches Archiv des Auswärtigen Amts, Bonn, Germany.

34. *Deer River News*, 6 April 1944, p. 1; *Deer River News*, 23 March 1944, p. 1; Teufel, ed., "Site Survey to Inactivation," 1945, Chapter 3, sec. F; *Drahtpost* (Algona German POW base camp newspaper), 28 January 1945, p. 15.

35. *Drahtpost* (Algona German POW base camp newspaper), 28 January 1945, p. 15; "Records of the Office of the Provost Marshal General," Minnesota Branch Camp #404, Deer River, Record Group 389, National Archives, Washington, D.C.; Schwieger Report 3 July 1944, 3.

36. *Deer River News*, 22 June 1944, p. 1.

37. "Records of the Office of the Provost Marshal General," Minnesota Branch Camp #404, Deer River, Special Orders, 1944, Record Group 389, National Archives, Washington, D.C.; *Grand Rapids Herald-Review*, 22 May 1972, p. 2; Dawson Report, 6. "PW's" in the first sentence was modernized to "POWs."

38. *Grand Rapids Herald-Review*, 11 October 1944, p. 1; Robert Devore, "Our Pampered Prisoners of War," *Collier's*, 14 October 1944, 14, 57.

39. *Deer River News*, 3 May 1945, p. 1.

40. *Drahtpost* (Algona German POW base camp newspaper), 28 January 1945, p. 15.

41. Ibid.; Schwieger Report, 3 July 1944, 4.

42. *Deer River News*, 3 May 1945, p. 1; *Deer River News*, 10 May 1945, p. 1; *Mankato Free Press*, 3 May 1945, p. 1; *Grand Rapids Herald-Review*, 16 May 1945, p. 1; A. L. LaFreniere to Arthur Lobdell, 12 May 1945. Transcript in the A. T. Lobdell Manuscript Collection.

43. *Drahtpost* (Algona German POW base camp newspaper), 25 March 1945, p. 10; *Drahtpost* (Algona German POW base camp newspaper), 15 April

1945, pp. 1–20; "ICRC visit from Schnyder at Deer River," 14 September 1945, Politisches Archiv des Auswärtigen Amts, Bonn, Germany.

44. "ICRC visit from Schnyder at Deer River," 14 September 1945, Politisches Archiv des Auswärtigen Amts, Bonn, Germany; "ICRC visit from Schnyder at Algona," 12 September 1945, Politisches Archiv des Auswärtigen Amts, Bonn, Germany.

45. *Drahtpost* (Algona German POW base camp newspaper), 28 January 1945, p. 15; "Records of the Office of the Provost Marshal General," Minnesota Branch Camp #404, Record Group 389, National Archives, Washington, D.C.

46. "ICRC visit from Schnyder at Deer River," 14 September 1945, Politisches Archiv des Auswärtigen Amts, Bonn, Germany.

47. *Deer River News*, 20 December 1945, p. 1; *Grand Rapids Herald-Review*, 26 December 1945, p. 1; *Deer River News*, 27 December 1945, p. 1.

48. *Grand Rapids Herald-Review*, 17 January 1945, p. 1; *Drahtpost* (Algona German POW base camp newspaper), 28 January 1945, p. 20.

49. Werner Schmiedeberg to Simmons, 18 August 1996.

50. *Grand Rapids Herald-Review*, 24 January 1945, p. 1.

51. Werner Schmiedeberg to Simmons, 31 July 1996; 18 August 1996.

Epilogue

1. Pluth, "Prisoner of War Employment," 298; "Report on the Minnesota Farm Labor Program, 1945," 2; *Norman County Index*, 22 November 1945, p. 1.

2. "Report on the Minnesota Farm Labor Program, 1945," 9; Pluth, "Prisoner of War Employment," 302; *Norman County Index*, 22 November 1945, p. 1; "Announcement from Public Relations Office at Base Camp in Algona, Iowa," August 1945, A. T. Lobdell Manuscript Collection; "Listing of Contractor POW Production," A. T. Lobdell Manuscript Collection.

3. Robins, "Minnesota's POW Camps," 74–75.

4. Pluth, "Prisoner of War Employment," 293, 298, 302–3; *East Grand Forks Weekly Record*, 6 August 1943, p. 1; *Minneapolis Morning Tribune*, 4 August 1943, p. 1; *Minneapolis Morning Tribune*, 6 August 1943, p. 16.

5. Odegard Interview; Denzene and Jackson, *The Hollandale Story*, 3–4; Terry Shoptaugh, Wayne Gudmundson, and Karin Anderson, *The Growers: Sugar in the Valley* (Moorhead: Moorhead State University. Prairie Documents Photographic Book Series, 1993), 19.

6. *Montgomery: From "The Big Woods" to the Kolacky Capital, 1856–1976* (Montgomery's Bicentennial Committee, 1976), 69.

7. *New Ulm Daily Journal*, 6 August 1975, p. 4.

8. Beverly Buck to *Look Magazine*, 2 February 1970; Anthony Blais, interview by Beverly Buck, personal discussion, summer 1970; Preuhs, "Prisoner of War Camp No. 10," 1–3.

9. Werner Schmiedeberg to Simmons, 18 August 1996.

10. Hong Interviews.

Bibliography

Letters written to Henry (Hank) Peterson in Moorhead and presently located at the Northwest Minnesota History Center were translated by a member of the Department of Foreign Languages at Moorhead State University. French-language documents from the International Red Cross were translated by Jane Stull and Frank Lamouraux. All other translations were made by the author.

Newspapers

Ah La Ha Sa (Albert Lea High School paper)
Albert Lea Evening Tribune
Austin Daily Herald
Barnsville Record-Review
Beardsley News
Bemidji Sentinel
Bird Island Union
Blue Earth County Enterprise (Mapleton)
Blue Earth Post
Cannon Falls Beacon
Cass County Pioneer (Walker)
Chicago Tribune
Clinton Advocate
Cokato Enterprise
Cottonwood Current
Country Press (Moorhead)
Crookston Daily Times
Dakota County Tribune (Farmington)
Deer River News
Detroit News and Free Press
Drahtpost (Algona German POW Base Camp Newspaper)
Duluth Herald
Duluth News-Tribune
East Grand Forks Weekly Record
Fairmont Daily Sentinel
Faribault County Register (Blue Earth)
Faribault Daily News Republican and Pilot
Faribault Journal

Gaylord Hub
Goodhue County Tribune (Goodhue)
Graceville Enterprise
Grand Rapids Herald-Review
Howard Lake Herald
Itasca County Independent (Grand Rapids)
Jackson County Pilot (Jackson)
Jordon Independent
Kenyon Leader
Kossuth County Advance (Algona, Iowa)
Lagerzeitung (Algona German POW Base Camp Newspaper)
Le Center Leader
Le Sueur News-Herald
Lewiston Journal
Madison Lake Times
Manitou Messenger (St. Olaf College)
Mankato Free Press
Midwest Labor (Duluth)
Minneapolis Daily Times
Minneapolis Morning Tribune
Minneapolis Star Journal
Minneapolis Star Tribune
Minneapolis Sunday Tribune
Minnesota Labor (Minneapolis)
Montgomery Messenger
Moorhead Daily News
Morgan Messenger
New Ulm Daily Journal
New Ulm Review
Norman County Index (Ada)
Northfield Independent
Northfield News
Olivia Times Journal
Ortonville Independent
Owatonna Daily People's Press
Park Rapids Enterprise
Plainview News
Princeton Union
Red Lake Falls Gazette
Redwood Falls Gazette

Rochester Post-Bulletin
St. Charles Press
St. James Courier
St. Paul Dispatch
St. Peter Herald
Sanborn Sentinel
Sleepy Eye Herald-Dispatch
Springfield Advance-Press
Steele County Photo News (Owatonna)
Tägliche Volkszeitung-Tribüne (St. Paul)
Truman Tribune
Wabasso Standard
Walnut Grove Tribune
Warren Sheaf
Waseca Herald
Watonwan County Plaindealer (St. James)
Wells Mirror
Winnebago Times
Winona Republican-Herald
Winona Sunday News
Winthrop News

Journals and Periodicals

Bloch, Cordelia. "When I Was in Prison You Visited Me: Teenage Experience Leads to Prison Visitation Ministry." *Journey*, quarterly publication of Franciscan Sisters of Little Falls, Minnesota (winter 1986).

Buecker, Thomas R. "Nazi Influence at the Fort Robinson Prisoner of War Camp during World War II." *Nebraska History* 73 (spring 1992).

Clark, Penny. "Farm Work and Friendship: The German Prisoner of War Camp at Lake Wabaunsee." *Emporia State Research Studies* 36 (winter 1988).

Coker, Kathy Roe. "World War II Prisoners of War in Georgia: German Memories of Camp Gordon, 1943–1945." *Georgia Historical Quarterly* 76 (winter 1992).

Devore, Robert. "Our Pampered Prisoners of War." *Collier's*, 14 October 1944.

Ehrmann, Henry W. "An Experiment in Political Education: The Prisoner-of-War Schools in the United States." *Social Research* 14 (September 1947).

Fay, Sidney B. "German Prisoners of War." *Current History* 8 (March 1945).

Fincher, Jack. "By Convention, the Enemy Within Never Did Without." *Smithsonian,* June 1995.

Frisch, Carlienne. "German Prisoners in Minnesota Were 'Good Workers.'" *Land Magazine*, 18 June 1981.

Lobdell, George H. "Minnesota's 1944 PW Escape: Down the Mississippi in the Lili Marlene #10." *Minnesota History* 54 (fall 1994).

Mason, John Brown. "German Prisoners of War in the United States." *American Journal of International Law* 39 (1945).

McKnight, Maxwell S. "The Employment of Prisoners of War in the United States." *International Labour Review* 50 (July 1944).

Miller, Duane Ernest. "Barbed-Wire Farm Laborers: Michigan's Prisoner of War Experience during World War II." *Michigan History* 73 (September/October 1989).

O'Brien, Patrick G., Thomas D. Isern, and R. Daniel Lumley. "Stalag Sunflower: German Prisoners of War in Kansas." *Kansas History* 7 (autumn 1984).

"Our Growing Prison Camps: How U.S. Treats War Captives." *National Week,* 28 May 1943.

Peihl, Mark. "POWs Work at Moorhead Truck Farm." *Clay County Historical Society Newsletter* (March/April 1991).

Pluth, Edward J. "Prisoner of War Employment in Minnesota during World War II." *Minnesota History* 44 (winter 1975).

"Potatoes, Peat and Prisoners of War." *Isanti County Traveler* 10 (summer 1995).

Robins, Jim. "Minnesota's POW Camps." *Minneapolis St. Paul Magazine,* January 1986.

Stuart, Graham H. "War Prisoners and Internees in the United States." *American Foreign Service Journal* 21 (October 1944).

"The Conditions of Employment of Prisoners of War: The Geneva Convention of 1929 and Its Application." *International Labour Review* 47 (February 1943).

Books

Baily, Ronald H. *Prisoners of War.* Chicago: Time-Life Books, 1981.

Bischof, Günter and Stephen Ambrose, eds. *Eisenhower and the German POWs: Facts against Falsehood.* Baton Rouge: Louisiana State University Press, 1992.

Cokato's First Century, 1878–1978. Cokato Centennial Committee, 1979.

Denzene, Georges, and Beverly J. Jackson. *The Hollandale Story: 1918–1950.* Freeborn County Historical Society, 1989.

Hartshorne, M. Holmes. *Kierkegaard, Godly Deceiver: The Nature and Meaning of his Pseudonymous Writings.* New York: Columbia University Press, 1990.

History of Rice and Steele Counties Minnesota. Vol. 2. Chicago: H.C. Cooper and Co., 1918.

Hopkins, Charles Howard. *History of the YMCA in North America.* New York: Association Press, 1951.

―――. *John R. Mott 1865–1955.* Grand Rapids: William B. Eerdmans Publishing Company, 1979.

Huber, Max. *Das Internationale Rote Kreuz: Idee und Wirklichkeit* (The International Red Cross: Idea and Reality). Zürich: Max Niehans Verlag, 1951.

International Committee of the Red Cross. *Inter Arma Caritas: The Work of the International Red Cross during the Second World War.* Geneva: International Committee of the Red Cross, 1947.

Joyce, James Avery. *Red Cross International and the Strategy of Peace.* New York: Oceana Publications, Inc., 1959.

Keefer, Louis E. *Italian Prisoners of War in America, 1942–1946: Captives or Allies?* New York: Praeger Publishers, 1992.

Koop, Allen V. *Stark Decency: German Prisoners of War in a New England Village.* Hanover, NH: University Press of New England, 1988.

Krammer, Arnold. *Nazi Prisoners of War in America.* New York: Stein and Day Publishers, 1979.

Lewis, George G., and John Mewha. *History of Prisoner of War Utilization by the United States Army, 1776–1945.* Washington, D.C.: Department of the Army, 1955.

Malantschuk, Gregor. *Kierkegaard's Thought.* Princeton: Princeton University Press, 1971.

Maschke, Erich, ed. *Zur Geschichte der deutschen Kriegsgefangenen des Zweiten Weltkrieges* (To the History of the German Prisoners of War of World War Two). Vol. 10/1, *Die deutschen Kriegsgefangenen in amerikanischer Hand: USA* (The German Prisoners of War in American Captivity: USA) by Hermann Jung. Munich: Verlag Ernst und Werner Gieseking, 1972.

Maschke, Erich, ed. *Zur Geschichte der deutschen Kriegsgefangenen des Zweiten Weltkrieges* (To the History of the German Prisoners of War of World War Two). Vol. 14, *Geist und Kultur der deutschen Kriegsgefangenen im Westen* (Spiritual and Cultural Activities of German Prisoners of War in the West) by Kurt Böhme. Munich: Verlag Ernst und Werner Gieseking, 1972.

Maschke, Erich, ed. *Zur Geschichte der deutschen Kriegsgefangenen des Zweiten Weltkrieges* (To the History of the German Prisoners of War of World War Two). Vol. 15, *Die deutschen Kriegsgefangenen des Zweiten Weltkrieges: Eine Zusammenfassung* (The German Prisoners of War of World War Two: A Summary) by Erich Maschke, Kurt Böhme, Diether Cartellieri, Werner Ratza, Hergard Robel, Emil Schieche, and Helmut Wolff. Munich: Verlag Ernst und Werner Gieseking, 1974.

May, Lowell A. *Camp Concordia: German POWs in the Midwest.* Manhattan, Kansas: Sunflower University Press, 1995.

MIS-Northwest Association. *Unsung Heroes, Military Intelligence Service: Past, Present, Future.* Seattle: MIS-Northwest Association, 1996.

Montgomery: From 'The Big Woods' to the Kolacky Capital, 1856–1976. Montgomery's Bicentennial Committee, 1976.

Mullen, John Douglas. *Kierkegaard's Philosophy: Self-Deception and Cowardice in the Present Age.* New York: Times Mirror, 1981.

Powell, Allan Kent. *Splinters of a Nation: German Prisoners of War in Utah.* Salt Lake City: University of Utah Press, 1989.

Radicalism in MN, 1900–1960: A Survey of Selected Sources/20th-Century Radicalism in Minnesota Project, Carl Ross, project director. St. Paul: Minnesota State Historical Society Press, 1994.

Robin, Ron Theodore. *The Barbed-Wire College: Reeducating German POWs in the United States during World War II.* Princeton: Princeton University Press, 1995.

Searle, R. Newell. *Whitewater: The Valley of Promise.* Minnesota State Heritage Series, #2, 1977.

Shoptaugh, Terry, Wayne Gudmundson, and Karin Anderson. *The Growers: Sugar in the Valley.* Moorhead: Moorhead State University. Prairie Documents Photographic Book Series, 1993.

Svoboda, Frank D. *Looking Back: A History of Agriculture in Renville County, Minnesota*. Renville County Historical Society, 1976.

Wells Centennial Steering Committee 1869–1969, 1969.

Wilcox, Walter W. *The Farmer in the Second World War*. Ames, Iowa: Iowa State College Press, 1947.

Unpublished Materials

I. Monographs

Dahms, Steven Victor. "The Work of the Lutheran Church–Missouri Synod and Its Pastors and Congregations among German Prisoners of War in the United States during World War II." Thesis, University of Wisconsin–Oshkosh, May 1989.

Manley, John E. "Administration and Relationships of War Prisoners Aid of the YMCA in the United States during World War II." World Alliance File #18, Kautz Family YMCA Archives, St. Paul, Minnesota.

Pluth, Edward J. "The Administration and Operation of German Prisoner of War Camps in the United States during World War II." Ph.D. diss., Ball State University, 1970.

Preuhs, Elroy. "Algona Prisoner of War Camp No. 10 Whitewater State Park." 1976, Whitewater State Park Archives, St. Charles, Minnesota.

Speakman, Cummins E. Jr. "Re-education of German Prisoners of War in the United States during World War II." Thesis, University of Virginia, June 1948.

Teufel, Kurt C., ed. "The History of Camp Concordia from Site Survey to Inactivation." 1945, Federal Records Center, Kansas City, Missouri.

Vulliet, Andre. "Preliminary Report of the War Prisoners Aid Young Men's Christian Associations during World War II." 1946, World Alliance File #18, National YMCA Archives, St. Paul, Minnesota.

Zwagerman, Kelly. "A Study of German Prisoner of War Labor in Faribault, Minnesota during World War Two." Graduate research paper, Mankato State University, December 1989.

II. Documents

"Advisory Group Selected to Aid Farm Help Chief." 26 February 1943, Minnesota Farm Help Coordinating Committee Newsletter, HD 1775f.M6A 5 1943, Minnesota State Historical Society, St. Paul, MN.

Arthur T. Lobdell Manuscript Collection, G. H. Lobdell, Curator, Chandler, AZ.

————. Announcement from Public Relations Office at Base Camp in Algona, Iowa. August 1945.

————. Listing of Contractor POW Production.

————. POW Labor Report, 15 September, 28 September 1945.

————. Standard Operating Procedure for Prisoner of War Branch Camps, Prisoner of War Camp, Algona, Iowa, circa July 1944.

————. Moorhead Investigation File, 1944 and 1945.

"Big Stone County Annual Report 1944." 1944, Big Stone County Extension Office.

"Big Stone County Annual Report 1945." 1945, Big Stone County Extension Office.

"Brown County Annual Report 1943." 1943, Brown County Extension Office.

"Brown County Annual Report 1945." 1945, Brown County Extension Office.

"Clay County Annual Report 1944." 1944, Clay County Extension Office.

"Clay County Annual Report 1945." 1945, Clay County Extension Office.

"Convention Relative to the Treatment of Prisoners of War. Geneva, 27 July 1929."

"Cooperative Agreement between Agricultural Extension Service of the University of Minnesota and War Manpower Commission for Furnishing Facilities and Services." 1944, File "R," Farm Labor Program WWII, appendix A, University of Minnesota Archives, Minneapolis, MN.

"District Court of the United States No. 1108." R7, U5, S8, Box 29, 1108-2, National Archives–Central Plains Region. Kansas City, Mo.

"Faribault City Council Minutes." 23 May 1944, Faribault City Council.

"Faribault County Annual Report 1945." 1945, Faribault County Extension Office.

"Farm Help Plan Based on Local Administration." 14 March 1943, Minnesota Farm Help Coordinating Committee Newsletter, HD 1775f.M6A 5 1943, Minnesota State Historical Society, St. Paul, MN.

"Farm Labor Conference at Morris." 7 March 1943, Minnesota Farm Help Coordinating Committee Newsletter, HD 1775f.M6A 5 1943, Minnesota State Historical Society, St. Paul, MN.

"George Taylor Address Book." 1943, Dorothy Steinbeisser, Olivia, MN.

"Historical Notes." 3 December 1981, Brown County Historical Society.

"ICRC Visits." Zehnder at Algona, 8 March 1945; Fairmont, 9 March 1945; New Ulm, 9 March 1945; Owatonna, 10 March 1945;

Clarinda, Iowa, 15, 16 March 1945; Schnyder at Algona, 12 September 1945; Faribault, 13 September 1945; Montgomery, 13 September 1945; Owatonna, 13 September 1945; Bena, 14 September 1945; Deer River, 14 September 1945. Politisches Archiv des Auswärtigen Amts, Bonn, Germany.

"Jackson County Annual Report 1943." 1943, Jackson County Extension Office.

"Jackson County Annual Report 1945." 1945, Jackson County Extension Office.

"Le Sueur County Annual Report 1944." 1944, Le Sueur County Extension Office.

"Le Sueur County Annual Report 1945." 1945, Le Sueur County Extension Office.

"Lyon County Annual Report 1945." 1945, Lyon County Extension Office.

"Mankato Meet Lays Foundation Farm Help Drive." 7 March 1943, Minnesota Farm Help Coordinating Committee Newsletter, HD 1775f.M6A 5 1943, Minnesota State Historical Society, St. Paul, MN.

"Marshall County Annual Report 1944." 1944, Marshall County Extension Office.

"Marshall County Annual Report 1945." 1945, Marshall County Extension Office.

"Mille Lacs County Annual Report 1943." 1943, Mille Lacs County Extension Office.

"Minnesota Set to Begin Drive for Farm Help." 28 February 1943, Minnesota Farm Help Coordinating Committee Newsletter, HD 1775f.M6A 5 1943, Minnesota State Historical Society, St. Paul, MN.

"Norman County Annual Report 1944." 1944, Norman County Extension Office.

"Norman County Annual Report 1945." 1945, Norman County Extension Office.

"Olmsted County Annual Report 1945." 1945, Olmsted County Extension Office.

Records of the Office of the Provost Marshal General, Record Group 389, National Archives, Washington, D.C.

————. Algona Branch Camps. July 1944; August 1944; January 1945; February 1945; March 1945; May 1945.

————. Branch Camp #401, Remer. 1944.

————. Branch Camp #401, Remer, Current Work Detail Lists. 1944.

— ————. Branch Camp #401, Remer, Report on P.O.W. Mail for April 1944.

————. Branch Camp #402, Bena, Report of Logging Operations. 22 May 1944.

— ————. Branch Camp #402, Bena. 1944.

————. Branch Camp #404, Deer River, Report of Logging Operations. 20 May 1944.

————. Branch Camp #404, Deer River, Special Orders. 1944.

————. Branch Camp #404, Deer River. 1944.

————. Dawson Report. 29 September 1944.

————. Lt. Colonel A. T. Lobdell to Commanding General, 7th Service Command, 26 August 1944. Box 2745.

————. Officers in Branch Camps. 1944–1945.

————. Schwieger Report. 3 July 1944.

————. Schwieger Report. 24 June 1945.

————. Semi-Monthly Reports on Prisoners of War, 1 August 1945; 16 October 1945; 30 October 1945; 15 December 1945, 1 January 1946.

————. Special Use Permit. 19 June 1944.

————. YMCA Visits by Hong. Remer, 12 June 1944; Bena, 12, 13 June 1944; Owatonna and Faribault, 26 June 1944; Montgomery, 24 July 1944; New Ulm, 24 July 1944; Moorhead, 4 August 1944; Ortonville, 4 August 1944; Faribault, 9 August 1944; Howard Lake, 12 August 1944; Algona, 17, 18 October and 3 November 1944; Owatonna, 21 November 1944; Fairmont, 28 January 1945; Faribault, 22 May 1945; Owatonna, 9 August 1945; Wells, 10 August 1945.

————. Weekly Reports on Prisoners of War. 1 November 1944; 8 November 1944; 16 November 1944; 23 November 1944.

"Renville County Annual Report 1943." 1943, Renville County Extension Office.

"Renville County Annual Report 1944." 1944, Renville County Extension Office.

"Renville County Annual Report 1945." 1945, Renville County Extension Office.

"Report on the Minnesota Farm Labor Program, 1943." Minnesota Agricultural Extension Service, University of Minnesota Archives, St. Paul, Minnesota.

"Report on the Minnesota Farm Labor Program, 1944." Minnesota Agricultural Extension Service, University of Minnesota Archives, St. Paul, Minnesota.

"Report on the Minnesota Farm Labor Program, 1945." Minnesota Agricultural Extension Service, University of Minnesota Archives, St. Paul, Minnesota.

"Scott County Annual Report 1944." 1944, Scott County Extension Office.

"Scott County Annual Report 1945." 1945, Scott County Extension Office.

"State Can Get War Prisoners for Farm Work." 23 June 1943, Minnesota Farm Help Coordinating Committee Newsletter, HD 1775f.M6A 5 1943, Minnesota State Historical Society, St. Paul, MN.

"State Set to Mobilize its Farm Workers." 10 April 1943, Minnesota Farm Help Coordinating Committee Newsletter, HD 1775f.M6A 5 1943, Minnesota State Historical Society, St. Paul, MN.

"The International Committee of the Red Cross and the Second World War." 1998, Geneva: The International Committee of the Red Cross [http://www.icrc.ch/unicc/icrcnews].

"The Rotary Wheel." 23 August 1944, Fargo Rotary Club Newsletter.

"Timber Producers Association Bulletin #79." 1 December 1943, IID 9750.T58, Minnesota State Historical Society, St. Paul, Minnesota.

"Wabasha County Annual Report 1944." 1944, Wabasha County Extension Office.

"Wabasha County Annual Report 1945." 1945, Wabasha County Extension Office.

"War Manpower Commission Records." 25 February 1944, visit by Irving S. Anderson to Remer, Record Group #211, National Archives, Washington, D.C.

"Watonwan County Annual Report 1945." 1945, Watonwan County Extension Office.

"West Polk County Annual Report 1944." 1944, West Polk County Extension Office.

"West Polk County Annual Report 1945." 1945, West Polk County Extension Office.

"Winona County Annual Report 1944." 1944, Winona County Extension Office.

"World War II POW Camps." WCCO Dimension, 10 February 1991. Transcript available at WCCO Television, Minneapolis, Minnesota.

"Wright County Annual Report 1944." 1944, Wright County Extension Office.

"Wright County Annual Report 1945." 1945, Wright County Extension Office.

III. Interviews

Bakko, Lorenzo. Interview by author. Tape recording. Owatonna, Minnesota, 3 May 1994.

Becker, Karl. Interview by author. Personal discussion. Owatonna, Minnesota, 9 August 1994.

Blais, Anthony. Interview by Beverly Buck. Personal discussion. Summer 1970.

Clark, Loren. Interview by LaDona Conrads, 30 December 1973. Interview S262, transcript. Northwest Minnesota Historical Center Collections, Livingston Lord Library. Moorhead State University, Moorhead, MN.

Coupanger, Mildred. Interview by author. Personal discussion. Notes in author's possession. Elmore, Minnesota, 20 October 1995.

Crouch, Charles. Interview by author. Tape recording. Sleepy Eye, Minnesota, 19 April 1994.

Drury, Florence. Interview by Mark Peihl. Tape recording. Moorhead, MN, 25 February 1991, Clay County Historical Society, Moorhead, MN.

Funke, Alex. Interview by author. Tape recording. Bielefeld, Germany, 21 February 1995.

Henkel, Friedhelm. Interview by author. Tape recording. Hatzbach, Germany, 12 February 1995.

Hong, Howard. Interview by author. Tape recording. Northfield, Minnesota, 3 May 1994.

Hong, Howard. Interview by author. Tape recording. Hovland, Minnesota, 10 September 1995.

Horn, Paul. Interview by Gloria Thompson, 11 January 1973. Interview S267, transcript. Northwest Minnesota Historical Center Collections, Livingston Lord Library. Moorhead State University, Moorhead, MN.

Johnson, Edgar. Interview by Brenda Moerer, 9 February 1974. Interview S259, transcript. Northwest Minnesota Historical Center Collections, Livingston Lord Library. Moorhead State University, Moorhead, MN.

Knauer, Werner. Interview by author. Personal discussion. Notes in author's possession. Kronach, Germany, 13, 14 February 1995.

Kohleick, Ernst. Interview by author. Tape recording. Wuppertal, Germany, 24 February 1995.

Koivunen, Ilmar. Interview by Irene Paull. Tape recording. Cass Bay, Oregon, August 1968, OH20, Minnesota State Historical Society.

Kubat, Evelyn. Interview by author. Tape recording. Owatonna, Minnesota, 3 May 1994.

Lenz, Mrs. Immanuel. Interview by author. Tape recording. Olivia, Minnesota, 30 December 1989.

Matz, Harold. Interview by Norma Matz. Tape recording. Wells, Minnesota, June 1994, Faribault County Historical Society, Wells, MN.

Murray, Winifred. Interview by author. Tape recording. Bird Island, Minnesota, 27 March 1990.

Myers, Harold. Interview by Beverly Buck. Personal discussion. Summer 1970.

Myers, Mrs. Walter. Interview by Beverly Buck. Personal discussion. Summer 1970.

Neber, Alfred. Interview by author. Tape recording. Kindenheim, Germany, 20 July 1991.

Neber, Alfred. Interview by author. Personal discussion. Notes in author's possession. Kindenheim, Germany, 2 March 1995.

Odegard, Robert. Interview by author. Tape recording. Roseville, Minnesota, 13 April 1994.

Peterson, Henry. Interview by Gloria Thompson, 11 January 1973. Interview S267, transcript. Northwest Minnesota Historical Center Collections, Livingston Lord Library. Moorhead State University, Moorhead, MN.

Rasokat, Kurt. Interview by author. Personal discussion. Notes in author's possession. Bielefeld, Germany, 22, 23 February 1995.

Rauenhorst, George. Interview by author. Personal discussion. Notes in author's possession. Olivia, Minnesota, 13 June 1992.

Schultz, Roy W. Interview by Mark Peihl. Phone interview, 27 February 1991, Clay County Historical Society, Moorhead, MN.

Spartz, Elmer. Interview by Beverly Buck. Personal discussion. Summer 1970.

Stadther, Lawrence. Interview by author. Personal discussion. Olivia, Minnesota, July 1995.

Swentkosfke, Mahlon. Interview by Beverly Buck. Personal discussion. Summer 1970.

Waldschmidt, Heinrich. Interview by author. Tape recording. Hatzbach, Germany, 12 February 1995.

Welker, Hans. Interview by author. Phone interview. Olivia, Minnesota, 8 October 1994.

IV. Letters

Bakko, Lorenzo, to author, 12 April 1994.

Becker, Karl, to author, 1 January 1994.

Bloch, Cordelia, to author, 26 April 1995.

Buck, Beverly, to Look Magazine, 2 February 1970. Transcript in the hand of Beverly Buck, Effie, MN.

Carlson, Carl, to Beverly Buck, March 1970. Transcript in the hand of Beverly Buck, Effie, MN.

Coupangei, Mildred, to author, 17 April 1995.

Delin, Gerald, to author, 17 May, 11 August, 1 September 1995.

Fleshner, Harvey, to author, 7 December 1995; 17 September 1996.

Georgiwold, Folrath, to Henry Peterson, 22 May 1948. Transcript in Northwest Minnesota Historical Center, Moorhead, MN.

Hamer, Shirley, to author, 4 March 1996.

Heuer, Myron, to author, 14 August 1994; 16 July 1994; 12 September 1994.

Hong, Howard, to author, 25 September 1998.

Jeske, Muriel, to author, 25 January 1994.

Kratzheller, Hans, to author, 9 September 1995, 10 April 1996.

Kubat, Evelyn, to author, 28 January 1993; 26 April 1994.

LaFreniere, A. L., to Arthur Lobdell, 12 May 1945. Transcript in A. T. Lobdell Manuscript Collection, Arizona.

Lobdell, Arthur, to V. Tobler, 1 July 1944. Transcript in A. T. Lobdell Manuscript Collection, Arizona.

Lobdell, George H., to author, 26 July 1995; 29 February 1996; 24 August, 2 September 1998; 31 July 1999.

Massing, Hermann, to author, 11 August 1993.

Mueller, Horst, to Henry Peterson, 1 September 1947; 4 March 1948. Transcripts in Northwest Minnesota Historical Center, Moorhead, MN.

Müller, Joachim, to Henry Peterson, 12 December 1947. Transcript in Northwest Minnesota Historical Center, Moorhead, MN.

Rockvam, Eileen, to author, 7 July 1994.

Sauer, Alois, to Henry Peterson, 1 September 1948. Transcript in Northwest Minnesota Historical Center, Moorhead, MN.

Schmiedeberg, Werner, to author, 31 July, 18 August, 18 September, 1 November 1996.

Thaner, Klaus, to author, 25 February 1991.

Unknown, to Henry Peterson, 14 November 1947. Transcript in Northwest Minnesota Historical Center, Moorhead, MN.

Waldschmidt, Heinrich, to Coupanger family, 20, 23 November 1946; 21 February, 4 April, 10 August, 3 November, 24 December 1947; 8 March, 26 April, 1 November 1948; 8 March, 25 November 1949; 5 April, 6 June 1950; 15 October, 15 November 1951; 8 February 1952. Transcripts in the hand of Mildred Coupanger, Elmore, MN.

Wdowig, Franz, to Henry Peterson, 8 September 1948. Transcript in Northwest Minnesota Historical Center, Moorhead, MN.

Welker, Hans, to author, 2 January 1996.

Index